Pax Avalon

ConflictRevolution

STEVEN "REECE" FRIESEN

Herald Press

Waterloo, Ontario
Scottdale, Pennsylv...

Library and Archives Canada Cataloguing in Publication

Friesen, Steven, 1978-
    Pax Avalon : conflict revolution / Steven "Reece" Friesen.

ISBN 978-0-8361-9444-9

    I. Title.

PN6733.F75P39 2008   741.5'971   C2008-904908-X

PAX AVALON: CONFLICT REVOLUTION

Canadiana Entry Number: C2008-904908-X
Library of Congress Catalog Card Number: 2008934075
International Standard Book Number: 978-0-8361-9444-9
Printed in Canada
Cover by Steven "Reece" Friesen

15 14 13 12 11 10 09 08   10 9 8 7 6 5 4 3 2 1

To order or request information please call 1-800-245-7894
or visit www.heraldpress.com.

Euripedes, a playwright in ancient Greece, once said, "Short is the joy that guilty pleasure brings." He was right, of course -- the things we know are wrong can never *really* satisfy us. Still, sometimes the thing we write off as a guilty pleasure just needs a little tweaking.

I grew up reading comic books in a home where reading was encouraged but comic books were not. My parents didn't forbid me to buy and read comics, but they were disappointed that I would waste my time on something that promoted mindless violence, sarcastic attitudes, and women wearing material tighter than spandex. I was torn -- I loved the stories, I loved the pictures, I loved the idea of superhuman abilities (flight, above all), *and* -- I loved my parents. So I went through these phases where I would clean out my room (AKA, throw my comics away), but after a while, I would just go out and buy more. Then I tried drawing comics. It all started out as tracing, then finishing incomplete tracings by hand, then my own first awkward creations. It was electric! Oh, don't get me wrong, I was a horrible artist, but still I was completely hooked -- and feeling guilty about the whole thing. I'd been taught, and myself believed, that God created people as special beings and that human life was incredibly precious. I also came to understand that God gives us gifts -- gifts that are meant to be used. Therein lay my problem. I was developing a gift from God for drawing his creations beating the *tar* out of each other. I couldn't reconcile the two ideas, so I asked God to take this guilty pleasure of mine away... or make it into something good.

Pax Avalon is that "something good." It is drawn in the style of the books that I loved when I was growing up: superhero comics. It is influenced by the fantastic artists whose work has inspired me over the years: Jim Lee, Michael Turner, John Byrne, J. Scott Campbell (no doubt you'll see a classic pose or two of theirs in my work), and many others. It is *like* the comic books that I used to read in my childhood in many ways, except for one thing -- violence is *not* the solution. Oh, there is fighting in this book -- I couldn't try to convince you that there are other ways to deal with problems if I refused to consider the merits of typical conflict solving methods. However, violence does not stand alone as an option, nor does it get the luxury of a quick curtain. There are consequences to our actions, and the entire comic book medium tends to skip over the aftershocks to the victory parade -- a complete collateral damage blindspot.

So, those of you who *love* comic books -- I hope you enjoy the art and the story. I hope that it entertains you but also challenges you. Those of you who pick this up because you believe as I do and want to be supportive -- I expect you also will be challenged, but in a different way. This medium may seem strange to you and perhaps even a little shocking. There are a few things you should know in order to understand what you're reading here. First of all, the currency of this medium is *power* -- the ability to change the way things are going. To change it for the *better* is the mark of heroism. Simply wanting to change things doesn't make a person a hero -- they must have the power to back it up. And simply having the power isn't enough -- villains have power but use it for evil and selfish means. OK, so the currency of comics is power, but the *symbol* of that power is curves. Muscular curves for the men, and provocative curves for the women. That is why you don't see flabby dudes in capes or big-boned women in magical tiaras. The promotion of unrealistic and even exploitive body images has been a justified criticism since this medium began, but it is also inseparably linked to the language of comic books ("power" and "change"). *This* comic book is an attempt to speak that language in a way that does not objectify women or reduce men to the sum of their (body) parts, but it *is* still a comic book. So the clothing *is* form fitting and the characters *are* in good shape (they have the power to effect change), but in much more modest ways than you'll see in most graphic artwork. This is the difficult task of communicating through art, but it's one that I feel is worth undertaking.

Finally, you'll notice an asterix (*) every so often as you're reading through *Pax Avalon: ConflictRevolution*. If you check the back of the book, you'll find a page titled "Thinking It Through." Look for the number of the page you were just on and you'll find some notes about the idea(s) presented there. If you'd like to respond to these ideas or throw a comment or two of your own out there, drop by WWW.PAXAVALON.COM and join in the conversation with other readers. I'm especially curious about your responses to the "aftermath" question on the final page. Anyway ...

Enjoy the world of Pax Avalon!

STEVEN "REECE" FRIESEN

CHAPTER ONE

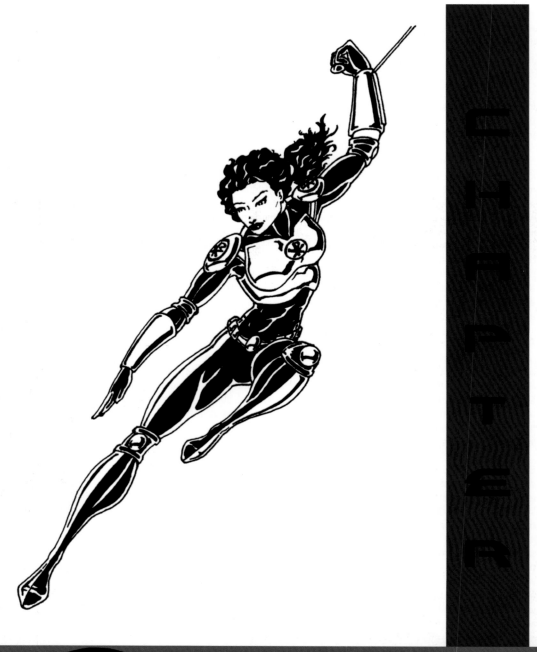

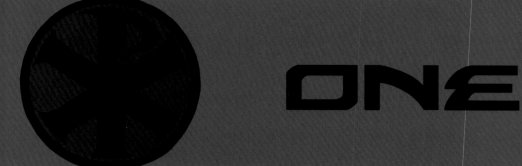

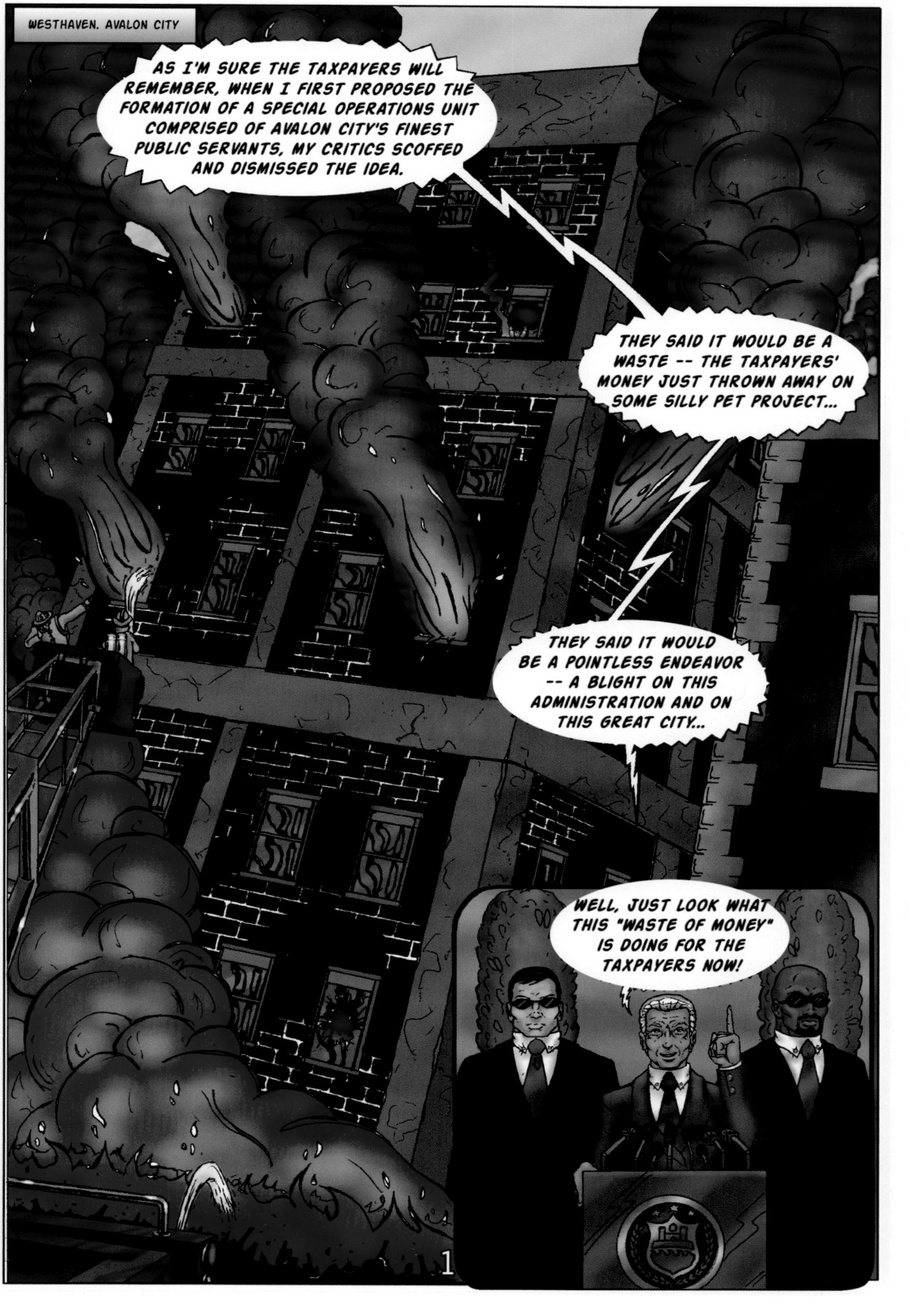
WESTHAVEN. AVALON CITY
AS I'M SURE THE TAXPAYERS WILL REMEMBER, WHEN I FIRST PROPOSED THE FORMATION OF A SPECIAL OPERATIONS UNIT COMPRISED OF AVALON CITY'S FINEST PUBLIC SERVANTS, MY CRITICS SCOFFED AND DISMISSED THE IDEA.
THEY SAID IT WOULD BE A WASTE -- THE TAXPAYERS' MONEY JUST THROWN AWAY ON SOME SILLY PET PROJECT...
THEY SAID IT WOULD BE A POINTLESS ENDEAVOR -- A BLIGHT ON THIS ADMINISTRATION AND ON THIS GREAT CITY...
WELL, JUST LOOK WHAT THIS "WASTE OF MONEY" IS DOING FOR THE TAXPAYERS NOW!

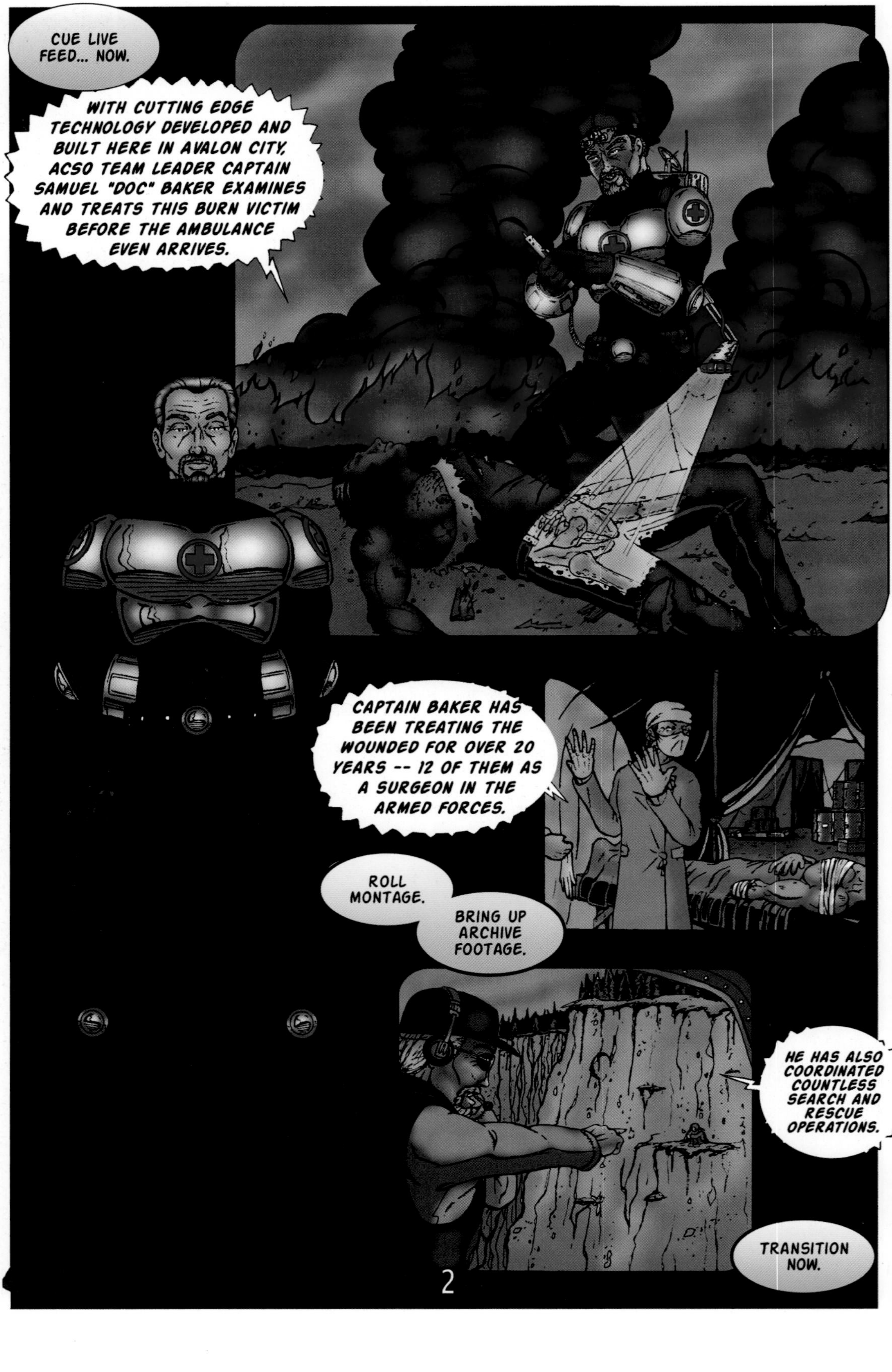

CUE LIVE FEED... NOW.
WITH CUTTING EDGE TECHNOLOGY DEVELOPED AND BUILT HERE IN AVALON CITY, ACSO TEAM LEADER CAPTAIN SAMUEL "DOC" BAKER EXAMINES AND TREATS THIS BURN VICTIM BEFORE THE AMBULANCE EVEN ARRIVES.
CAPTAIN BAKER HAS BEEN TREATING THE WOUNDED FOR OVER 20 YEARS -- 12 OF THEM AS A SURGEON IN THE ARMED FORCES.
ROLL MONTAGE.
BRING UP ARCHIVE FOOTAGE.
HE HAS ALSO COORDINATED COUNTLESS SEARCH AND RESCUE OPERATIONS.
TRANSITION NOW.

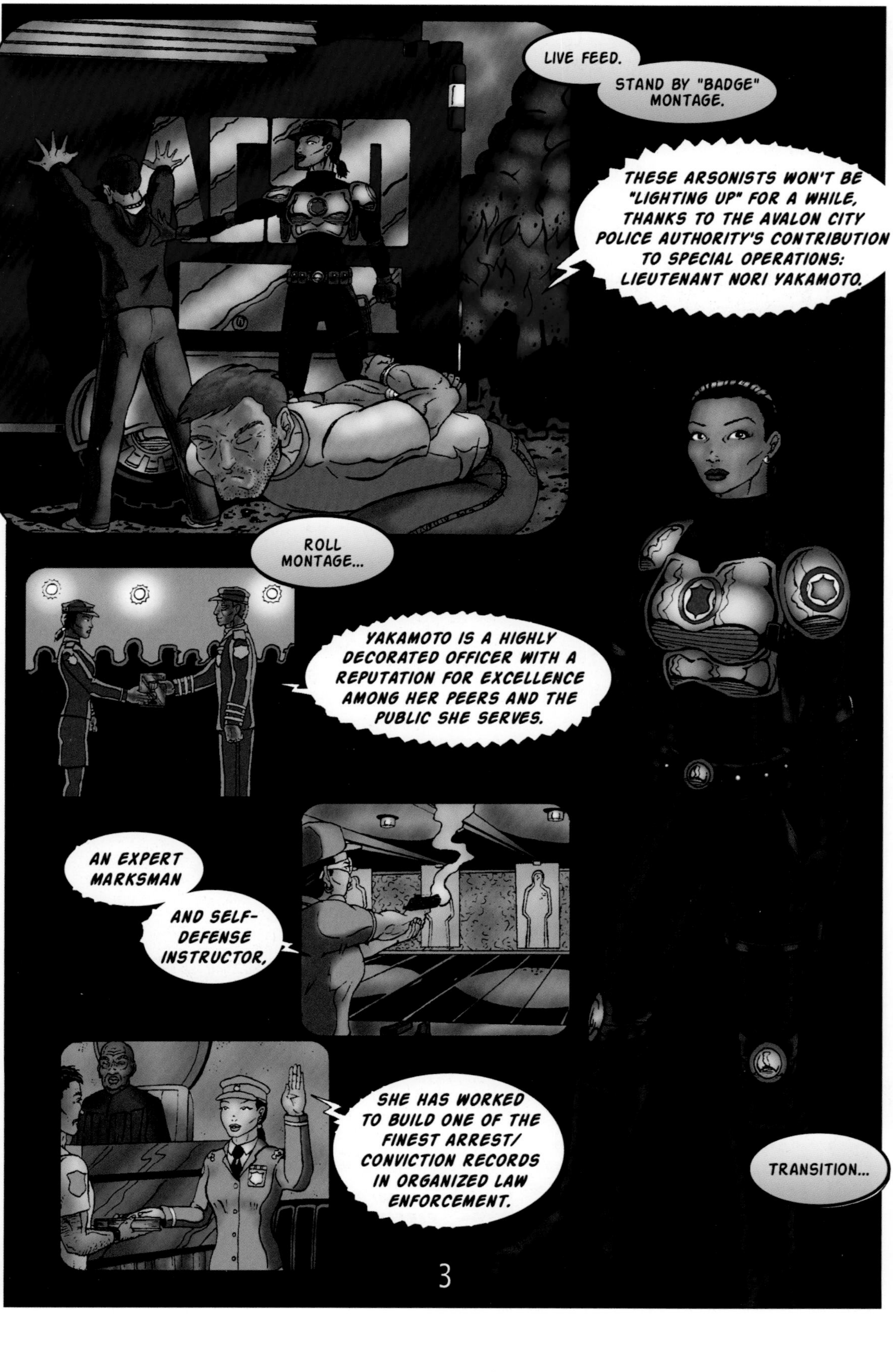
LIVE FEED.
STAND BY "BADGE" MONTAGE.
THESE ARSONISTS WON'T BE "LIGHTING UP" FOR A WHILE, THANKS TO THE AVALON CITY POLICE AUTHORITY'S CONTRIBUTION TO SPECIAL OPERATIONS: LIEUTENANT NORI YAKAMOTO.
ROLL MONTAGE...
YAKAMOTO IS A HIGHLY DECORATED OFFICER WITH A REPUTATION FOR EXCELLENCE AMONG HER PEERS AND THE PUBLIC SHE SERVES.
AN EXPERT MARKSMAN
AND SELF-DEFENSE INSTRUCTOR,
SHE HAS WORKED TO BUILD ONE OF THE FINEST ARREST/ CONVICTION RECORDS IN ORGANIZED LAW ENFORCEMENT.
TRANSITION...

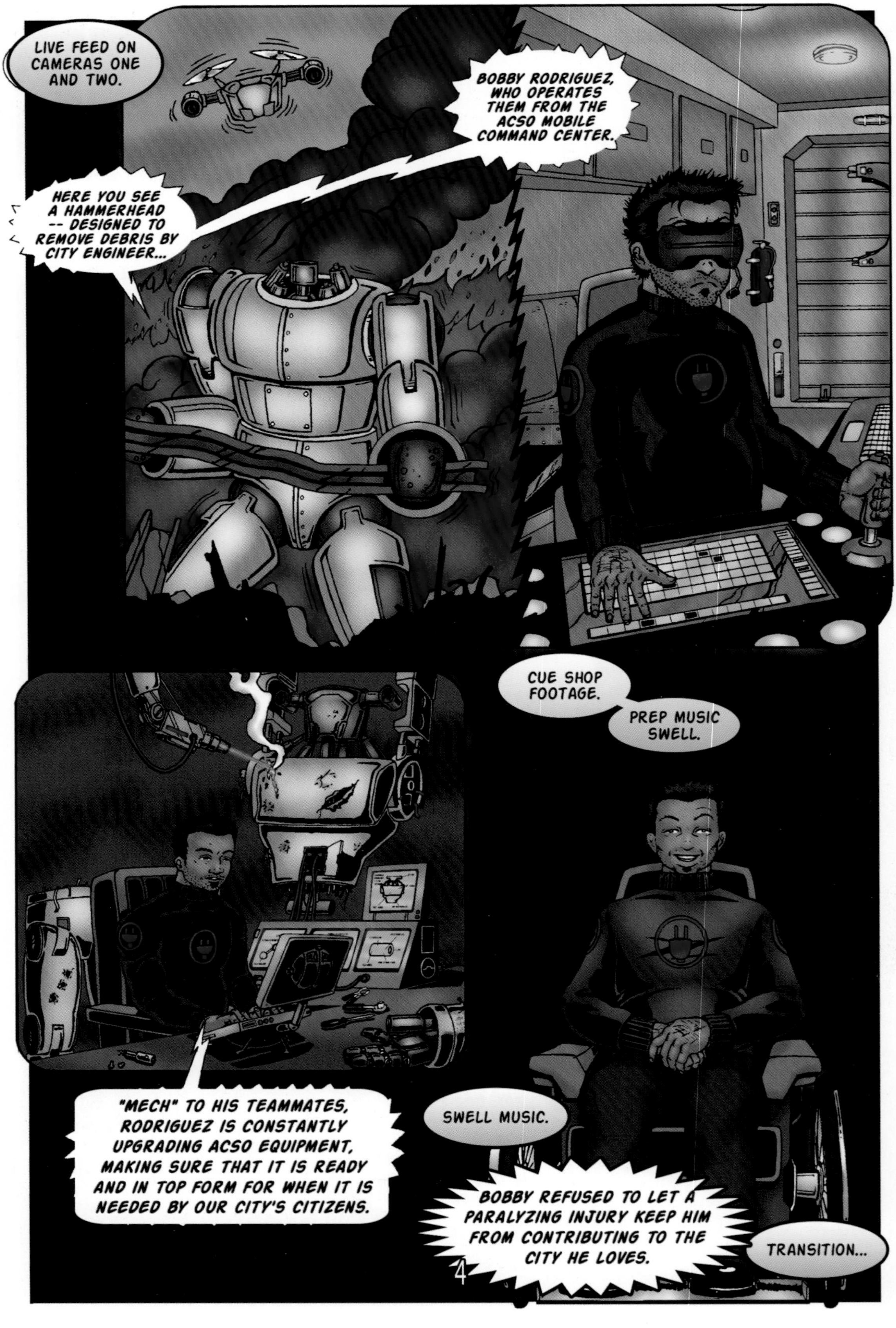
LIVE FEED ON CAMERAS ONE AND TWO.
BOBBY RODRIGUEZ, WHO OPERATES THEM FROM THE ACSO MOBILE COMMAND CENTER.
HERE YOU SEE A HAMMERHEAD -- DESIGNED TO REMOVE DEBRIS BY CITY ENGINEER...
CUE SHOP FOOTAGE.
PREP MUSIC SWELL.
"MECH" TO HIS TEAMMATES, RODRIGUEZ IS CONSTANTLY UPGRADING ACSO EQUIPMENT, MAKING SURE THAT IT IS READY AND IN TOP FORM FOR WHEN IT IS NEEDED BY OUR CITY'S CITIZENS.
SWELL MUSIC.
BOBBY REFUSED TO LET A PARALYZING INJURY KEEP HIM FROM CONTRIBUTING TO THE CITY HE LOVES.
TRANSITION...

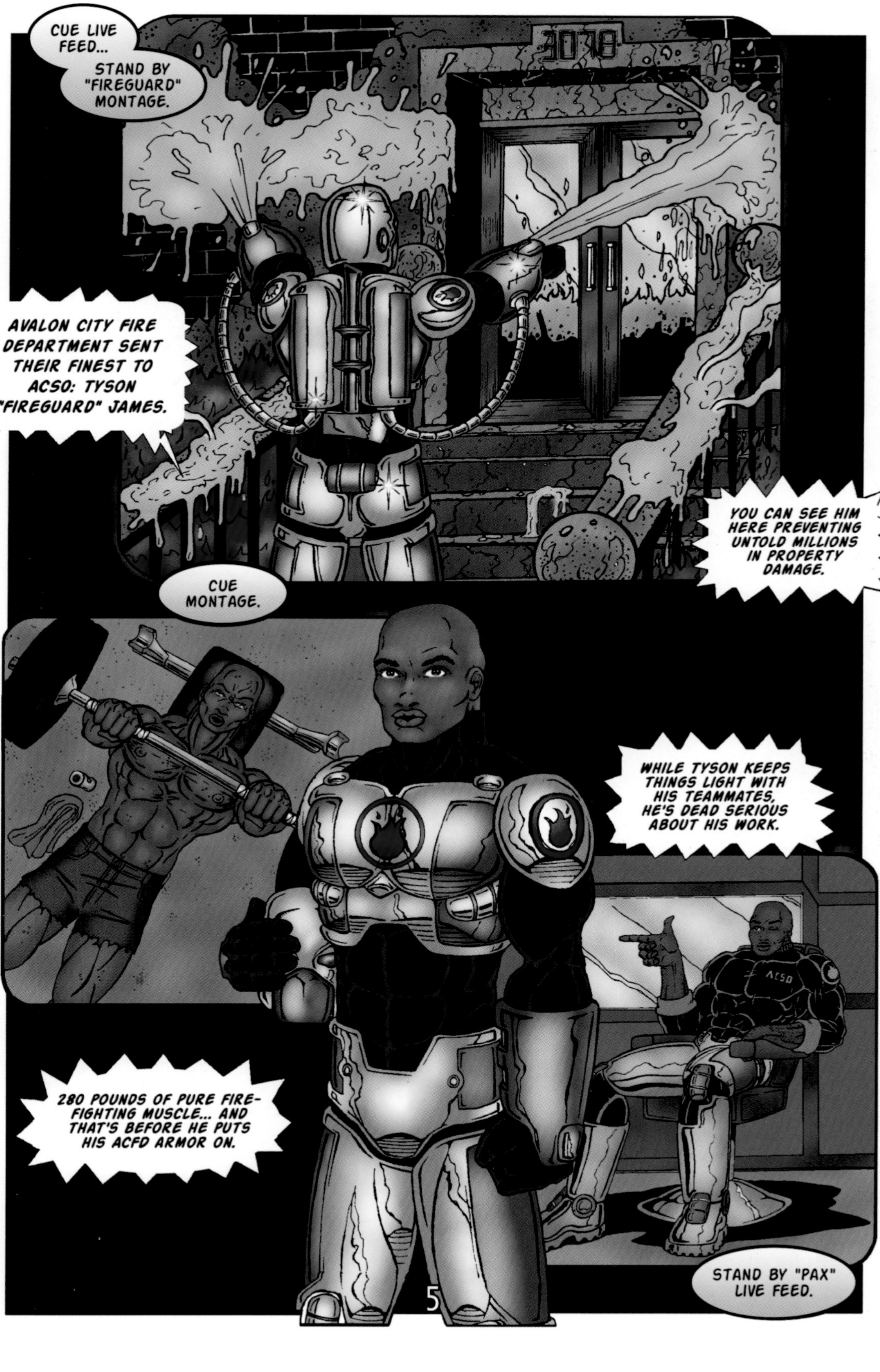
3078
CUE LIVE FEED...
STAND BY "FIREGUARD" MONTAGE.
AVALON CITY FIRE DEPARTMENT SENT THEIR FINEST TO ACSO: TYSON "FIREGUARD" JAMES.
YOU CAN SEE HIM HERE PREVENTING UNTOLD MILLIONS IN PROPERTY DAMAGE.
CUE MONTAGE.
WHILE TYSON KEEPS THINGS LIGHT WITH HIS TEAMMATES, HE'S DEAD SERIOUS ABOUT HIS WORK.
ACSO
280 POUNDS OF PURE FIRE-FIGHTING MUSCLE... AND THAT'S BEFORE HE PUTS HIS ACFD ARMOR ON.
STAND BY "PAX" LIVE FEED.

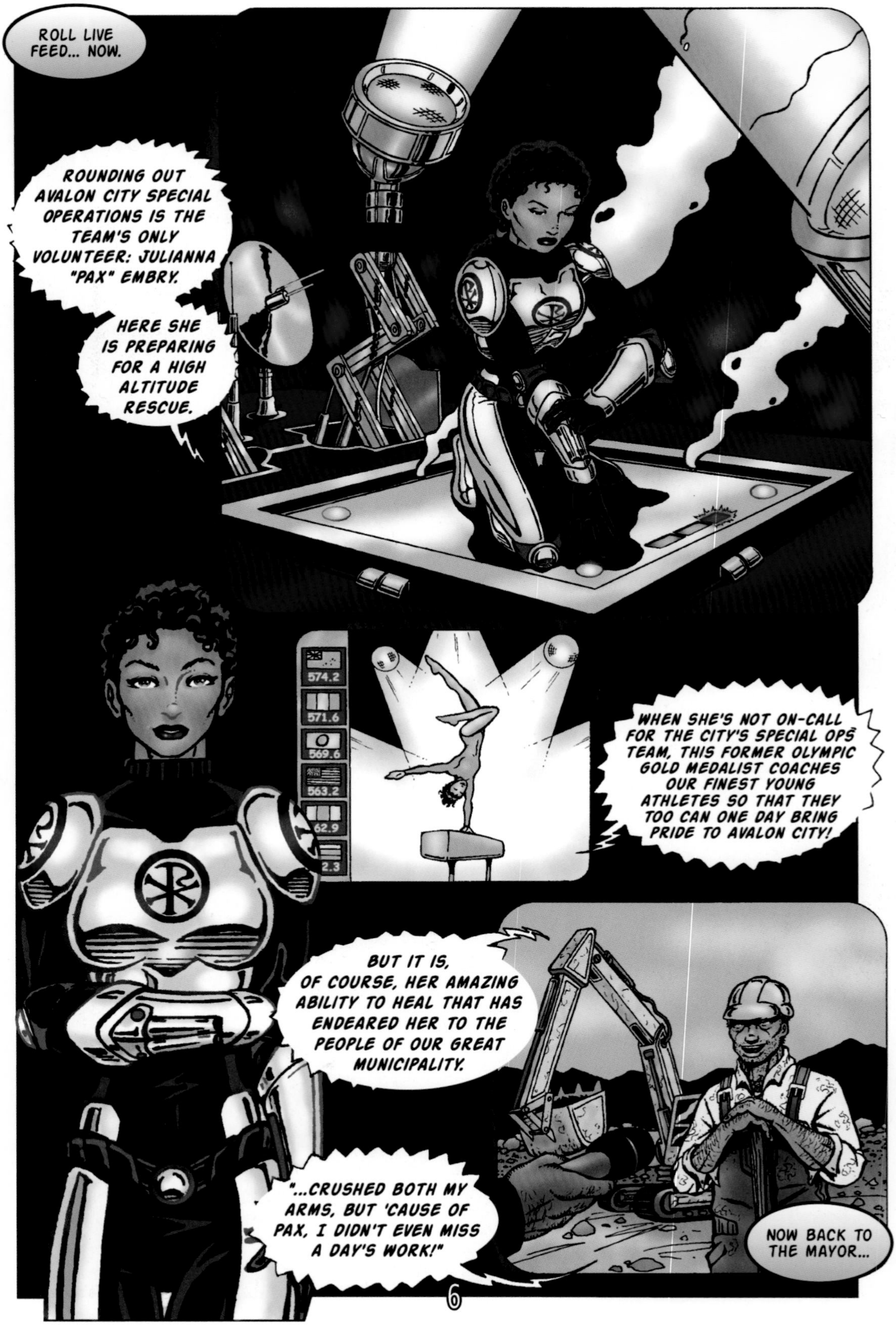
ROLL LIVE FEED... NOW.
ROUNDING OUT AVALON CITY SPECIAL OPERATIONS IS THE TEAM'S ONLY VOLUNTEER: JULIANNA "PAX" EMBRY.
HERE SHE IS PREPARING FOR A HIGH ALTITUDE RESCUE.
574.2
571.6
569.6
563.2
62.9
2.3
WHEN SHE'S NOT ON-CALL FOR THE CITY'S SPECIAL OPS TEAM, THIS FORMER OLYMPIC GOLD MEDALIST COACHES OUR FINEST YOUNG ATHLETES SO THAT THEY TOO CAN ONE DAY BRING PRIDE TO AVALON CITY!
BUT IT IS, OF COURSE, HER AMAZING ABILITY TO HEAL THAT HAS ENDEARED HER TO THE PEOPLE OF OUR GREAT MUNICIPALITY.
"...CRUSHED BOTH MY ARMS, BUT 'CAUSE OF PAX, I DIDN'T EVEN MISS A DAY'S WORK!"
NOW BACK TO THE MAYOR...

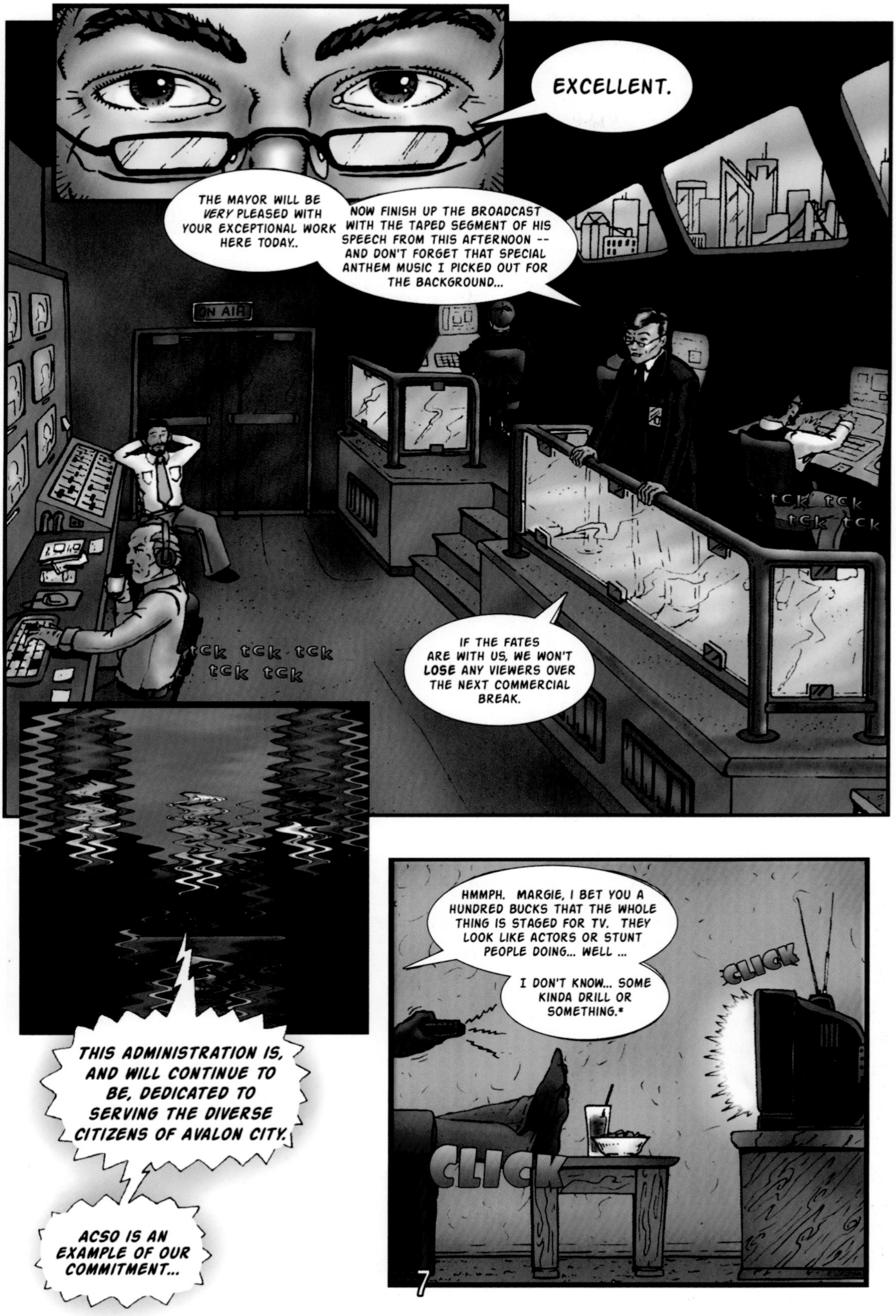
EXCELLENT.
THE MAYOR WILL BE VERY PLEASED WITH YOUR EXCEPTIONAL WORK HERE TODAY..
NOW FINISH UP THE BROADCAST WITH THE TAPED SEGMENT OF HIS SPEECH FROM THIS AFTERNOON -- AND DON'T FORGET THAT SPECIAL ANTHEM MUSIC I PICKED OUT FOR THE BACKGROUND...
ON AIR
tck tck
tck tck
tck tck tck
tck tck
IF THE FATES ARE WITH US, WE WON'T LOSE ANY VIEWERS OVER THE NEXT COMMERCIAL BREAK.
THIS ADMINISTRATION IS, AND WILL CONTINUE TO BE, DEDICATED TO SERVING THE DIVERSE CITIZENS OF AVALON CITY.
ACSO IS AN EXAMPLE OF OUR COMMITMENT...
HMMPH. MARGIE, I BET YOU A HUNDRED BUCKS THAT THE WHOLE THING IS STAGED FOR TV. THEY LOOK LIKE ACTORS OR STUNT PEOPLE DOING... WELL ...
I DON'T KNOW... SOME KINDA DRILL OR SOMETHING.*
CLICK
CLICK

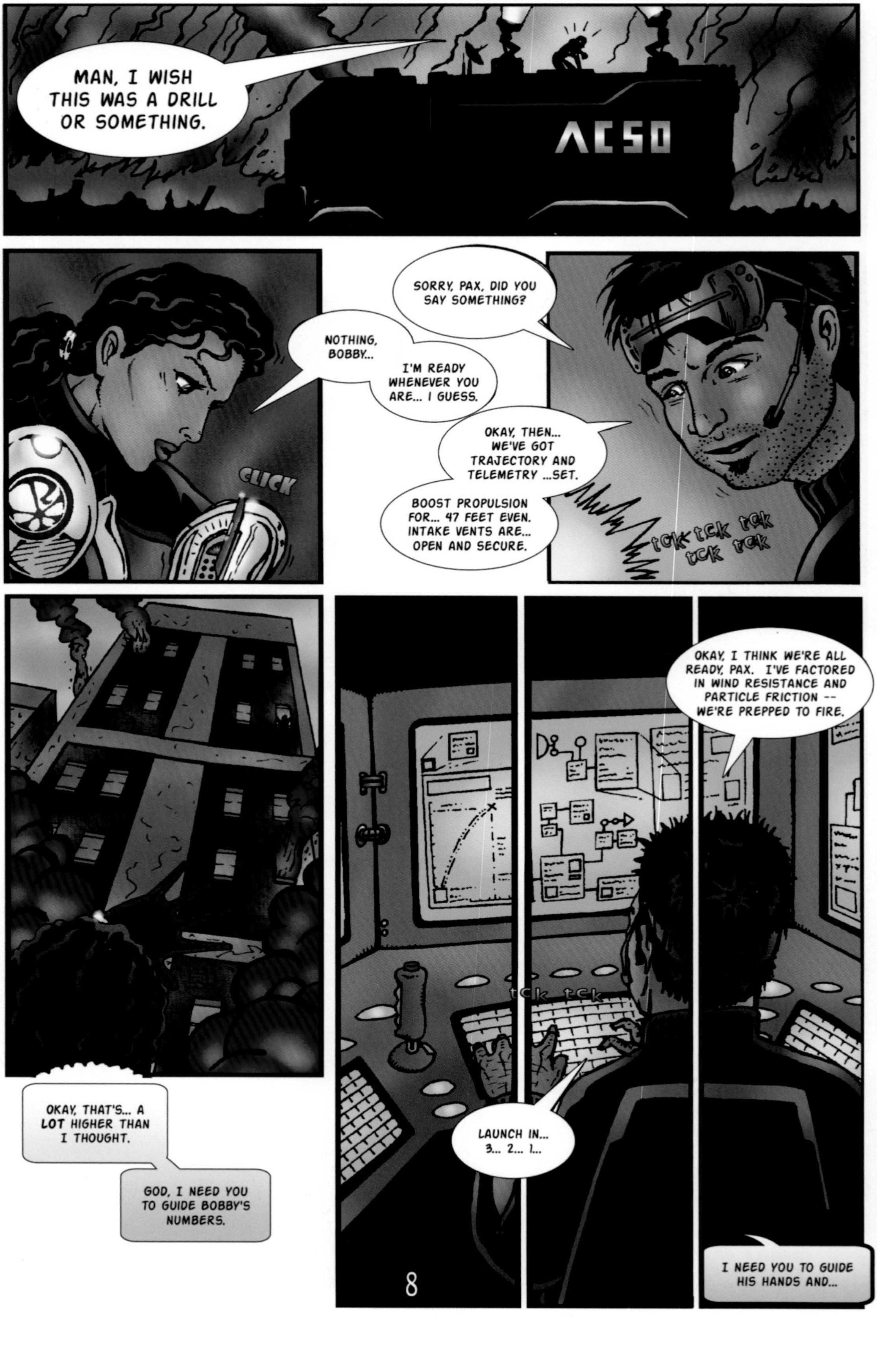
MAN, I WISH THIS WAS A DRILL OR SOMETHING.
ACSO
SORRY, PAX, DID YOU SAY SOMETHING?
NOTHING, BOBBY...
I'M READY WHENEVER YOU ARE... I GUESS.
CLICK
OKAY, THEN... WE'VE GOT TRAJECTORY AND TELEMETRY ...SET.
BOOST PROPULSION FOR... 47 FEET EVEN. INTAKE VENTS ARE... OPEN AND SECURE.
tck tck tck tck tck
OKAY, THAT'S... A **LOT** HIGHER THAN I THOUGHT.
GOD, I NEED YOU TO GUIDE BOBBY'S NUMBERS.
OKAY, I THINK WE'RE ALL READY, PAX. I'VE FACTORED IN WIND RESISTANCE AND PARTICLE FRICTION -- WE'RE PREPPED TO FIRE.
tck tck
LAUNCH IN... 3... 2... 1...
I NEED YOU TO GUIDE HIS HANDS AND...

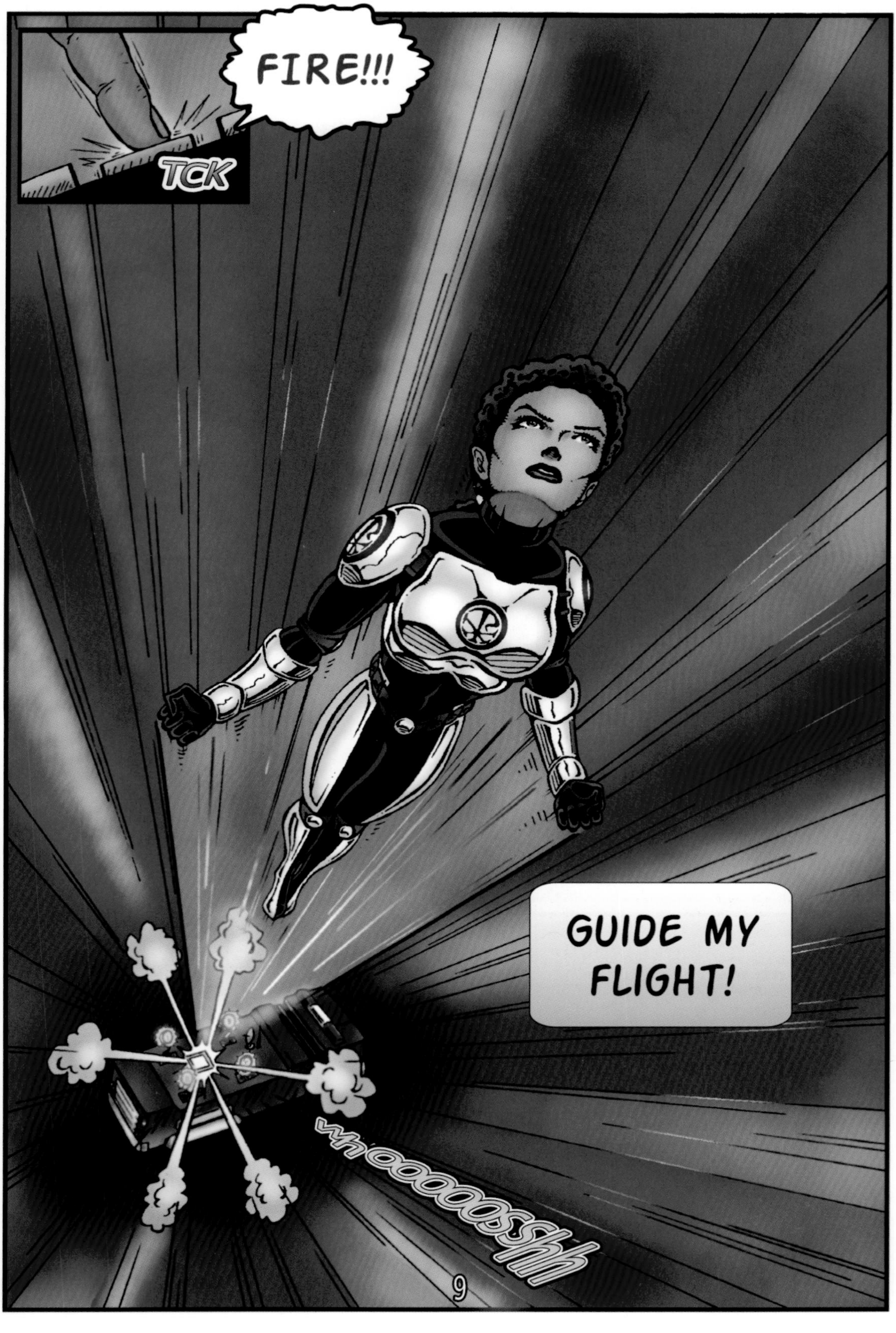
FIRE!!!
TCK
GUIDE MY FLIGHT!
whooooossshh

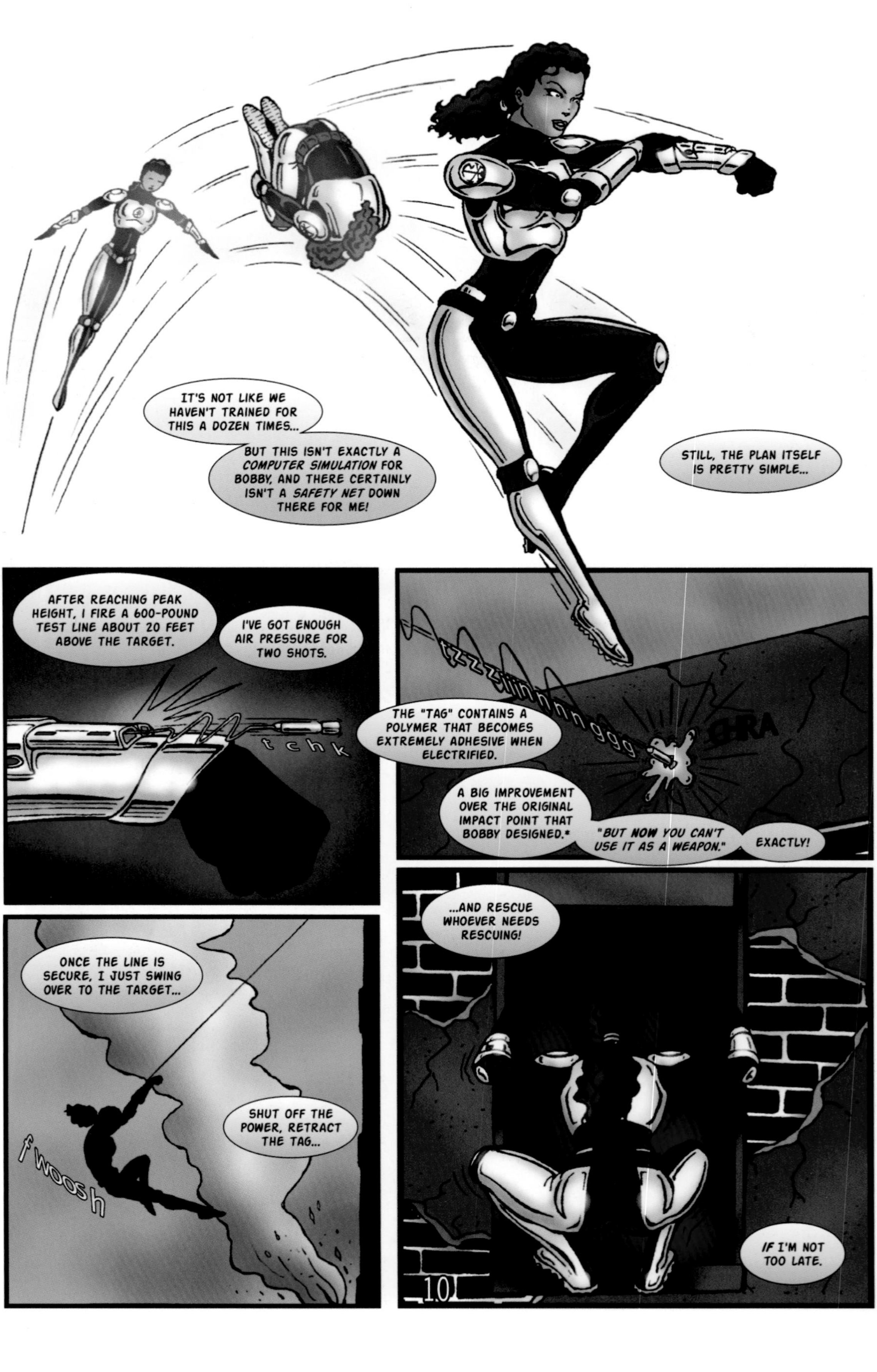

IT'S NOT LIKE WE HAVEN'T TRAINED FOR THIS A DOZEN TIMES...
BUT THIS ISN'T EXACTLY A *COMPUTER SIMULATION* FOR BOBBY, AND THERE CERTAINLY ISN'T A *SAFETY NET* DOWN THERE FOR ME!
STILL, THE PLAN ITSELF IS PRETTY SIMPLE...
AFTER REACHING PEAK HEIGHT, I FIRE A 600-POUND TEST LINE ABOUT 20 FEET ABOVE THE TARGET.
I'VE GOT ENOUGH AIR PRESSURE FOR TWO SHOTS.
tchk
THE "TAG" CONTAINS A POLYMER THAT BECOMES EXTREMELY ADHESIVE WHEN ELECTRIFIED.
A BIG IMPROVEMENT OVER THE ORIGINAL IMPACT POINT THAT BOBBY DESIGNED.*
"BUT NOW YOU CAN'T USE IT AS A WEAPON."
EXACTLY!
ONCE THE LINE IS SECURE, I JUST SWING OVER TO THE TARGET...
SHUT OFF THE POWER, RETRACT THE TAG...
fwoosh
...AND RESCUE WHOEVER NEEDS RESCUING!
IF I'M NOT TOO LATE.

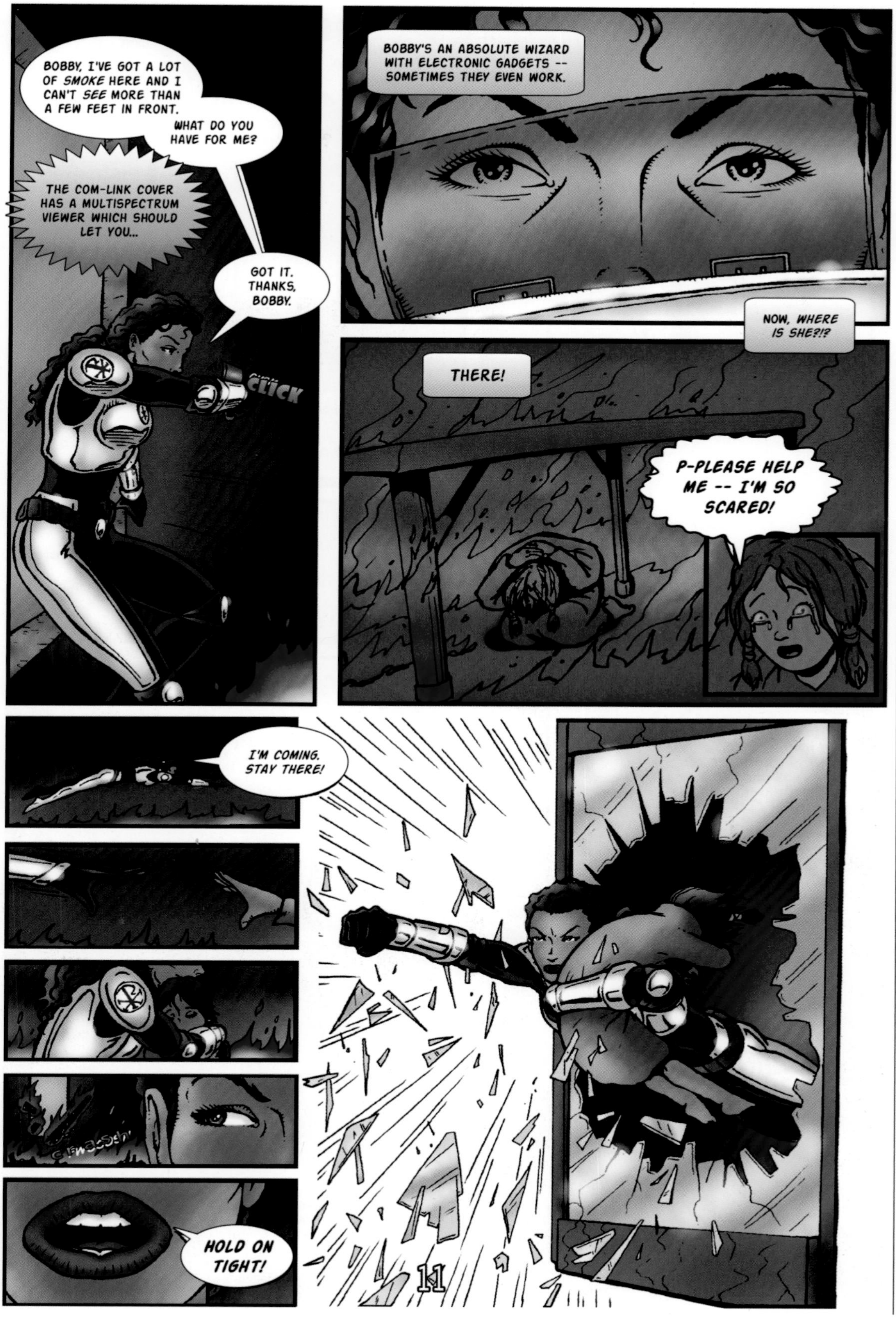
BOBBY, I'VE GOT A LOT OF SMOKE HERE AND I CAN'T SEE MORE THAN A FEW FEET IN FRONT.
WHAT DO YOU HAVE FOR ME?
THE COM-LINK COVER HAS A MULTISPECTRUM VIEWER WHICH SHOULD LET YOU...
GOT IT. THANKS, BOBBY.
CLICK
BOBBY'S AN ABSOLUTE WIZARD WITH ELECTRONIC GADGETS -- SOMETIMES THEY EVEN WORK.
NOW, WHERE IS SHE?!?
THERE!
P-PLEASE HELP ME -- I'M SO SCARED!
I'M COMING. STAY THERE!
HOLD ON TIGHT!

HEADS UP!

WE'RE COMING IN FAST!!

JAMIE!!!

THANK YOU... THANK YOU SO MUCH!

YOU'RE WELCOME.

I MEAN... I DON'T... KNOW WHAT I WOULD HAVE DONE...

IT'S OKAY. I UNDERSTAND...

PAX, I HAVE A MEDICAL EMERGENCY OVER HERE, AND I NEED YOUR HELP IMMEDIATELY!

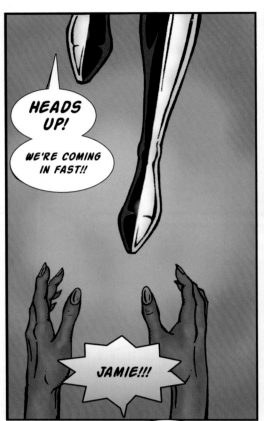

WHAT CAN I DO, DOC?

I'VE STABILIZED MOST OF THE OTHERS, BUT THIS MAN HAS **THIRD-DEGREE** BURNS ON HIS FACE AND ARMS. HE'S IN A LOT OF PAIN, AND THERE'S NOT MUCH I CAN DO.

HAVE YOU GIVEN HIM PAIN-KILLERS OR DRUGS OF ANY KIND? IT MIGHT NOT WORK IF YOU HAVE.

NO, I REMEMBERED THAT. LOOK, PAX, CAN YOU HANDLE THIRD-DEGREE BURNS? IT'S NOT PRETTY...

WHAT'S YOUR NAME?*

CAN YOU... HELP ME?

T... THOMAS.

12

WELL, THOMAS, I'VE NEVER TRIED TO TAKE ON AN INJURY LIKE THIS BEFORE, BUT HOLD ON A MOMENT...

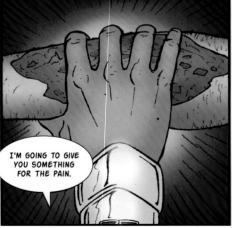

I'M GOING TO GIVE YOU SOMETHING FOR THE PAIN.

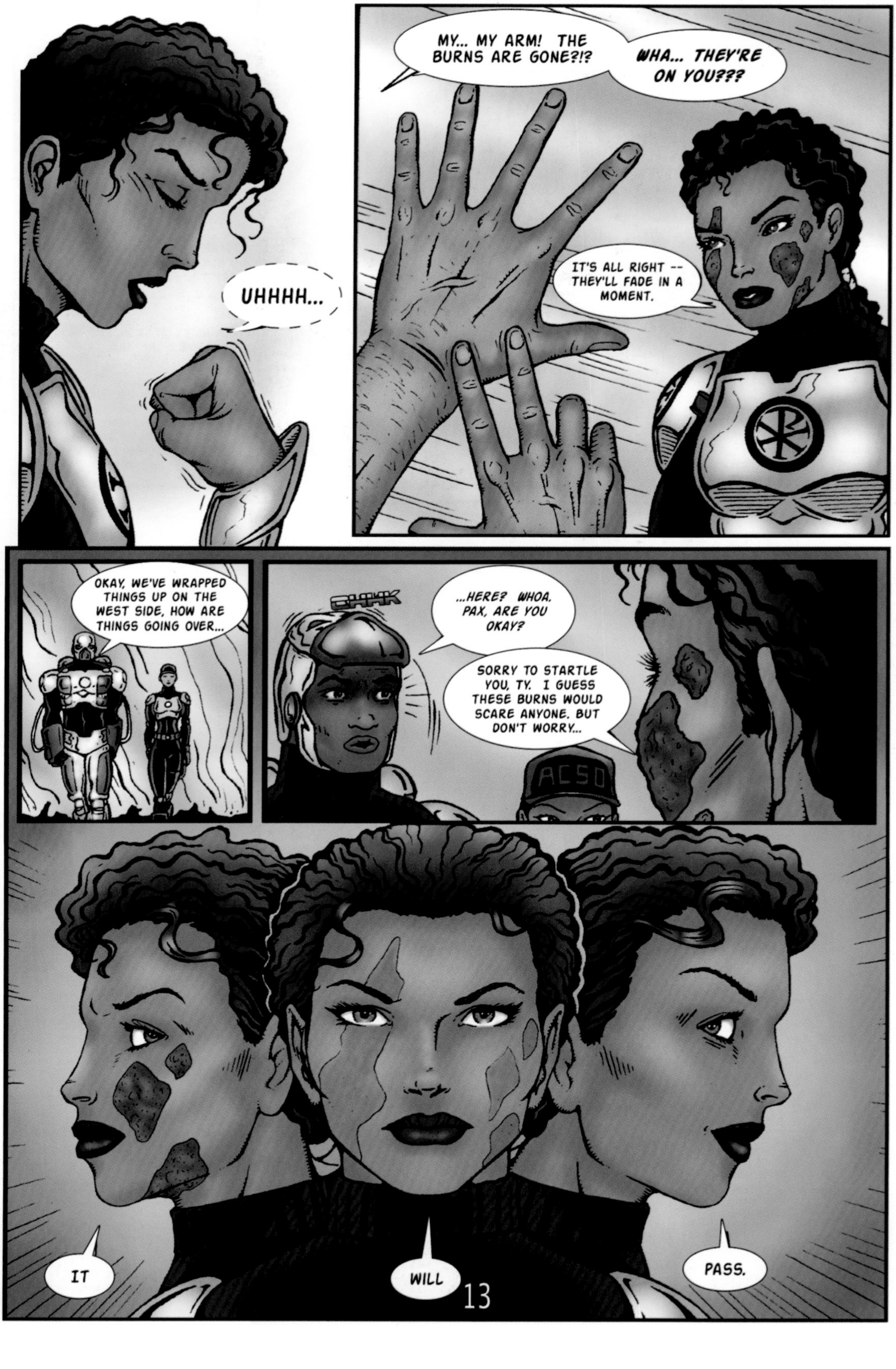
UHHHH...
MY... MY ARM! THE BURNS ARE GONE?!?
WHA... THEY'RE ON YOU???
IT'S ALL RIGHT -- THEY'LL FADE IN A MOMENT.
OKAY, WE'VE WRAPPED THINGS UP ON THE WEST SIDE, HOW ARE THINGS GOING OVER...
CHHK
...HERE? WHOA. PAX, ARE YOU OKAY?
SORRY TO STARTLE YOU, TY. I GUESS THESE BURNS WOULD SCARE ANYONE. BUT DON'T WORRY...
ACSD
IT
WILL
PASS.

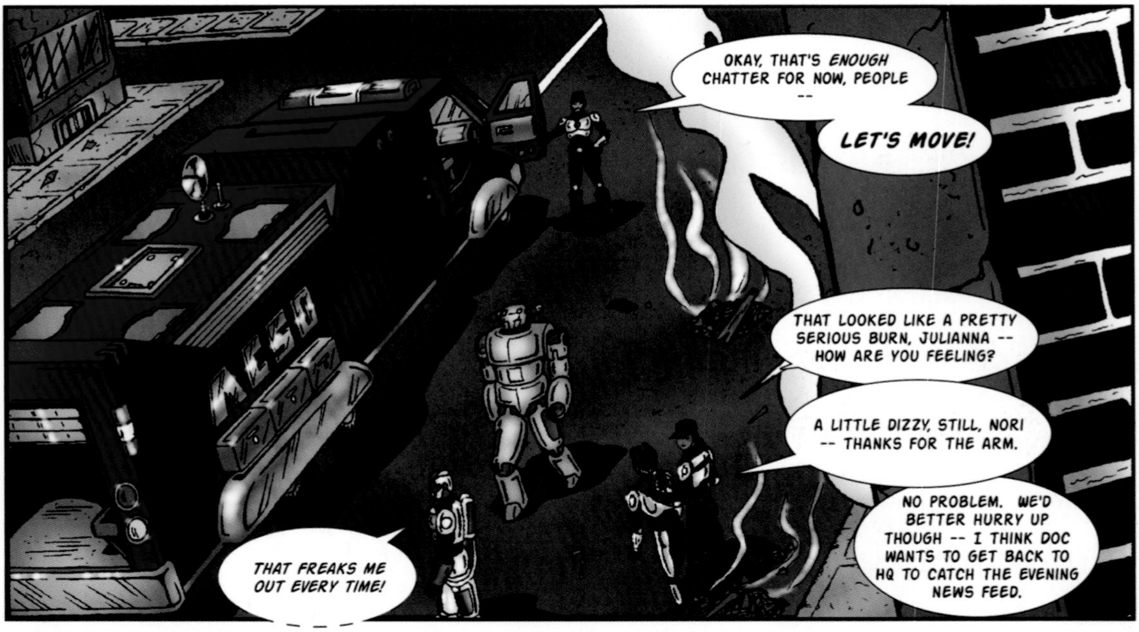
OKAY, THAT'S ENOUGH CHATTER FOR NOW, PEOPLE --
LET'S MOVE!
THAT LOOKED LIKE A PRETTY SERIOUS BURN, JULIANNA -- HOW ARE YOU FEELING?
A LITTLE DIZZY, STILL, NORI -- THANKS FOR THE ARM.
NO PROBLEM. WE'D BETTER HURRY UP THOUGH -- I THINK DOC WANTS TO GET BACK TO HQ TO CATCH THE EVENING NEWS FEED.
THAT FREAKS ME OUT EVERY TIME!

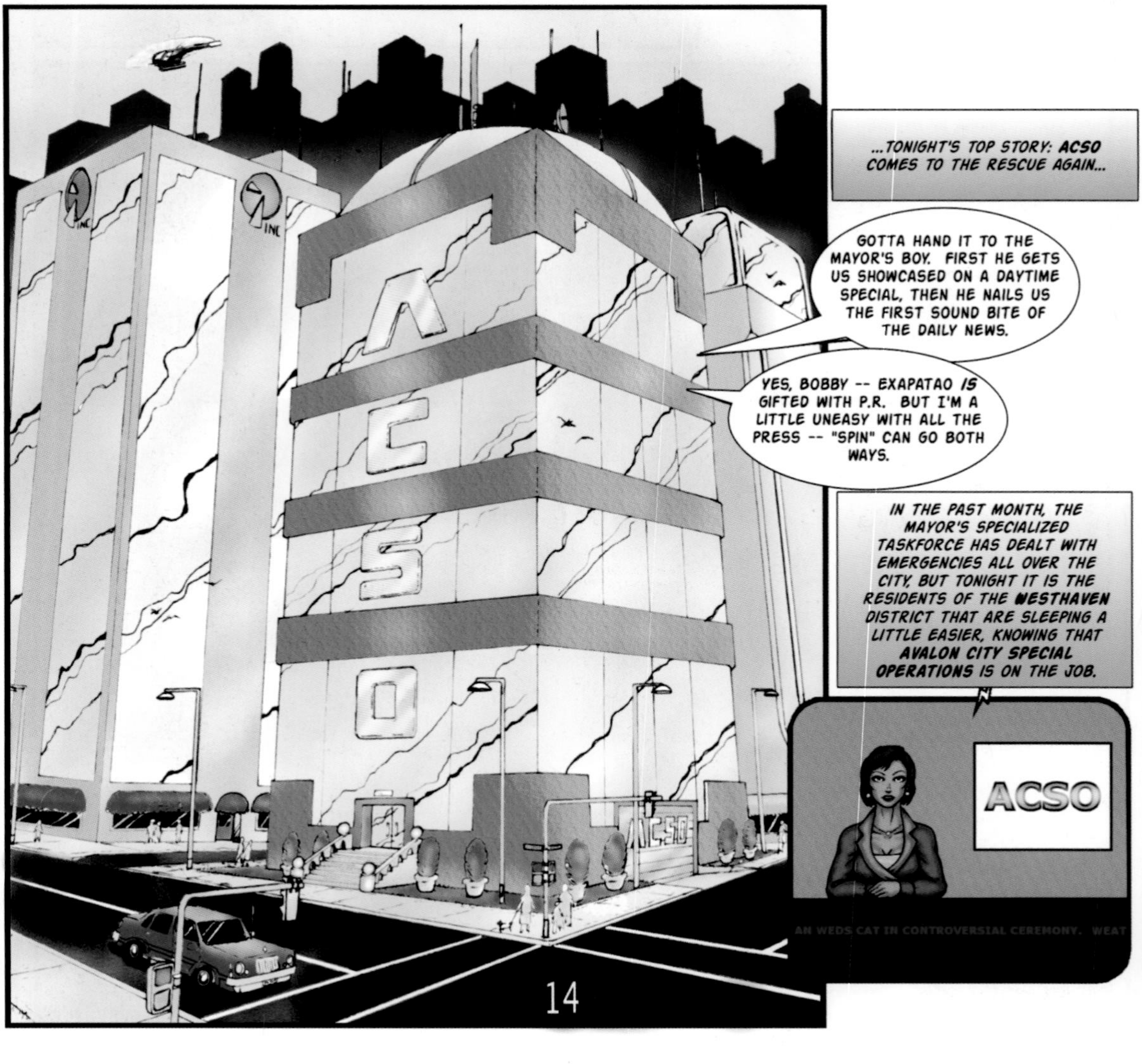
...TONIGHT'S TOP STORY: ACSO COMES TO THE RESCUE AGAIN...
GOTTA HAND IT TO THE MAYOR'S BOY. FIRST HE GETS US SHOWCASED ON A DAYTIME SPECIAL, THEN HE NAILS US THE FIRST SOUND BITE OF THE DAILY NEWS.
YES, BOBBY -- EXAPATAO IS GIFTED WITH P.R. BUT I'M A LITTLE UNEASY WITH ALL THE PRESS -- "SPIN" CAN GO BOTH WAYS.
IN THE PAST MONTH, THE MAYOR'S SPECIALIZED TASKFORCE HAS DEALT WITH EMERGENCIES ALL OVER THE CITY, BUT TONIGHT IT IS THE RESIDENTS OF THE WESTHAVEN DISTRICT THAT ARE SLEEPING A LITTLE EASIER, KNOWING THAT AVALON CITY SPECIAL OPERATIONS IS ON THE JOB.
ACSO
AN WEDS CAT IN CONTROVERSIAL CEREMONY. WEAT
ACSO

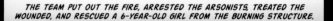

THE TEAM PUT OUT THE FIRE, ARRESTED THE ARSONISTS, TREATED THE WOUNDED, AND RESCUED A 6-YEAR-OLD GIRL FROM THE BURNING STRUCTURE.

BUT NOT *EVERYONE* IS HAPPY ABOUT ACSO'S INVOLVEMENT IN OPERATIONS AROUND THE CITY.

OH, YOU HAVE *GOT* TO BE KIDDING ME!

BE QUIET.

IT'S JUST... STUPID!

BE QUIET... *NOW.*

THIS IS THE FIFTH TIME THIS MONTH *ACSO* HAS *INTERVENED* IN EMERGENCY OPERATIONS AROUND THE CITY, PROMPTING CRITICISM FROM BOTH POLICE AND FIRE AUTHORITIES.

BUT AT A PRESS CONFERENCE THIS AFTERNOON, MAYOR STEVENSON *DEFENDED* HIS DECISION TO CREATE THE HYBRID EMERGENCY RESPONSE TEAM.

CAN YOU BELIEVE THESE PEOPLE!?! WE'RE OUT THERE RISKING OUR BUTTS...

BOBBY, SO HELP ME, IF YOU DON'T SHUT UP, *I WILL* ANESTHETIZE YOU.

"I DID NOT CREATE ACSO TO UNDERMINE THE EFFORTS OF THE FINE MEN AND WOMEN WHO SERVE AND PROTECT AVALON CITY BUT TO SUPPORT THEM WHEN OUR EXISTING RESOURCES ARE STRETCHED TO THEIR LIMITS."

"THIS IN MIND, I WILL *CONTINUE* TO ACTIVATE *ACSO* WHENEVER THE SITUATION WARRANTS IT. WE HAVE NO IDEA WHAT TOMORROW WILL BRING..."

15

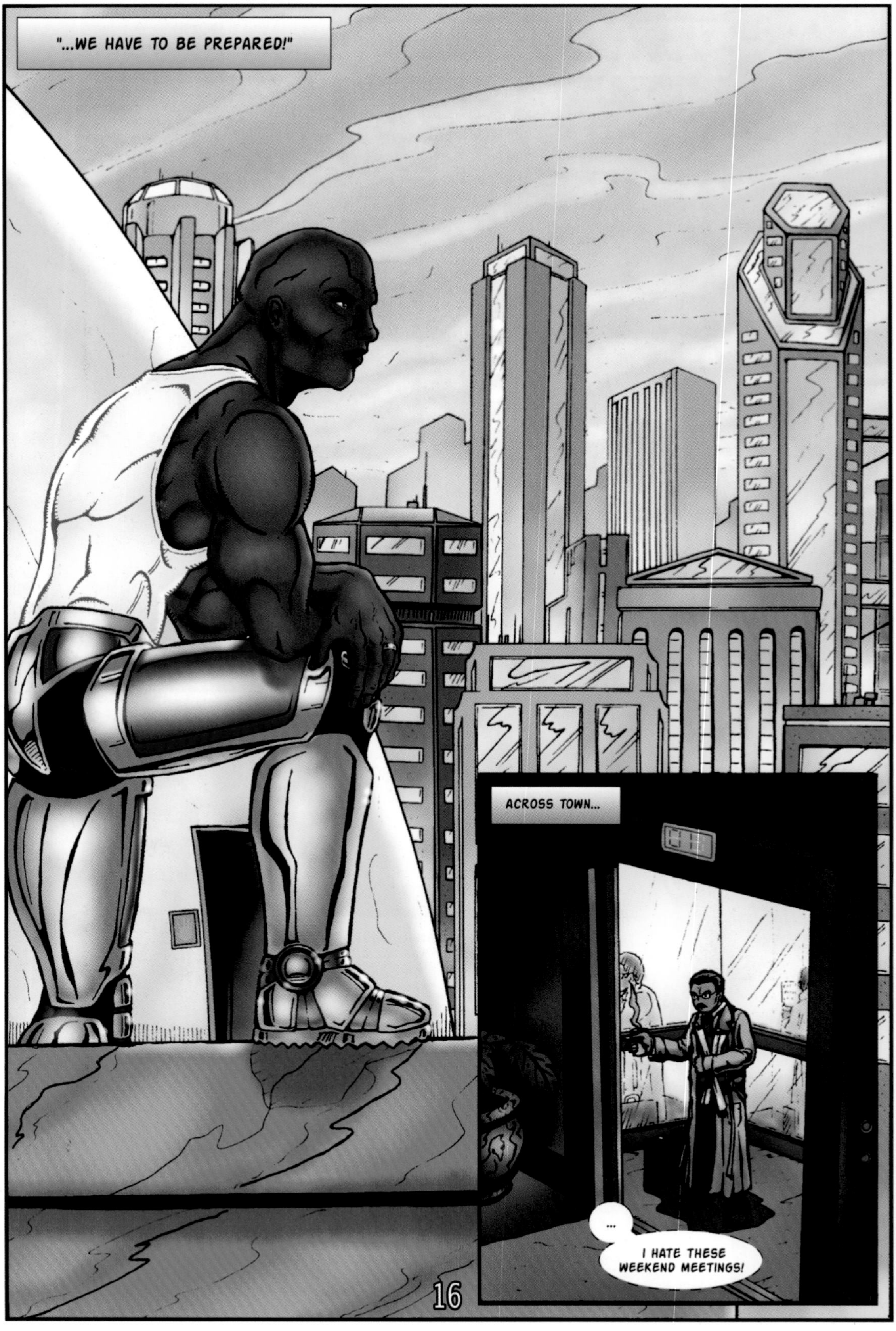
"...WE HAVE TO BE PREPARED!"
ACROSS TOWN...
...
I HATE THESE WEEKEND MEETINGS!

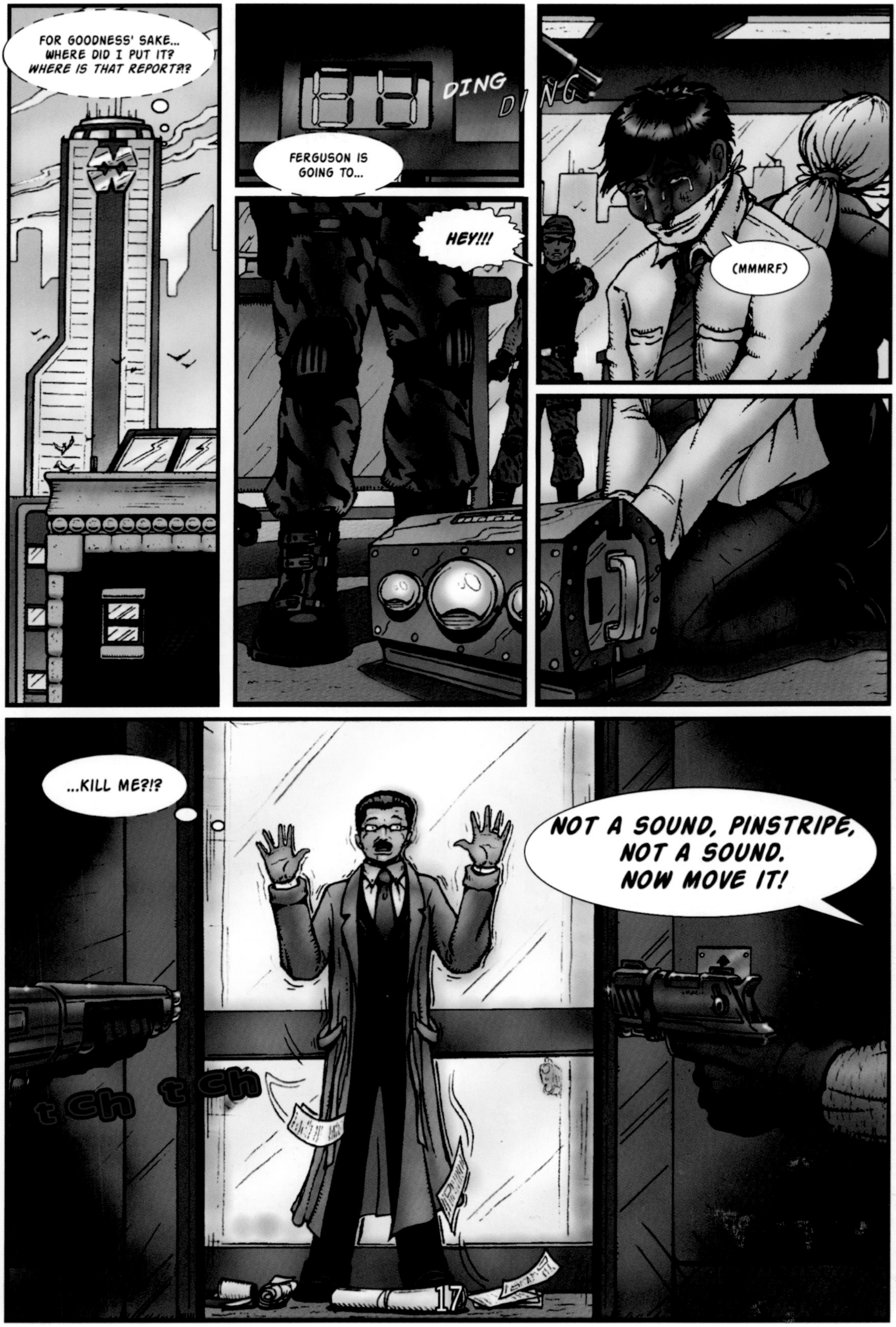
FOR GOODNESS' SAKE... WHERE DID I PUT IT? WHERE IS THAT REPORT?!?
DING
DING
FERGUSON IS GOING TO...
HEY!!!
(MMMRF)
...KILL ME?!?
NOT A SOUND, PINSTRIPE, NOT A SOUND. NOW MOVE IT!
t ch t ch

LATER THAT SAME DAY...

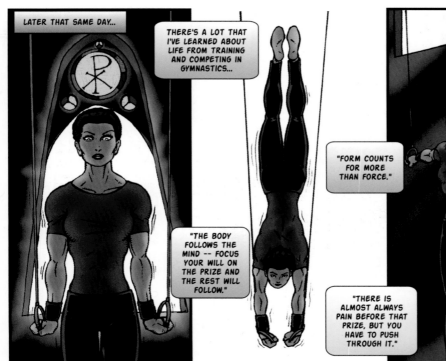

THERE'S A LOT THAT I'VE LEARNED ABOUT LIFE FROM TRAINING AND COMPETING IN GYMNASTICS...

"THE BODY FOLLOWS THE MIND -- FOCUS YOUR WILL ON THE PRIZE AND THE REST WILL FOLLOW."

"FORM COUNTS FOR MORE THAN FORCE."

"THERE IS ALMOST ALWAYS PAIN BEFORE THAT PRIZE, BUT YOU HAVE TO PUSH THROUGH IT."

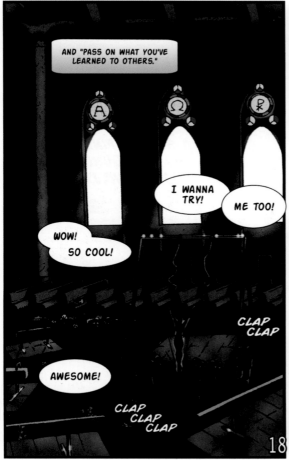

AND "PASS ON WHAT YOU'VE LEARNED TO OTHERS."

I WANNA TRY!

ME TOO!

WOW!

SO COOL!

CLAP CLAP

AWESOME!

CLAP CLAP CLAP

18

OK, NOW IT'S *YOUR* TURN TO TRY IT.

EACH OF YOU WORKS THE RINGS WITH ME FOR FIVE MINUTES.

WHEN YOU'RE NOT ON, YOU WORK THE HORSE OR THE BEAM WITH KEVIN AND LEANNE.

YES, MS. EMBRY.

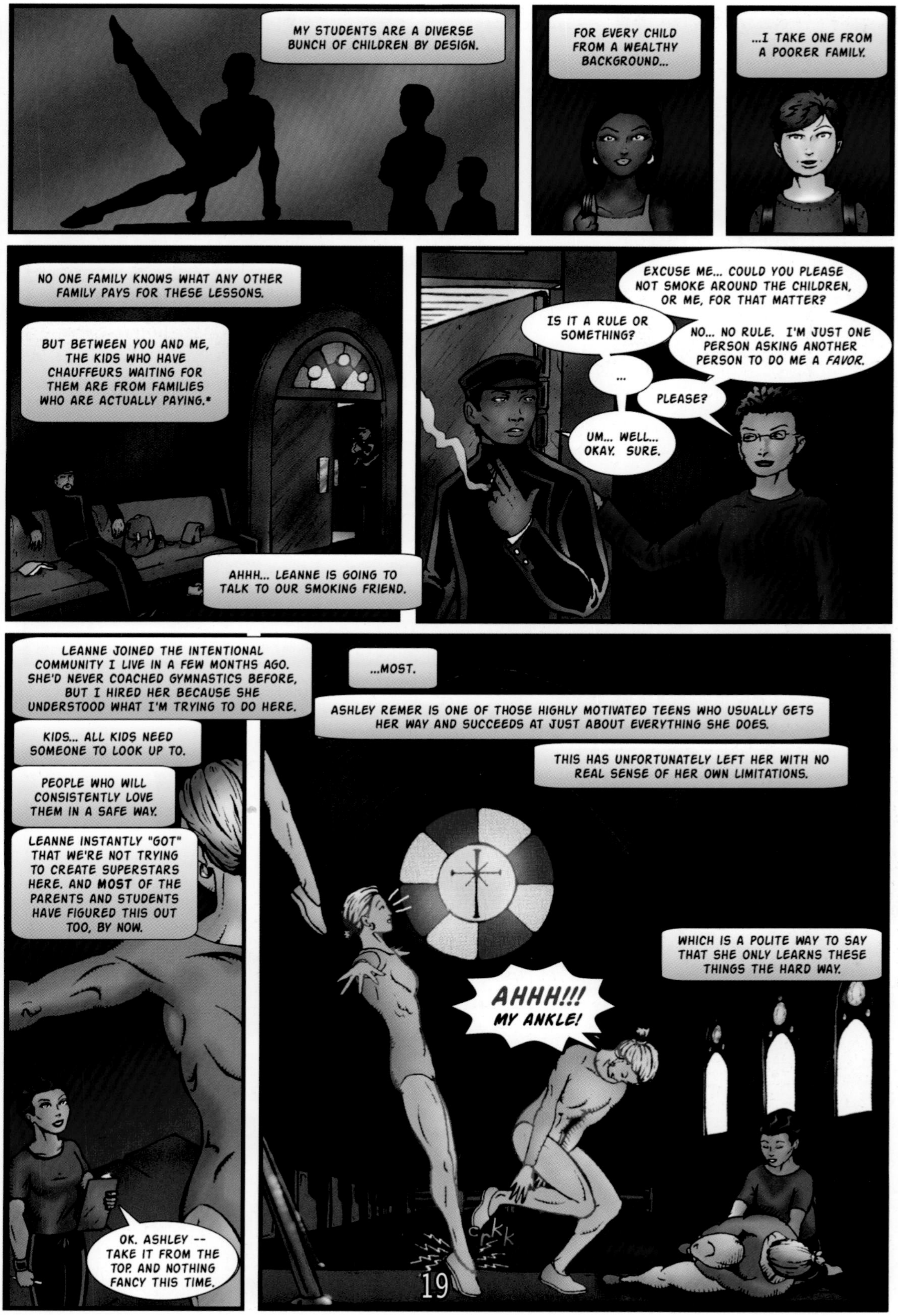
MY STUDENTS ARE A DIVERSE BUNCH OF CHILDREN BY DESIGN.
FOR EVERY CHILD FROM A WEALTHY BACKGROUND...
...I TAKE ONE FROM A POORER FAMILY.
NO ONE FAMILY KNOWS WHAT ANY OTHER FAMILY PAYS FOR THESE LESSONS.
BUT BETWEEN YOU AND ME, THE KIDS WHO HAVE CHAUFFEURS WAITING FOR THEM ARE FROM FAMILIES WHO ARE ACTUALLY PAYING.*
AHHH... LEANNE IS GOING TO TALK TO OUR SMOKING FRIEND.
EXCUSE ME... COULD YOU PLEASE NOT SMOKE AROUND THE CHILDREN, OR ME, FOR THAT MATTER?
IS IT A RULE OR SOMETHING?
NO... NO RULE. I'M JUST ONE PERSON ASKING ANOTHER PERSON TO DO ME A *FAVOR*.
...
PLEASE?
UM... WELL... OKAY. SURE.
LEANNE JOINED THE INTENTIONAL COMMUNITY I LIVE IN A FEW MONTHS AGO. SHE'D NEVER COACHED GYMNASTICS BEFORE, BUT I HIRED HER BECAUSE SHE UNDERSTOOD WHAT I'M TRYING TO DO HERE.
KIDS... ALL KIDS NEED SOMEONE TO LOOK UP TO.
PEOPLE WHO WILL CONSISTENTLY LOVE THEM IN A SAFE WAY.
LEANNE INSTANTLY "GOT" THAT WE'RE NOT TRYING TO CREATE SUPERSTARS HERE. AND **MOST** OF THE PARENTS AND STUDENTS HAVE FIGURED THIS OUT TOO, BY NOW.
OK. ASHLEY -- TAKE IT FROM THE TOP. AND NOTHING FANCY THIS TIME.
...MOST.
ASHLEY REMER IS ONE OF THOSE HIGHLY MOTIVATED TEENS WHO USUALLY GETS HER WAY AND SUCCEEDS AT JUST ABOUT EVERYTHING SHE DOES.
THIS HAS UNFORTUNATELY LEFT HER WITH NO REAL SENSE OF HER OWN LIMITATIONS.
WHICH IS A POLITE WAY TO SAY THAT SHE ONLY LEARNS THESE THINGS THE HARD WAY.
AHHH!!! MY ANKLE!
CRKK

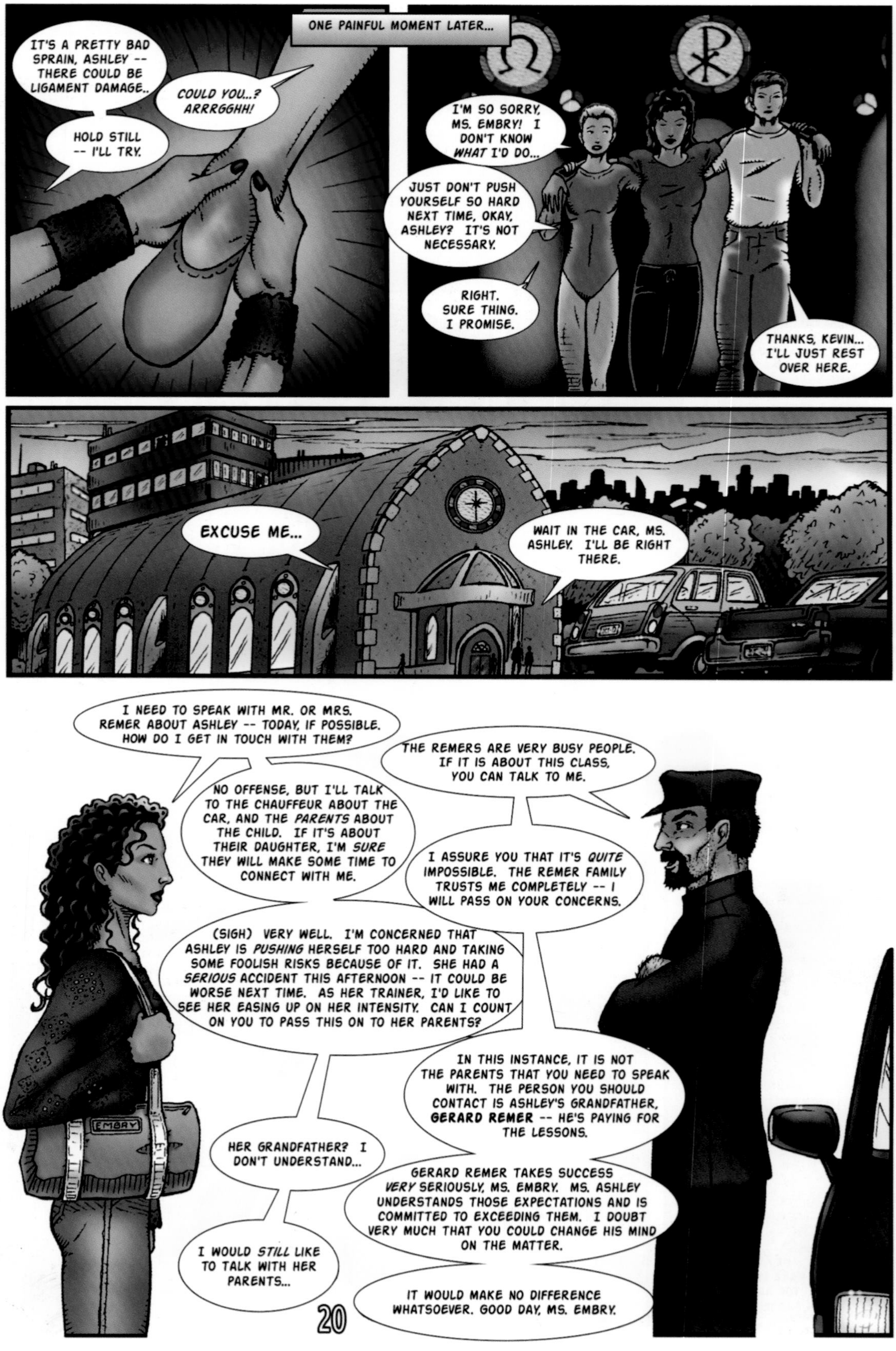
ONE PAINFUL MOMENT LATER...
IT'S A PRETTY BAD SPRAIN, ASHLEY -- THERE COULD BE LIGAMENT DAMAGE..
COULD YOU...? ARRRGGHH!
HOLD STILL -- I'LL TRY.
I'M SO SORRY, MS. EMBRY! I DON'T KNOW WHAT I'D DO...
JUST DON'T PUSH YOURSELF SO HARD NEXT TIME, OKAY, ASHLEY? IT'S NOT NECESSARY.
RIGHT. SURE THING. I PROMISE.
THANKS, KEVIN... I'LL JUST REST OVER HERE.
EXCUSE ME...
WAIT IN THE CAR, MS. ASHLEY. I'LL BE RIGHT THERE.
I NEED TO SPEAK WITH MR. OR MRS. REMER ABOUT ASHLEY -- TODAY, IF POSSIBLE. HOW DO I GET IN TOUCH WITH THEM?
THE REMERS ARE VERY BUSY PEOPLE. IF IT IS ABOUT THIS CLASS, YOU CAN TALK TO ME.
NO OFFENSE, BUT I'LL TALK TO THE CHAUFFEUR ABOUT THE CAR, AND THE PARENTS ABOUT THE CHILD. IF IT'S ABOUT THEIR DAUGHTER, I'M SURE THEY WILL MAKE SOME TIME TO CONNECT WITH ME.
I ASSURE YOU THAT IT'S QUITE IMPOSSIBLE. THE REMER FAMILY TRUSTS ME COMPLETELY -- I WILL PASS ON YOUR CONCERNS.
(SIGH) VERY WELL. I'M CONCERNED THAT ASHLEY IS PUSHING HERSELF TOO HARD AND TAKING SOME FOOLISH RISKS BECAUSE OF IT. SHE HAD A SERIOUS ACCIDENT THIS AFTERNOON -- IT COULD BE WORSE NEXT TIME. AS HER TRAINER, I'D LIKE TO SEE HER EASING UP ON HER INTENSITY. CAN I COUNT ON YOU TO PASS THIS ON TO HER PARENTS?
IN THIS INSTANCE, IT IS NOT THE PARENTS THAT YOU NEED TO SPEAK WITH. THE PERSON YOU SHOULD CONTACT IS ASHLEY'S GRANDFATHER, GERARD REMER -- HE'S PAYING FOR THE LESSONS.
HER GRANDFATHER? I DON'T UNDERSTAND...
GERARD REMER TAKES SUCCESS VERY SERIOUSLY, MS. EMBRY. MS. ASHLEY UNDERSTANDS THOSE EXPECTATIONS AND IS COMMITTED TO EXCEEDING THEM. I DOUBT VERY MUCH THAT YOU COULD CHANGE HIS MIND ON THE MATTER.
I WOULD STILL LIKE TO TALK WITH HER PARENTS...
IT WOULD MAKE NO DIFFERENCE WHATSOEVER. GOOD DAY, MS. EMBRY.
EMBRY

WELL, THAT DIDN'T GO VERY WELL.

VAROOOOM

LORD, I DON'T KNOW WHAT TO DO HERE.

PLEASE SHOW ME HOW TO REACH ASHLEY AND THE PEOPLE IN HER LIFE.

TEACH ME HOW TO RESPOND TO PEOPLE WHO ELEVATE ACCOMPLISHMENT OVER THE WELL-BEING OF OTHERS.

AMEN.

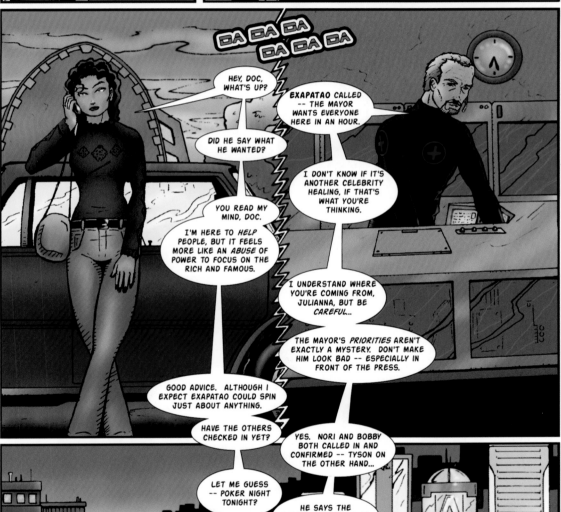

DA DA DA DA DA DA

HEY, DOC, WHAT'S UP?

EXAPATAO CALLED -- THE MAYOR WANTS EVERYONE HERE IN AN HOUR.

DID HE SAY WHAT HE WANTED?

I DON'T KNOW IF IT'S ANOTHER CELEBRITY HEALING, IF THAT'S WHAT YOU'RE THINKING.

YOU READ MY MIND, DOC.

I'M HERE TO HELP PEOPLE, BUT IT FEELS MORE LIKE AN ABUSE OF POWER TO FOCUS ON THE RICH AND FAMOUS.

I UNDERSTAND WHERE YOU'RE COMING FROM, JULIANNA, BUT BE CAREFUL...

THE MAYOR'S PRIORITIES AREN'T EXACTLY A MYSTERY. DON'T MAKE HIM LOOK BAD -- ESPECIALLY IN FRONT OF THE PRESS.

GOOD ADVICE. ALTHOUGH I EXPECT EXAPATAO COULD SPIN JUST ABOUT ANYTHING.

HAVE THE OTHERS CHECKED IN YET?

YES. NORI AND BOBBY BOTH CALLED IN AND CONFIRMED -- TYSON ON THE OTHER HAND...

LET ME GUESS -- POKER NIGHT TONIGHT?

HE SAYS THE AFTERNOON NAP HELPS HIS CONCENTRATION.

POOR BABY.

21

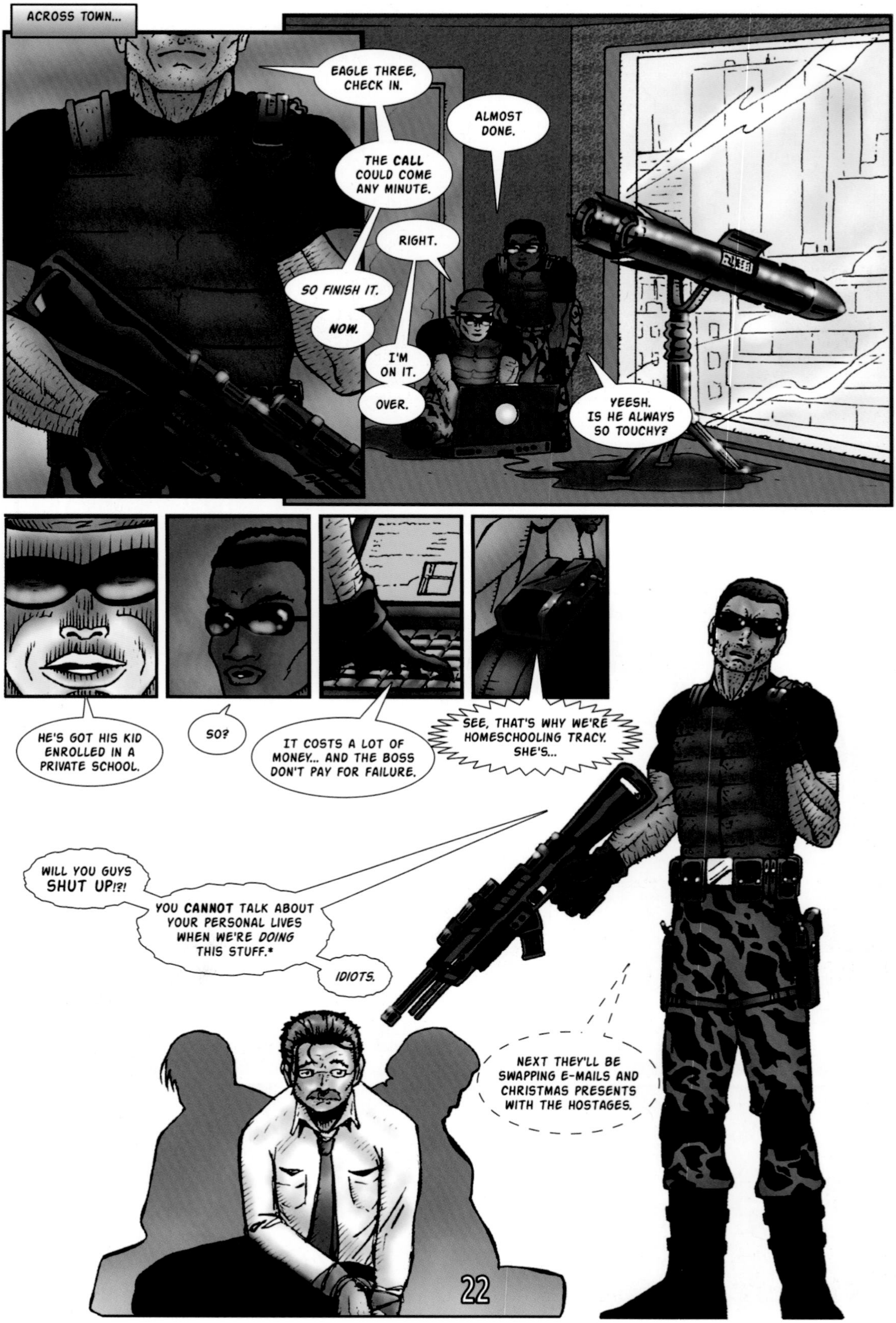
ACROSS TOWN...
EAGLE THREE, CHECK IN.
THE CALL COULD COME ANY MINUTE.
ALMOST DONE.
RIGHT.
SO FINISH IT.
NOW.
I'M ON IT.
OVER.
YEESH. IS HE ALWAYS SO TOUCHY?
HE'S GOT HIS KID ENROLLED IN A PRIVATE SCHOOL.
SO?
IT COSTS A LOT OF MONEY... AND THE BOSS DON'T PAY FOR FAILURE.
SEE, THAT'S WHY WE'RE HOMESCHOOLING TRACY. SHE'S...
WILL YOU GUYS SHUT UP!?!
YOU CANNOT TALK ABOUT YOUR PERSONAL LIVES WHEN WE'RE DOING THIS STUFF.*
IDIOTS.
NEXT THEY'LL BE SWAPPING E-MAILS AND CHRISTMAS PRESENTS WITH THE HOSTAGES.

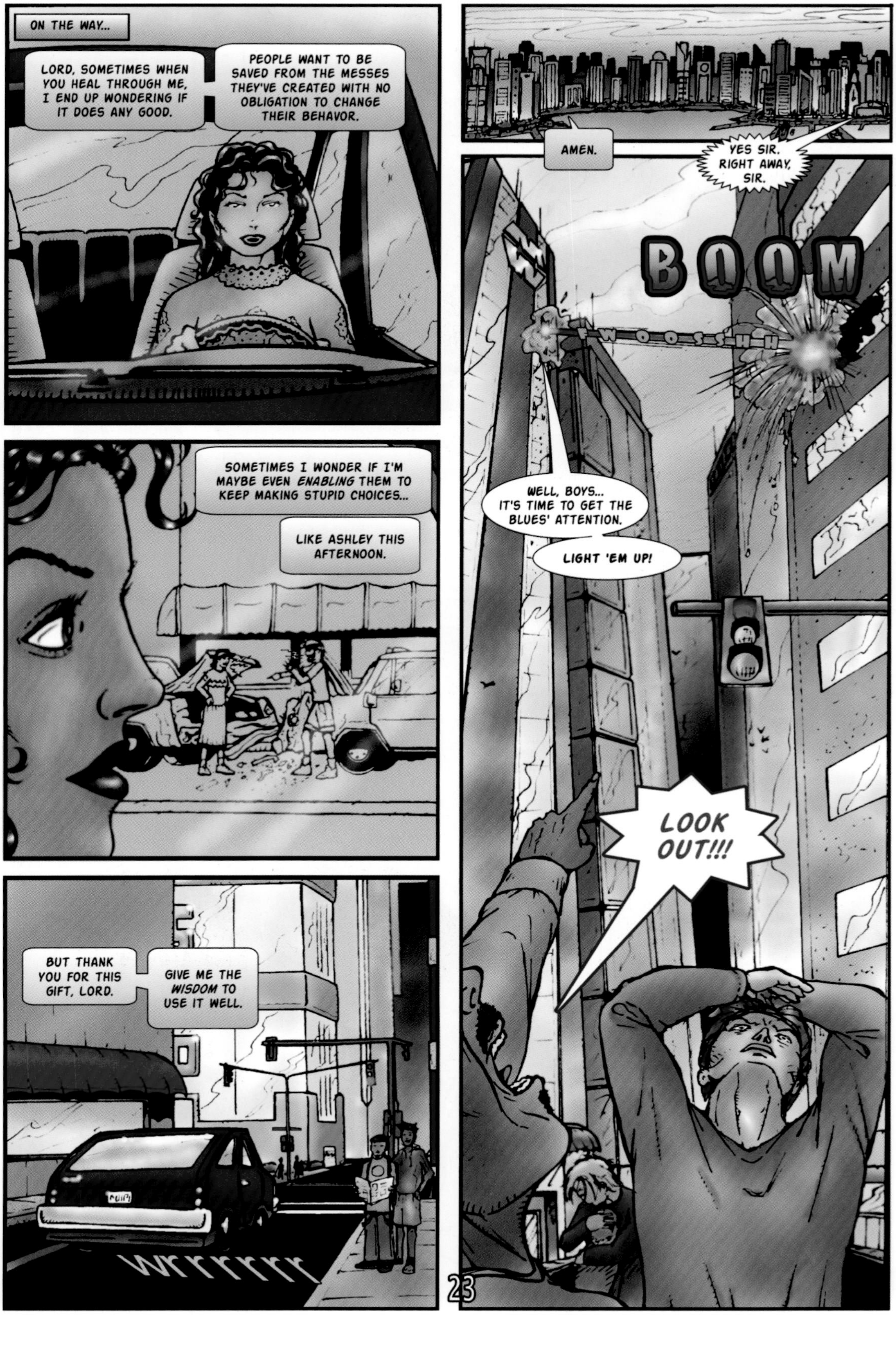
ON THE WAY...
LORD, SOMETIMES WHEN YOU HEAL THROUGH ME, I END UP WONDERING IF IT DOES ANY GOOD.
PEOPLE WANT TO BE SAVED FROM THE MESSES THEY'VE CREATED WITH NO OBLIGATION TO CHANGE THEIR BEHAVOR.
SOMETIMES I WONDER IF I'M MAYBE EVEN *ENABLING* THEM TO KEEP MAKING STUPID CHOICES...
LIKE ASHLEY THIS AFTERNOON.
BUT THANK YOU FOR THIS GIFT, LORD.
GIVE ME THE *WISDOM* TO USE IT WELL.
wrrrrrr
AMEN.
YES SIR. RIGHT AWAY, SIR.
BOOM
FWOOSSHH
WELL, BOYS... IT'S TIME TO GET THE BLUES' ATTENTION.
LIGHT 'EM UP!
LOOK OUT!!!

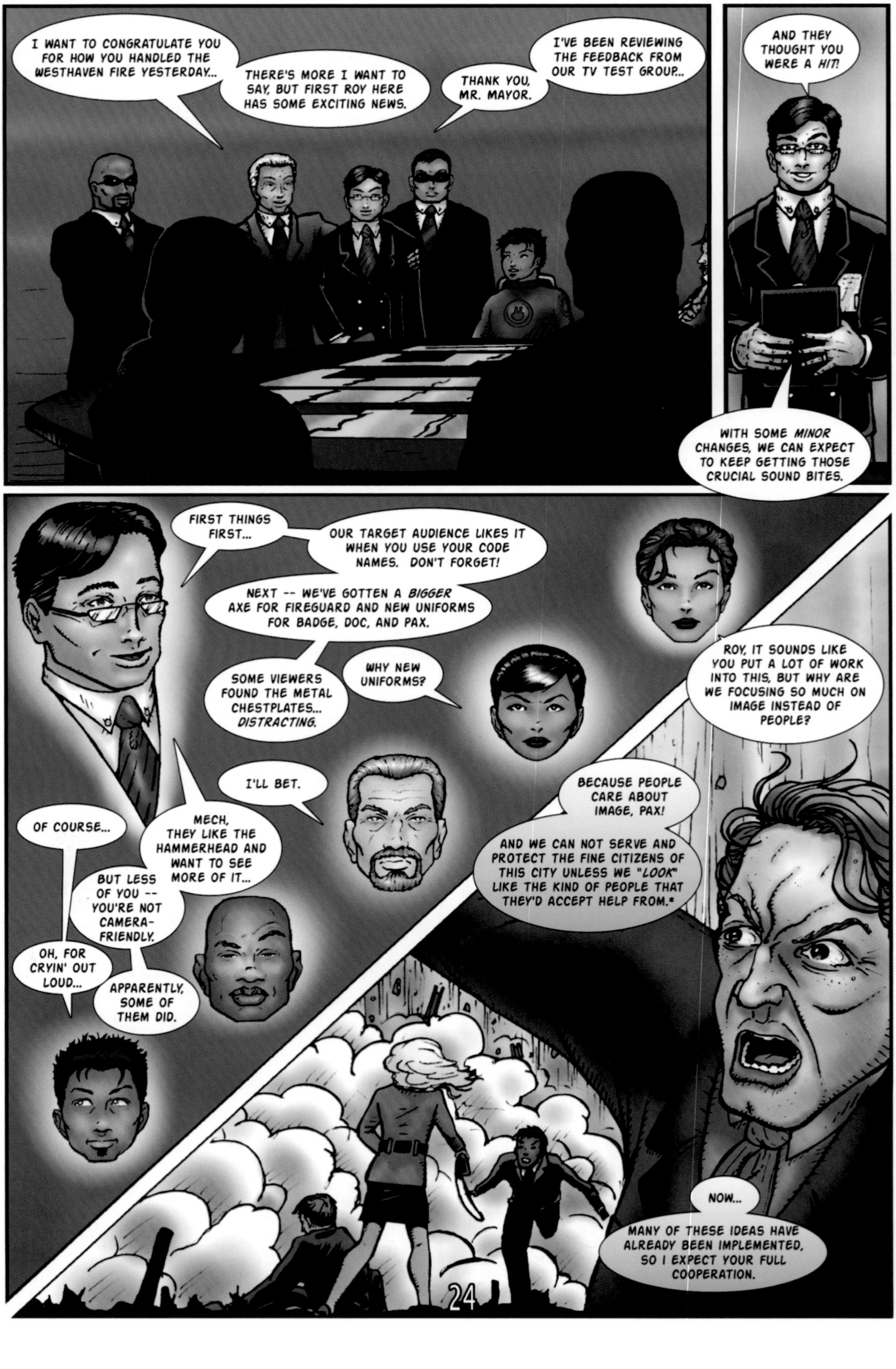
I WANT TO CONGRATULATE YOU FOR HOW YOU HANDLED THE WESTHAVEN FIRE YESTERDAY...
THERE'S MORE I WANT TO SAY, BUT FIRST ROY HERE HAS SOME EXCITING NEWS.
THANK YOU, MR. MAYOR.
I'VE BEEN REVIEWING THE FEEDBACK FROM OUR TV TEST GROUP...
AND THEY THOUGHT YOU WERE A *HIT*!
WITH SOME *MINOR* CHANGES, WE CAN EXPECT TO KEEP GETTING THOSE CRUCIAL SOUND BITES.
FIRST THINGS FIRST...
OUR TARGET AUDIENCE LIKES IT WHEN YOU USE YOUR CODE NAMES. DON'T FORGET!
NEXT -- WE'VE GOTTEN A *BIGGER* AXE FOR FIREGUARD AND NEW UNIFORMS FOR BADGE, DOC, AND PAX.
WHY NEW UNIFORMS?
SOME VIEWERS FOUND THE METAL CHESTPLATES... *DISTRACTING*.
I'LL BET.
MECH, THEY LIKE THE HAMMERHEAD AND WANT TO SEE MORE OF IT...
OF COURSE...
BUT LESS OF YOU -- YOU'RE NOT CAMERA-FRIENDLY.
OH, FOR CRYIN' OUT LOUD...
APPARENTLY, SOME OF THEM DID.
ROY, IT SOUNDS LIKE YOU PUT A LOT OF WORK INTO THIS, BUT WHY ARE WE FOCUSING SO MUCH ON IMAGE INSTEAD OF PEOPLE?
BECAUSE PEOPLE CARE ABOUT IMAGE, PAX!
AND WE CAN NOT SERVE AND PROTECT THE FINE CITIZENS OF THIS CITY UNLESS WE "*LOOK*" LIKE THE KIND OF PEOPLE THAT THEY'D ACCEPT HELP FROM.*
NOW...
MANY OF THESE IDEAS HAVE ALREADY BEEN IMPLEMENTED, SO I EXPECT YOUR FULL COOPERATION.

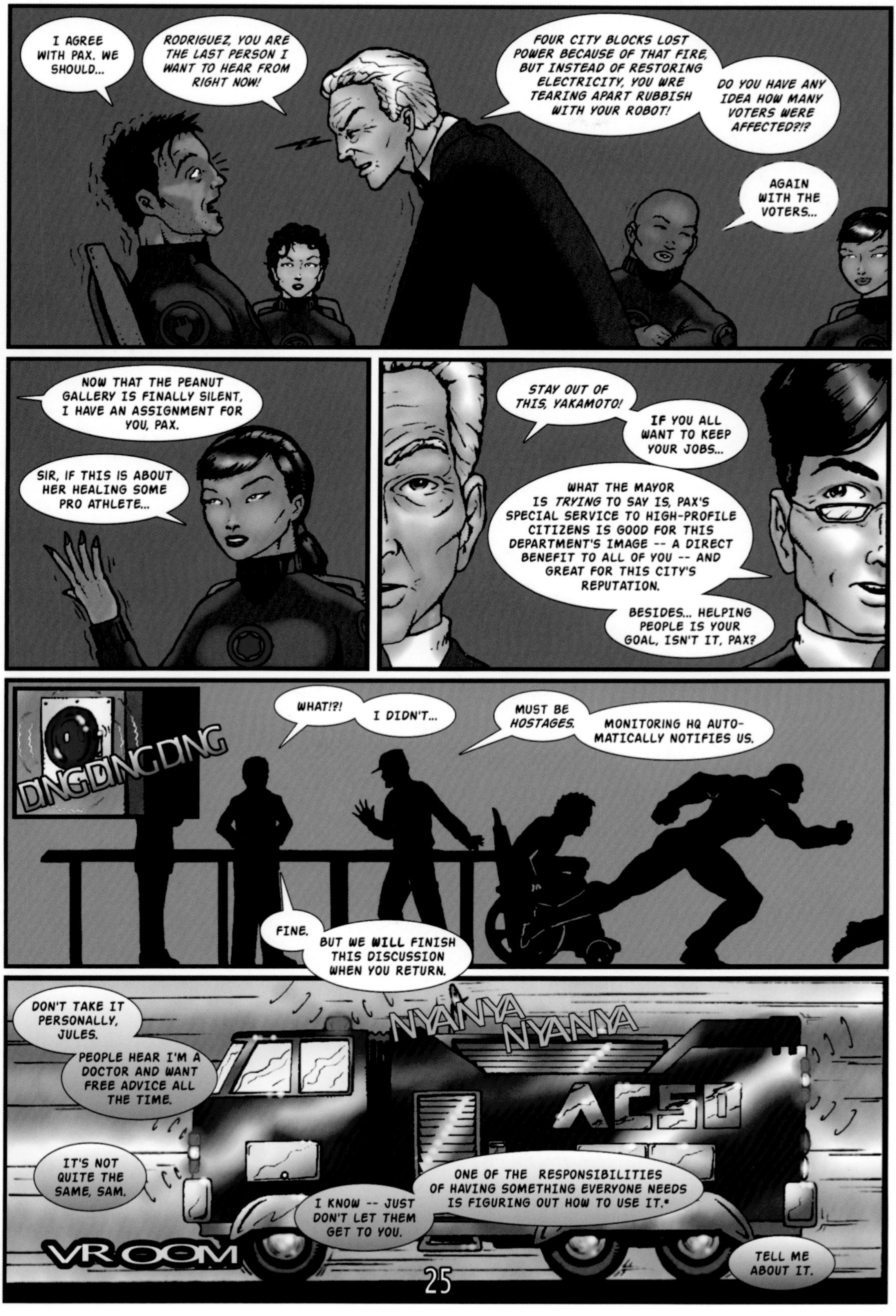
I AGREE WITH PAX. WE SHOULD...
RODRIGUEZ, YOU ARE THE LAST PERSON I WANT TO HEAR FROM RIGHT NOW!
FOUR CITY BLOCKS LOST POWER BECAUSE OF THAT FIRE, BUT INSTEAD OF RESTORING ELECTRICITY, YOU WRE TEARING APART RUBBISH WITH YOUR ROBOT!
DO YOU HAVE ANY IDEA HOW MANY VOTERS WERE AFFECTED?!?
AGAIN WITH THE VOTERS...
NOW THAT THE PEANUT GALLERY IS FINALLY SILENT, I HAVE AN ASSIGNMENT FOR YOU, PAX.
SIR, IF THIS IS ABOUT HER HEALING SOME PRO ATHLETE...
STAY OUT OF THIS, YAKAMOTO!
IF YOU ALL WANT TO KEEP YOUR JOBS...
WHAT THE MAYOR IS TRYING TO SAY IS, PAX'S SPECIAL SERVICE TO HIGH-PROFILE CITIZENS IS GOOD FOR THIS DEPARTMENT'S IMAGE -- A DIRECT BENEFIT TO ALL OF YOU -- AND GREAT FOR THIS CITY'S REPUTATION.
BESIDES... HELPING PEOPLE IS YOUR GOAL, ISN'T IT, PAX?
DINGDINGDING
WHAT!?!
I DIDN'T...
MUST BE HOSTAGES.
MONITORING HQ AUTOMATICALLY NOTIFIES US.
FINE.
BUT WE WILL FINISH THIS DISCUSSION WHEN YOU RETURN.
NYANYA NYANYA
ACSD
DON'T TAKE IT PERSONALLY, JULES.
PEOPLE HEAR I'M A DOCTOR AND WANT FREE ADVICE ALL THE TIME.
IT'S NOT QUITE THE SAME, SAM.
I KNOW -- JUST DON'T LET THEM GET TO YOU.
ONE OF THE RESPONSIBILITIES OF HAVING SOMETHING EVERYONE NEEDS IS FIGURING OUT HOW TO USE IT.*
TELL ME ABOUT IT.
VROOM

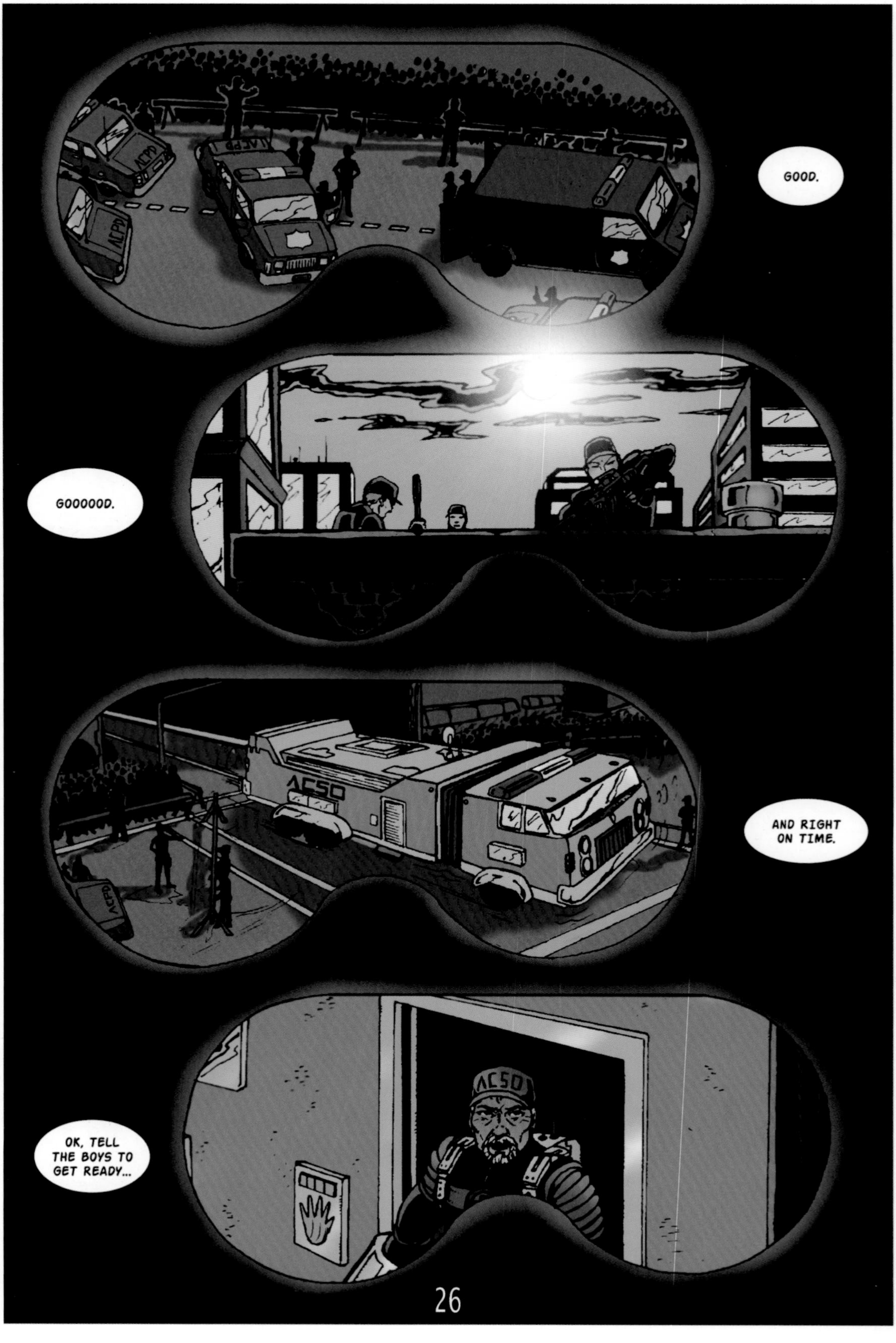
GOOD.
GOOOOOD.
AND RIGHT ON TIME.
OK, TELL THE BOYS TO GET READY...

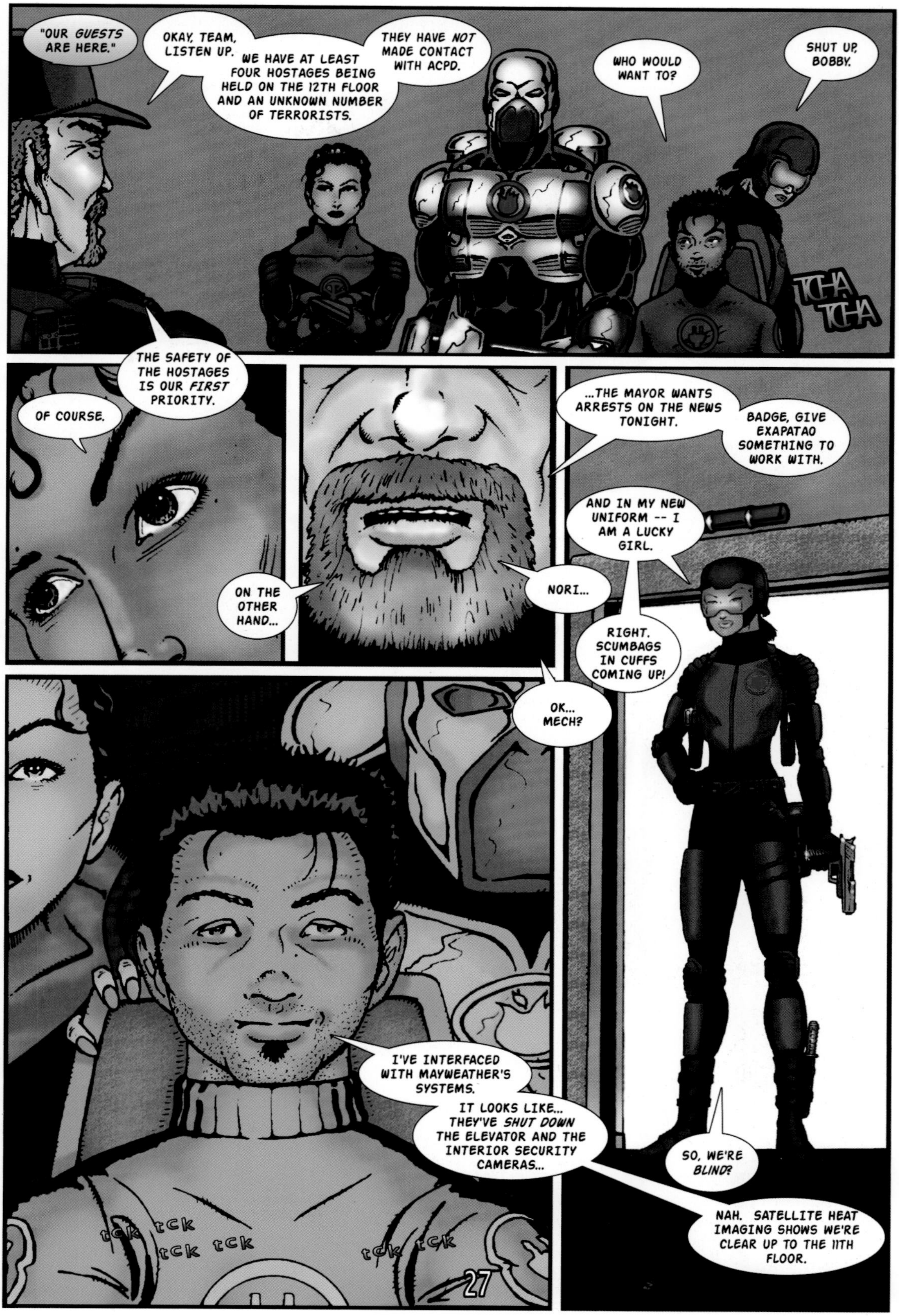
"OUR GUESTS ARE HERE."
OKAY, TEAM, LISTEN UP.
WE HAVE AT LEAST FOUR HOSTAGES BEING HELD ON THE 12TH FLOOR AND AN UNKNOWN NUMBER OF TERRORISTS.
THEY HAVE NOT MADE CONTACT WITH ACPD.
WHO WOULD WANT TO?
SHUT UP, BOBBY.
TCHA TCHA
THE SAFETY OF THE HOSTAGES IS OUR FIRST PRIORITY.
OF COURSE.
ON THE OTHER HAND...
NORI...
...THE MAYOR WANTS ARRESTS ON THE NEWS TONIGHT.
BADGE, GIVE EXAPATAO SOMETHING TO WORK WITH.
AND IN MY NEW UNIFORM -- I AM A LUCKY GIRL.
RIGHT. SCUMBAGS IN CUFFS COMING UP!
OK... MECH?
I'VE INTERFACED WITH MAYWEATHER'S SYSTEMS.
IT LOOKS LIKE... THEY'VE SHUT DOWN THE ELEVATOR AND THE INTERIOR SECURITY CAMERAS...
SO, WE'RE BLIND?
NAH. SATELLITE HEAT IMAGING SHOWS WE'RE CLEAR UP TO THE 11TH FLOOR.
tck tck tck tck tck tck

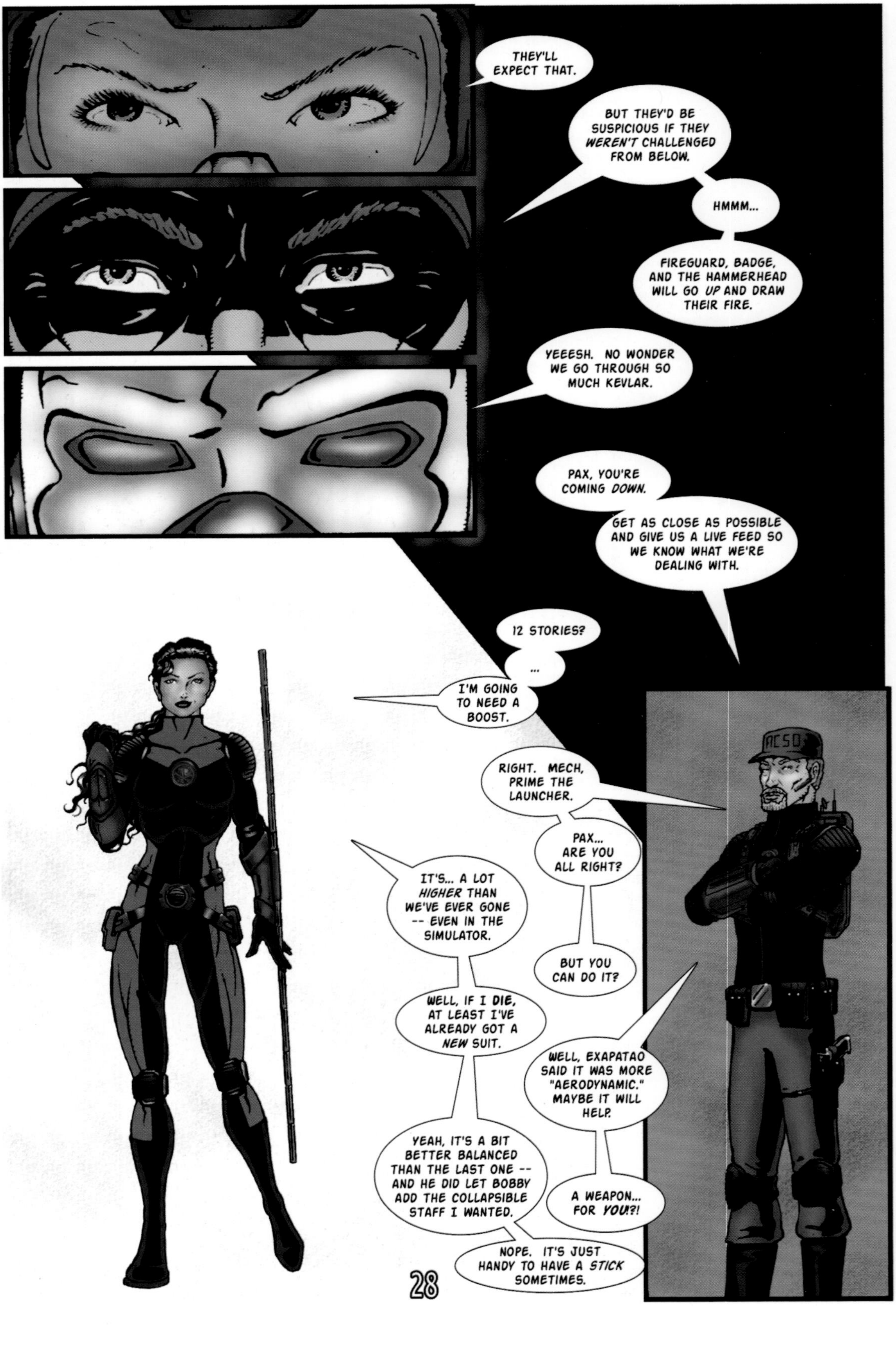
THEY'LL EXPECT THAT.
BUT THEY'D BE SUSPICIOUS IF THEY *WEREN'T* CHALLENGED FROM BELOW.
HMMM...
FIREGUARD, BADGE, AND THE HAMMERHEAD WILL GO *UP* AND DRAW THEIR FIRE.
YEEESH. NO WONDER WE GO THROUGH SO MUCH KEVLAR.
PAX, YOU'RE COMING *DOWN.*
GET AS CLOSE AS POSSIBLE AND GIVE US A LIVE FEED SO WE KNOW WHAT WE'RE DEALING WITH.
12 STORIES?
...
I'M GOING TO NEED A BOOST.
RIGHT. MECH, PRIME THE LAUNCHER.
PAX... ARE YOU ALL RIGHT?
IT'S... A LOT *HIGHER* THAN WE'VE EVER GONE -- EVEN IN THE SIMULATOR.
BUT YOU CAN DO IT?
WELL, IF I **DIE,** AT LEAST I'VE ALREADY GOT A *NEW* SUIT.
WELL, EXAPATAO SAID IT WAS MORE "AERODYNAMIC." MAYBE IT WILL HELP.
YEAH, IT'S A BIT BETTER BALANCED THAN THE LAST ONE -- AND HE DID LET BOBBY ADD THE COLLAPSIBLE STAFF I WANTED.
A WEAPON... FOR ***YOU***?!
NOPE. IT'S JUST HANDY TO HAVE A *STICK* SOMETIMES.
ACSO

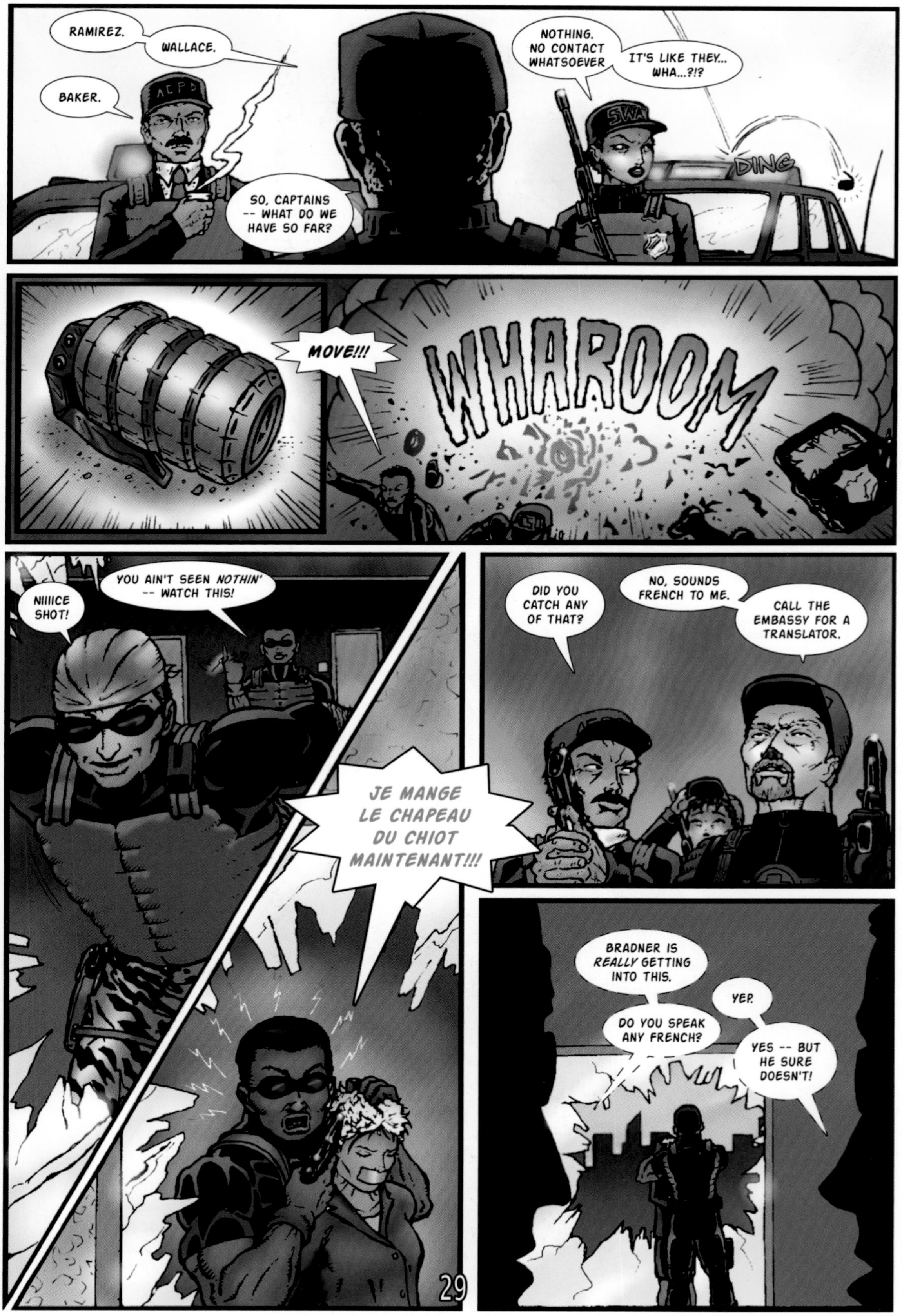
RAMIREZ.
WALLACE.
BAKER.
SO, CAPTAINS -- WHAT DO WE HAVE SO FAR?
NOTHING. NO CONTACT WHATSOEVER
IT'S LIKE THEY... WHA...?!?
DING
MOVE!!!
WHAROOM
NIIIICE SHOT!
YOU AIN'T SEEN *NOTHIN'* -- WATCH THIS!
JE MANGE LE CHAPEAU DU CHIOT MAINTENANT!!!
DID YOU CATCH ANY OF THAT?
NO, SOUNDS FRENCH TO ME.
CALL THE EMBASSY FOR A TRANSLATOR.
BRADNER IS *REALLY* GETTING INTO THIS.
YEP.
DO YOU SPEAK ANY FRENCH?
YES -- BUT HE SURE DOESN'T!

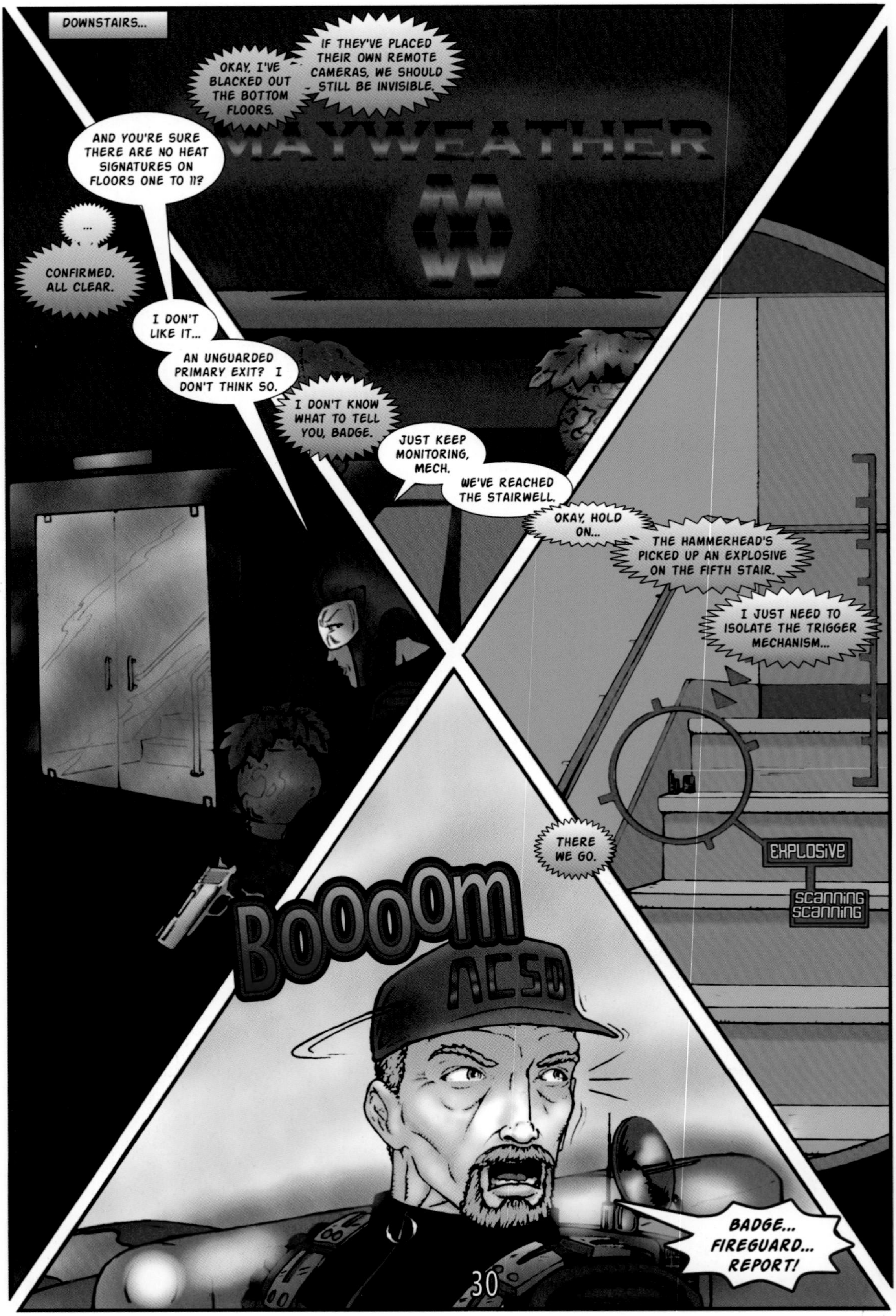
DOWNSTAIRS...
OKAY, I'VE BLACKED OUT THE BOTTOM FLOORS.
IF THEY'VE PLACED THEIR OWN REMOTE CAMERAS, WE SHOULD STILL BE INVISIBLE.
MAYWEATHER
AND YOU'RE SURE THERE ARE NO HEAT SIGNATURES ON FLOORS ONE TO 11?
...
CONFIRMED. ALL CLEAR.
I DON'T LIKE IT...
AN UNGUARDED PRIMARY EXIT? I DON'T THINK SO.
I DON'T KNOW WHAT TO TELL YOU, BADGE.
JUST KEEP MONITORING, MECH.
WE'VE REACHED THE STAIRWELL.
OKAY, HOLD ON...
THE HAMMERHEAD'S PICKED UP AN EXPLOSIVE ON THE FIFTH STAIR.
I JUST NEED TO ISOLATE THE TRIGGER MECHANISM...
EXPLOSIVE
SCANNING
SCANNING
THERE WE GO.
BOOOOOM
ACSD
BADGE... FIREGUARD... REPORT!

HEH HEH. SCRATCH A FEW OF AVALON CITY'S FINEST.

OKAY, PEOPLE -- LET'S KEEP TO THE SCHEDULE!

NO... WE'RE FINE, DOC...

THAT WAS RECKLESS, BOBBY!

YOU JUST DON'T WANT TO WASTE A GOOD EXPLOSIVE LIKE THAT.

BESIDES, NOW THEY THINK WE'RE WALL GRAVY!

GROSS. SAVE IT FOR YOUR GAMES.

IN MY GAMES, I'D USE THESE.

CHING

A LADDER, MECH.

JUST MAKE A LADDER, OKAY?

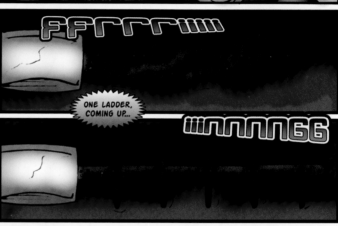

FFRRRRiiiii

ONE LADDER, COMING UP...

iiiNNNNN66

FIREGUARD, CAN YOU PULL THE HAMMERHEAD UP WHEN YOU FINISH HELPING BADGE?

LET'S... UGH... LEAVE HIM.*

DON'T TEMPT ME.

CREEAAAKK

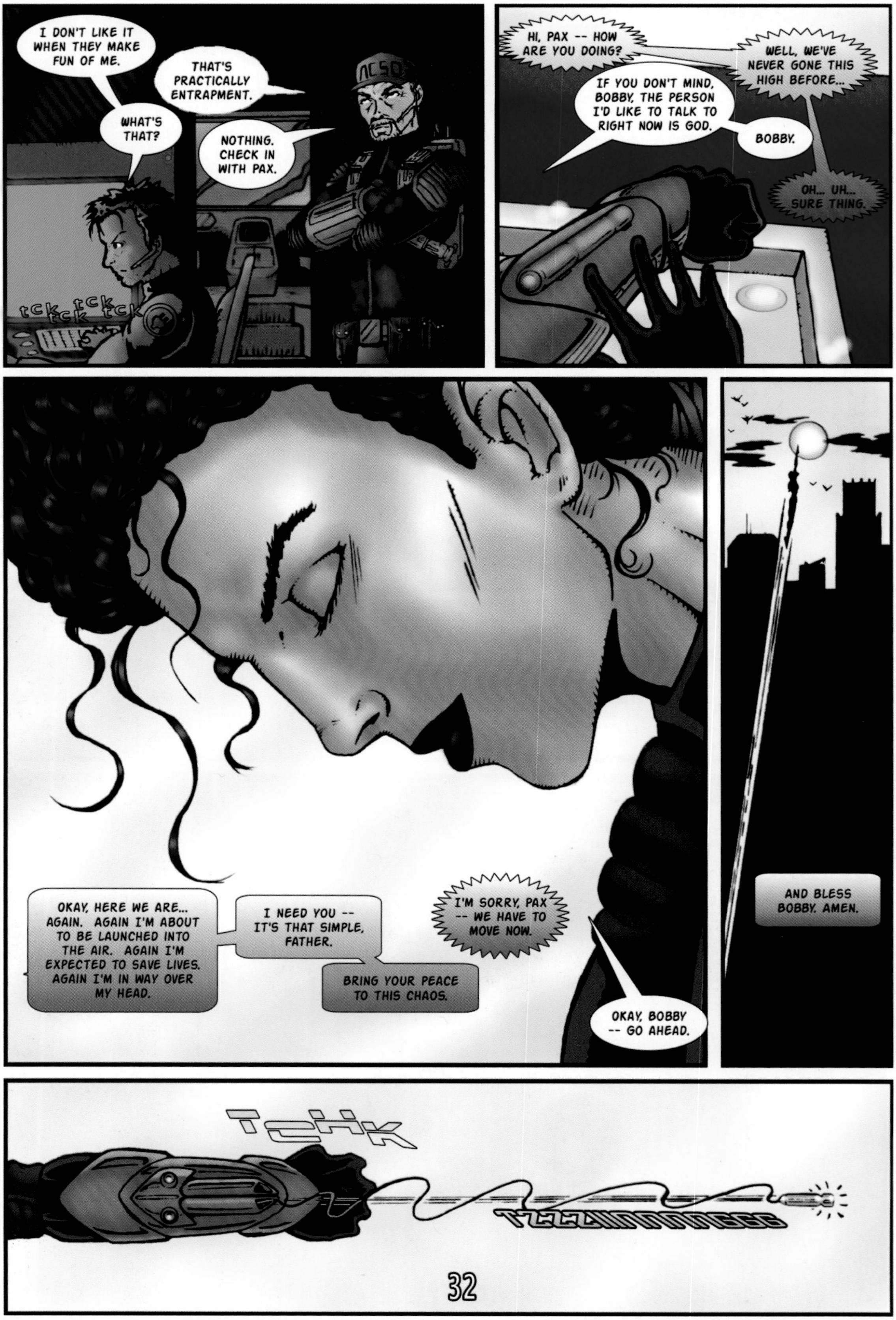
I DON'T LIKE IT WHEN THEY MAKE FUN OF ME.
THAT'S PRACTICALLY ENTRAPMENT.
WHAT'S THAT?
NOTHING. CHECK IN WITH PAX.
tck tck tck tck
HI, PAX -- HOW ARE YOU DOING?
WELL, WE'VE NEVER GONE THIS HIGH BEFORE...
IF YOU DON'T MIND, BOBBY, THE PERSON I'D LIKE TO TALK TO RIGHT NOW IS GOD.
BOBBY.
OH... UH... SURE THING.
OKAY, HERE WE ARE... AGAIN. AGAIN I'M ABOUT TO BE LAUNCHED INTO THE AIR. AGAIN I'M EXPECTED TO SAVE LIVES. AGAIN I'M IN WAY OVER MY HEAD.
I NEED YOU -- IT'S THAT SIMPLE, FATHER.
BRING YOUR PEACE TO THIS CHAOS.
I'M SORRY, PAX -- WE HAVE TO MOVE NOW.
OKAY, BOBBY -- GO AHEAD.
AND BLESS BOBBY. AMEN.
TCHK
TZZZIIINNNNGGG

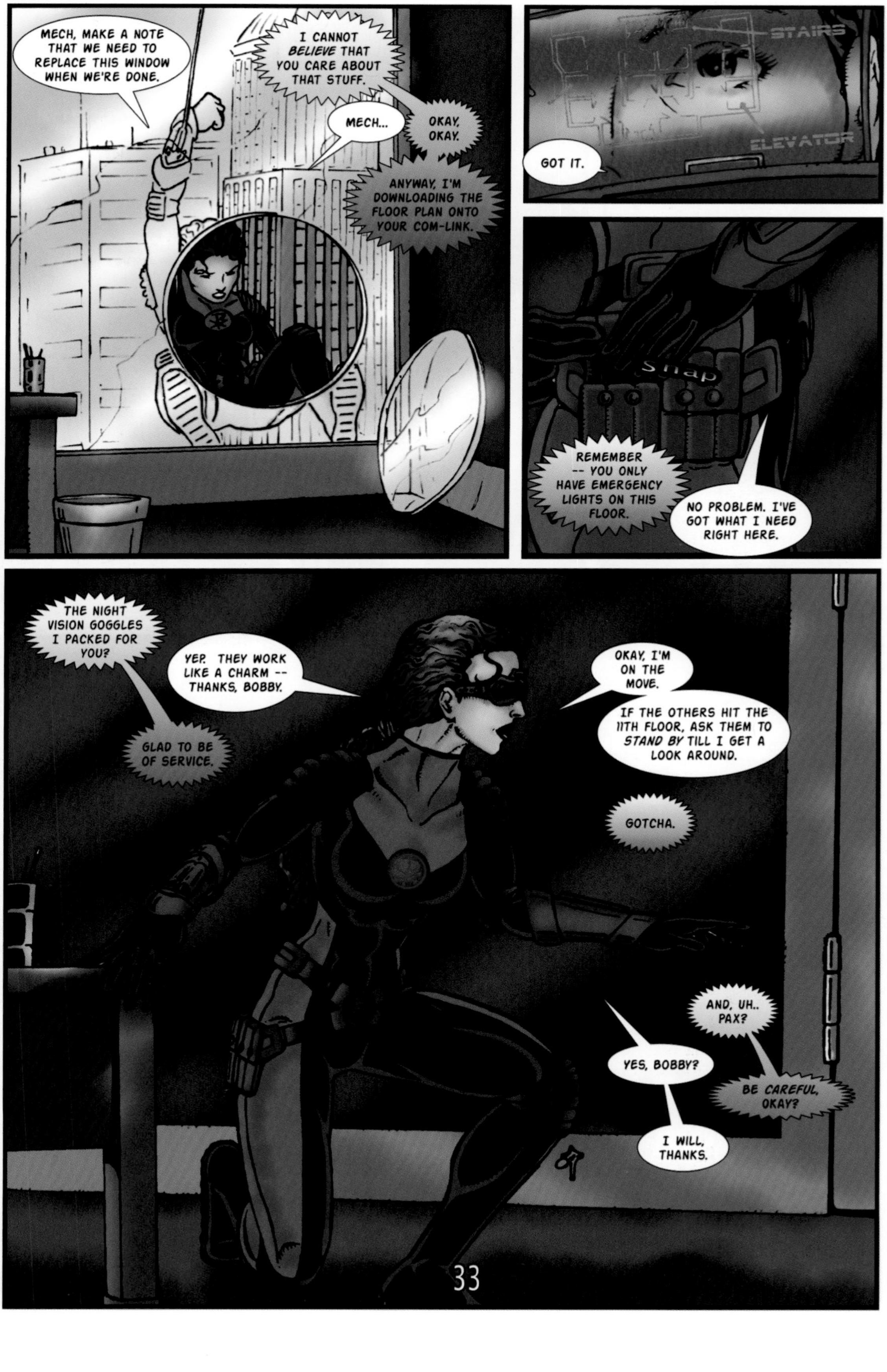
MECH, MAKE A NOTE THAT WE NEED TO REPLACE THIS WINDOW WHEN WE'RE DONE.
I CANNOT *BELIEVE* THAT YOU CARE ABOUT THAT STUFF.
MECH...
OKAY, OKAY.
ANYWAY, I'M DOWNLOADING THE FLOOR PLAN ONTO YOUR COM-LINK.
STAIRS
ELEVATOR
GOT IT.
SNAP
REMEMBER -- YOU ONLY HAVE EMERGENCY LIGHTS ON THIS FLOOR.
NO PROBLEM. I'VE GOT WHAT I NEED RIGHT HERE.
THE NIGHT VISION GOGGLES I PACKED FOR YOU?
YEP. THEY WORK LIKE A CHARM -- THANKS, BOBBY.
GLAD TO BE OF SERVICE.
OKAY, I'M ON THE MOVE.
IF THE OTHERS HIT THE 11TH FLOOR, ASK THEM TO *STAND BY* TILL I GET A LOOK AROUND.
GOTCHA.
AND, UH.. PAX?
YES, BOBBY?
BE *CAREFUL*, OKAY?
I WILL, THANKS.

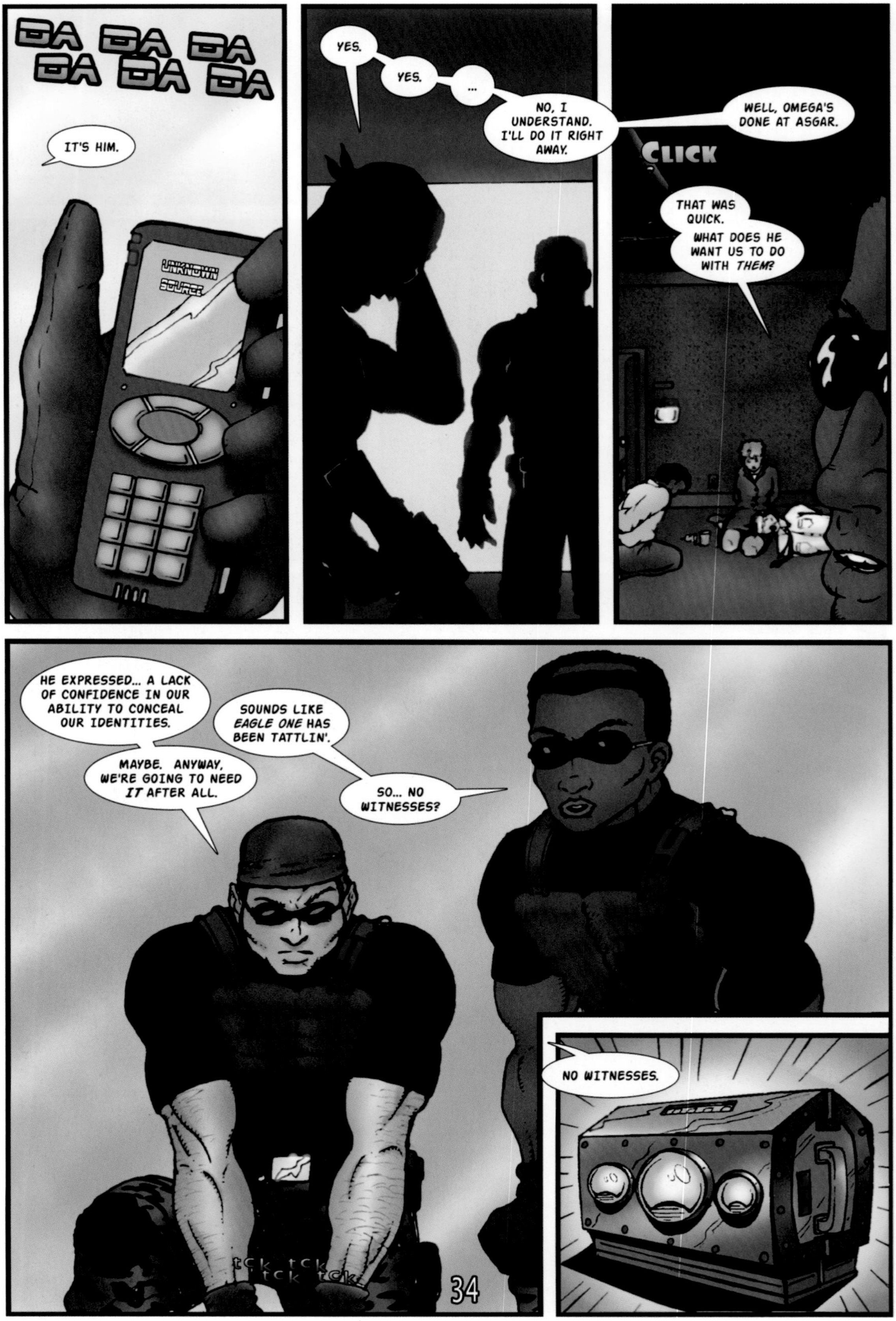
DA DA DA
DA DA DA
IT'S HIM.
UNKNOWN SOURCE
YES.
YES.
...
NO, I UNDERSTAND. I'LL DO IT RIGHT AWAY.
WELL, OMEGA'S DONE AT ASGAR.
CLICK
THAT WAS QUICK.
WHAT DOES HE WANT US TO DO WITH *THEM*?
HE EXPRESSED... A LACK OF CONFIDENCE IN OUR ABILITY TO CONCEAL OUR IDENTITIES.
SOUNDS LIKE *EAGLE ONE* HAS BEEN TATTLIN'.
MAYBE. ANYWAY, WE'RE GOING TO NEED *IT* AFTER ALL.
SO... NO WITNESSES?
NO WITNESSES.
tck tck
tck tck

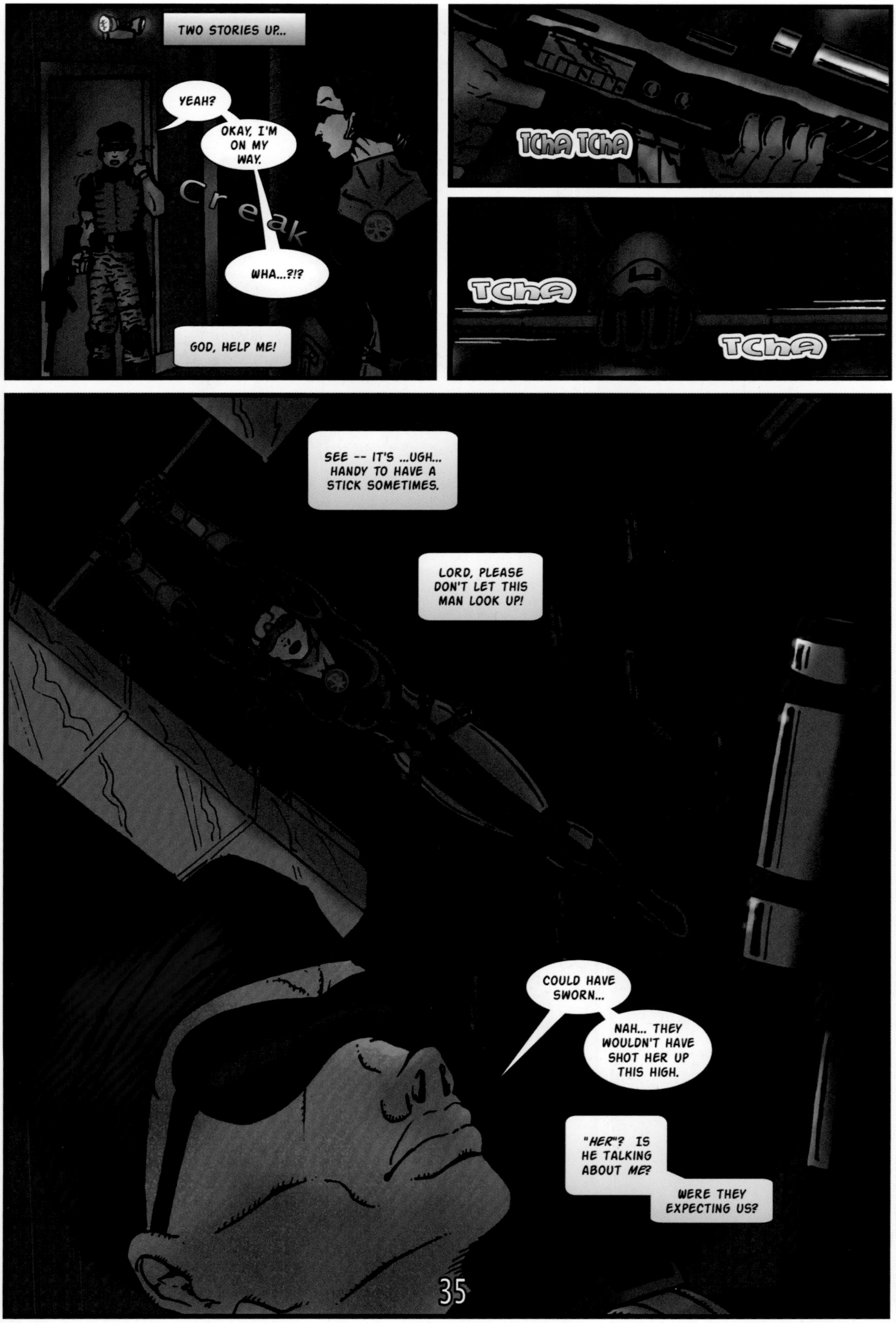

TWO STORIES UP...
YEAH?
OKAY, I'M ON MY WAY.
Creak
WHA...?!?
GOD, HELP ME!
TCHA TCHA
TCHA
TCHA
SEE -- IT'S ...UGH... HANDY TO HAVE A STICK SOMETIMES.
LORD, PLEASE DON'T LET THIS MAN LOOK UP!
COULD HAVE SWORN...
NAH... THEY WOULDN'T HAVE SHOT HER UP THIS HIGH.
"HER"? IS HE TALKING ABOUT ME?
WERE THEY EXPECTING US?

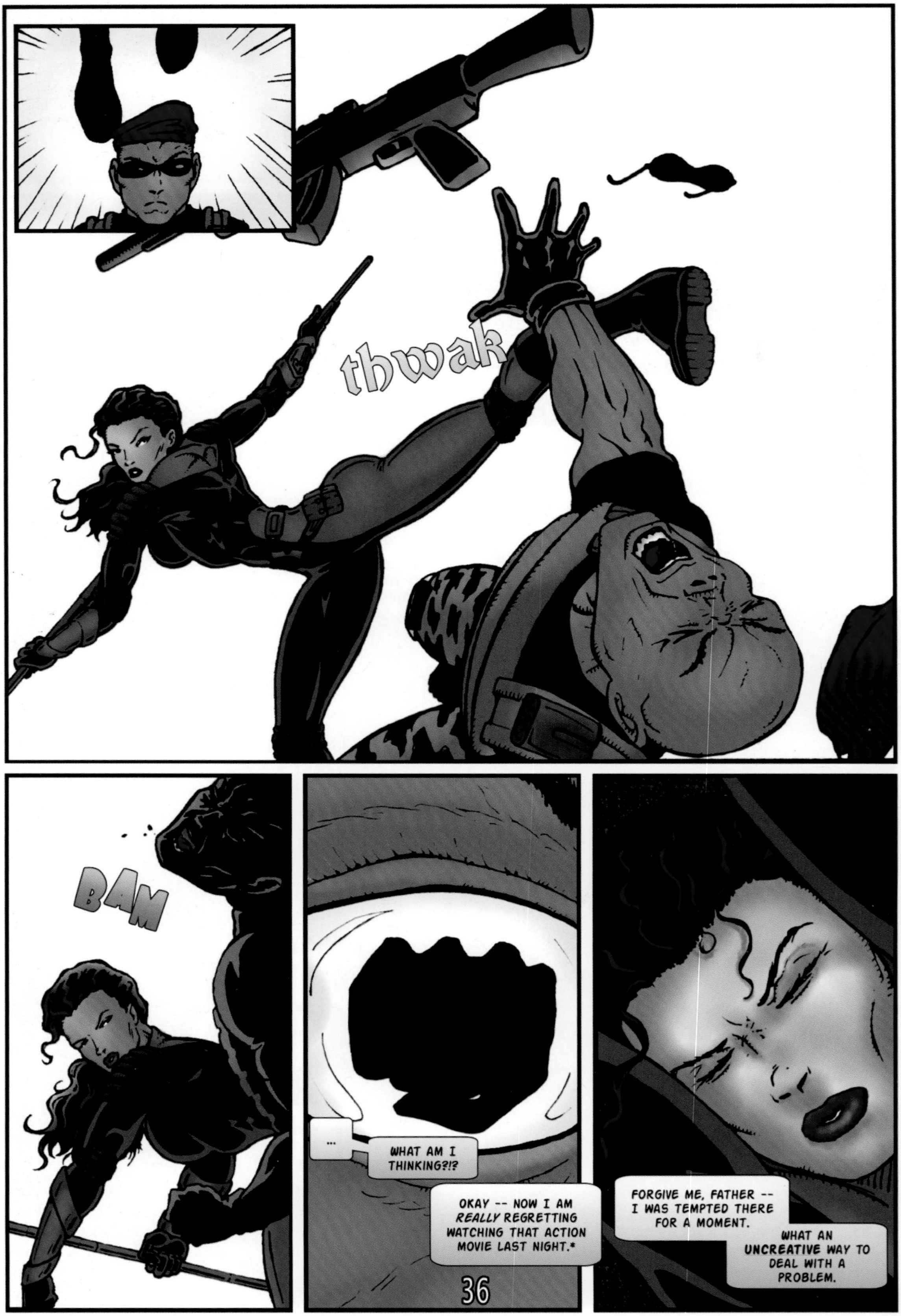
thwak
BAM
...
WHAT AM I THINKING?!?
OKAY -- NOW I AM *REALLY* REGRETTING WATCHING THAT ACTION MOVIE LAST NIGHT.*
FORGIVE ME, FATHER -- I WAS TEMPTED THERE FOR A MOMENT.
WHAT AN **UNCREATIVE** WAY TO DEAL WITH A PROBLEM.

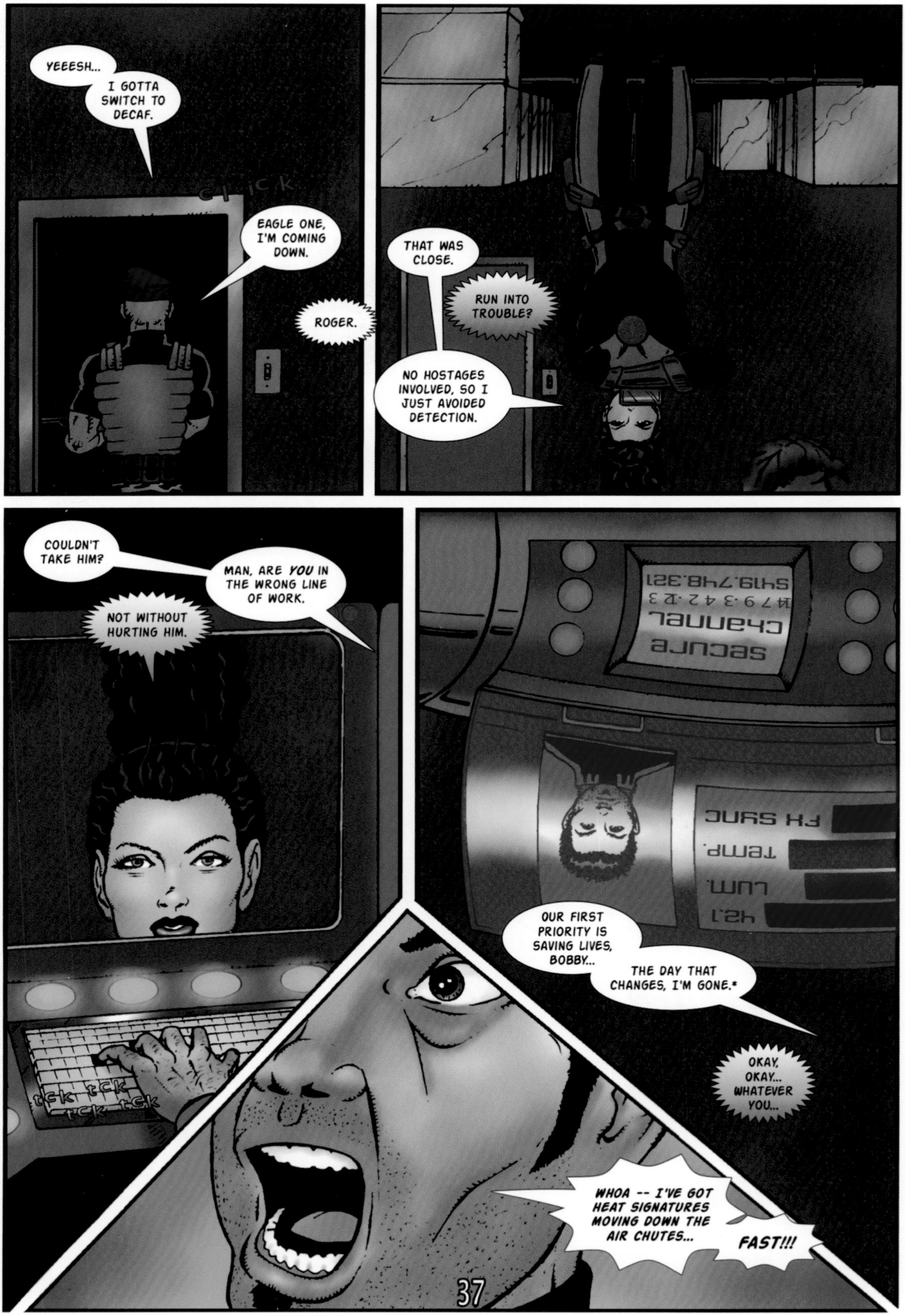
YEEESH... I GOTTA SWITCH TO DECAF.
click
EAGLE ONE, I'M COMING DOWN.
ROGER.
THAT WAS CLOSE.
RUN INTO TROUBLE?
NO HOSTAGES INVOLVED, SO I JUST AVOIDED DETECTION.
COULDN'T TAKE HIM?
NOT WITHOUT HURTING HIM.
MAN, ARE *YOU* IN THE WRONG LINE OF WORK.
tck tck tck tck
OUR FIRST PRIORITY IS SAVING LIVES, BOBBY...
THE DAY THAT CHANGES, I'M GONE.*
OKAY, OKAY... WHATEVER YOU...
WHOA -- I'VE GOT HEAT SIGNATURES MOVING DOWN THE AIR CHUTES...
FAST!!!

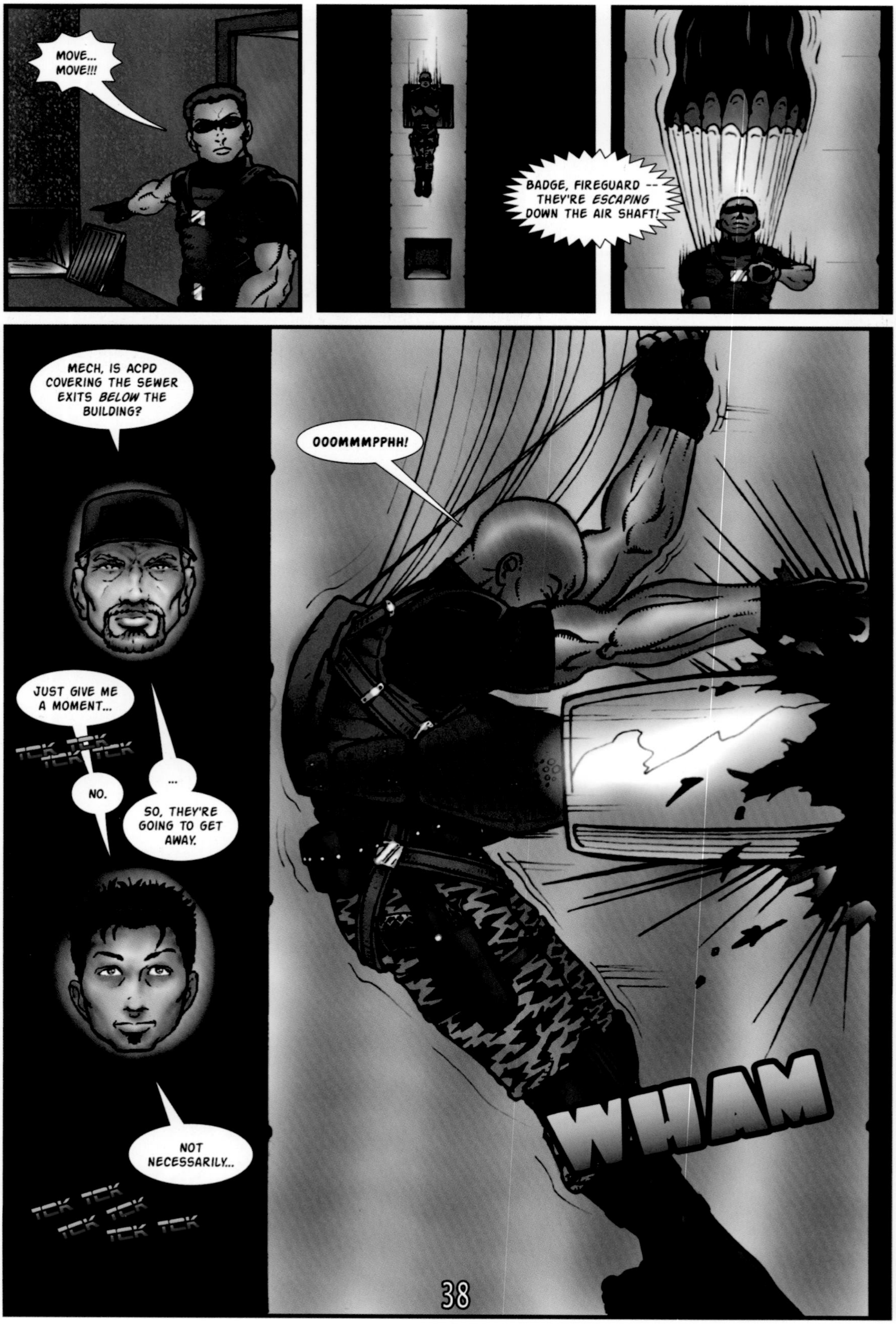
MOVE... MOVE!!!
BADGE, FIREGUARD -- THEY'RE *ESCAPING* DOWN THE AIR SHAFT!
MECH, IS ACPD COVERING THE SEWER EXITS *BELOW* THE BUILDING?
JUST GIVE ME A MOMENT...
TCK TCK TCK TCK
NO.
...
SO, THEY'RE GOING TO GET AWAY.
NOT NECESSARILY...
TCK TCK TCK TCK TCK TCK
OOOMMMPPHH!
WHAM

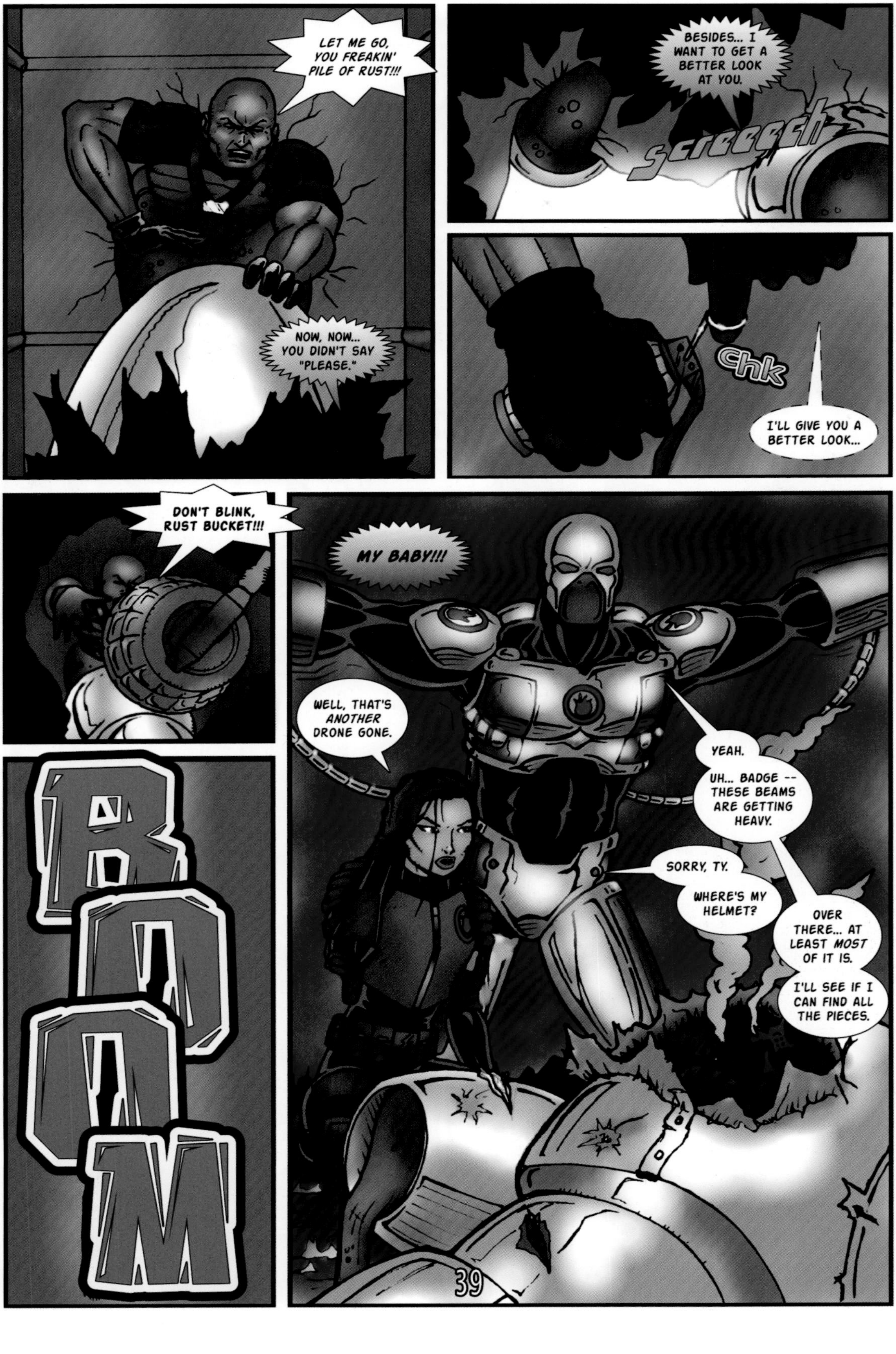
LET ME GO, YOU FREAKIN' PILE OF RUST!!!
NOW, NOW... YOU DIDN'T SAY "PLEASE."
BESIDES... I WANT TO GET A BETTER LOOK AT YOU.
Screeech
Chk
I'LL GIVE YOU A BETTER LOOK...
DON'T BLINK, RUST BUCKET!!!
BOOM
MY BABY!!!
WELL, THAT'S *ANOTHER* DRONE GONE.
YEAH.
UH... BADGE -- THESE BEAMS ARE GETTING HEAVY.
SORRY, TY.
WHERE'S MY HELMET?
OVER THERE... AT LEAST *MOST* OF IT IS.
I'LL SEE IF I CAN FIND ALL THE PIECES.

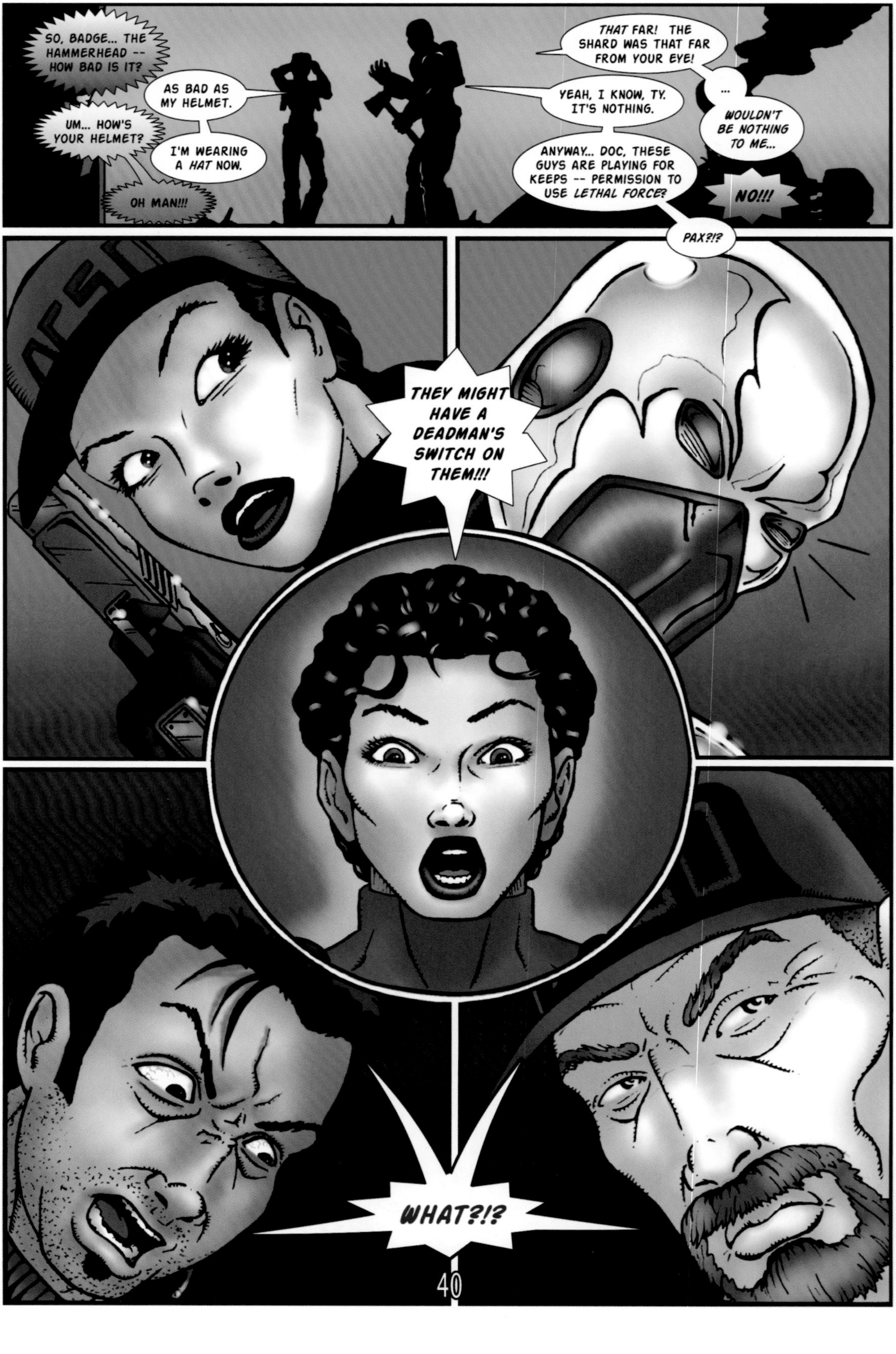
SO, BADGE... THE HAMMERHEAD -- HOW BAD IS IT?
AS BAD AS MY HELMET.
UM... HOW'S YOUR HELMET?
I'M WEARING A HAT NOW.
OH MAN!!!
YEAH, I KNOW, TY. IT'S NOTHING.
THAT FAR! THE SHARD WAS THAT FAR FROM YOUR EYE!
...
WOULDN'T BE NOTHING TO ME...
ANYWAY... DOC, THESE GUYS ARE PLAYING FOR KEEPS -- PERMISSION TO USE LETHAL FORCE?
NO!!!
PAX?!?
THEY MIGHT HAVE A DEADMAN'S SWITCH ON THEM!!!
WHAT?!?

TWO

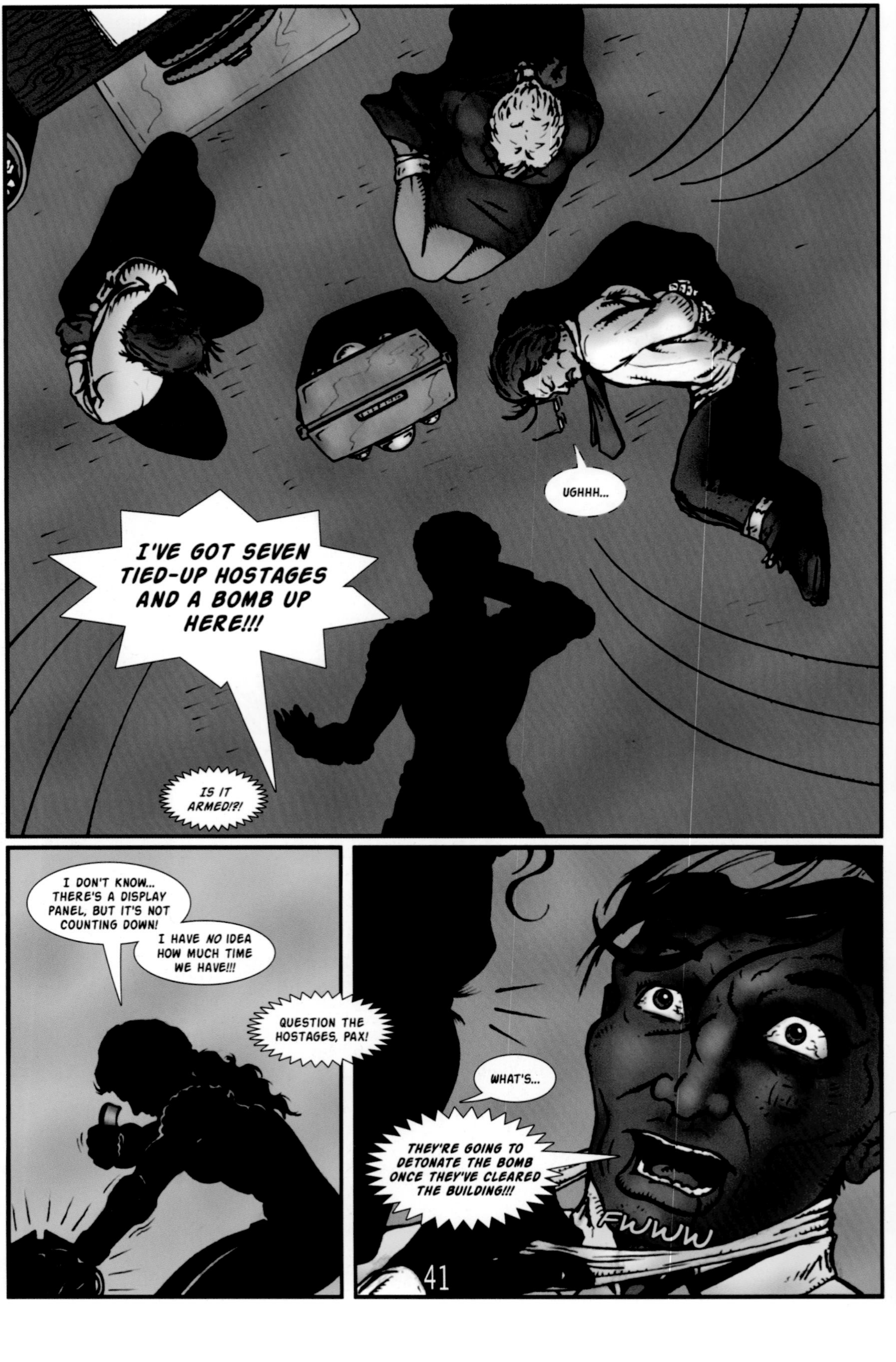
UGHHH...
I'VE GOT SEVEN TIED-UP HOSTAGES AND A BOMB UP HERE!!!
IS IT ARMED!?!
I DON'T KNOW... THERE'S A DISPLAY PANEL, BUT IT'S NOT COUNTING DOWN!
I HAVE NO IDEA HOW MUCH TIME WE HAVE!!!
QUESTION THE HOSTAGES, PAX!
WHAT'S...
THEY'RE GOING TO DETONATE THE BOMB ONCE THEY'VE CLEARED THE BUILDING!!!
FWWW

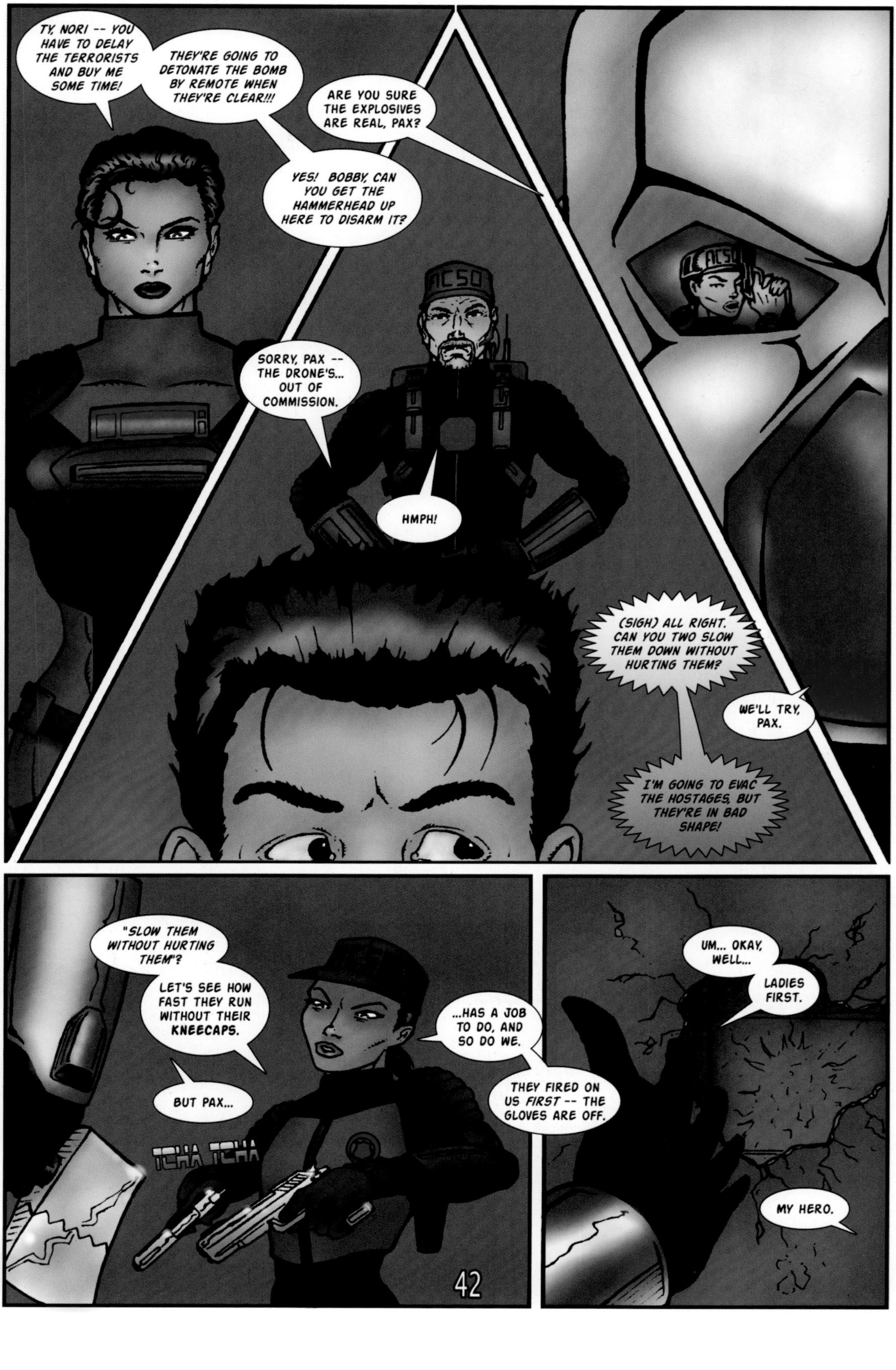
TY, NORI -- YOU HAVE TO DELAY THE TERRORISTS AND BUY ME SOME TIME!
THEY'RE GOING TO DETONATE THE BOMB BY REMOTE WHEN THEY'RE CLEAR!!!
ARE YOU SURE THE EXPLOSIVES ARE REAL, PAX?
YES! BOBBY, CAN YOU GET THE HAMMERHEAD UP HERE TO DISARM IT?
ACSO
SORRY, PAX -- THE DRONE'S... OUT OF COMMISSION.
HMPH!
(SIGH) ALL RIGHT. CAN YOU TWO SLOW THEM DOWN WITHOUT HURTING THEM?
WE'LL TRY, PAX.
I'M GOING TO EVAC THE HOSTAGES, BUT THEY'RE IN BAD SHAPE!
"SLOW THEM WITHOUT HURTING THEM"?
LET'S SEE HOW FAST THEY RUN WITHOUT THEIR KNEECAPS.
BUT PAX...
...HAS A JOB TO DO, AND SO DO WE.
THEY FIRED ON US FIRST -- THE GLOVES ARE OFF.
TCHA TCHA
UM... OKAY, WELL...
LADIES FIRST.
MY HERO.

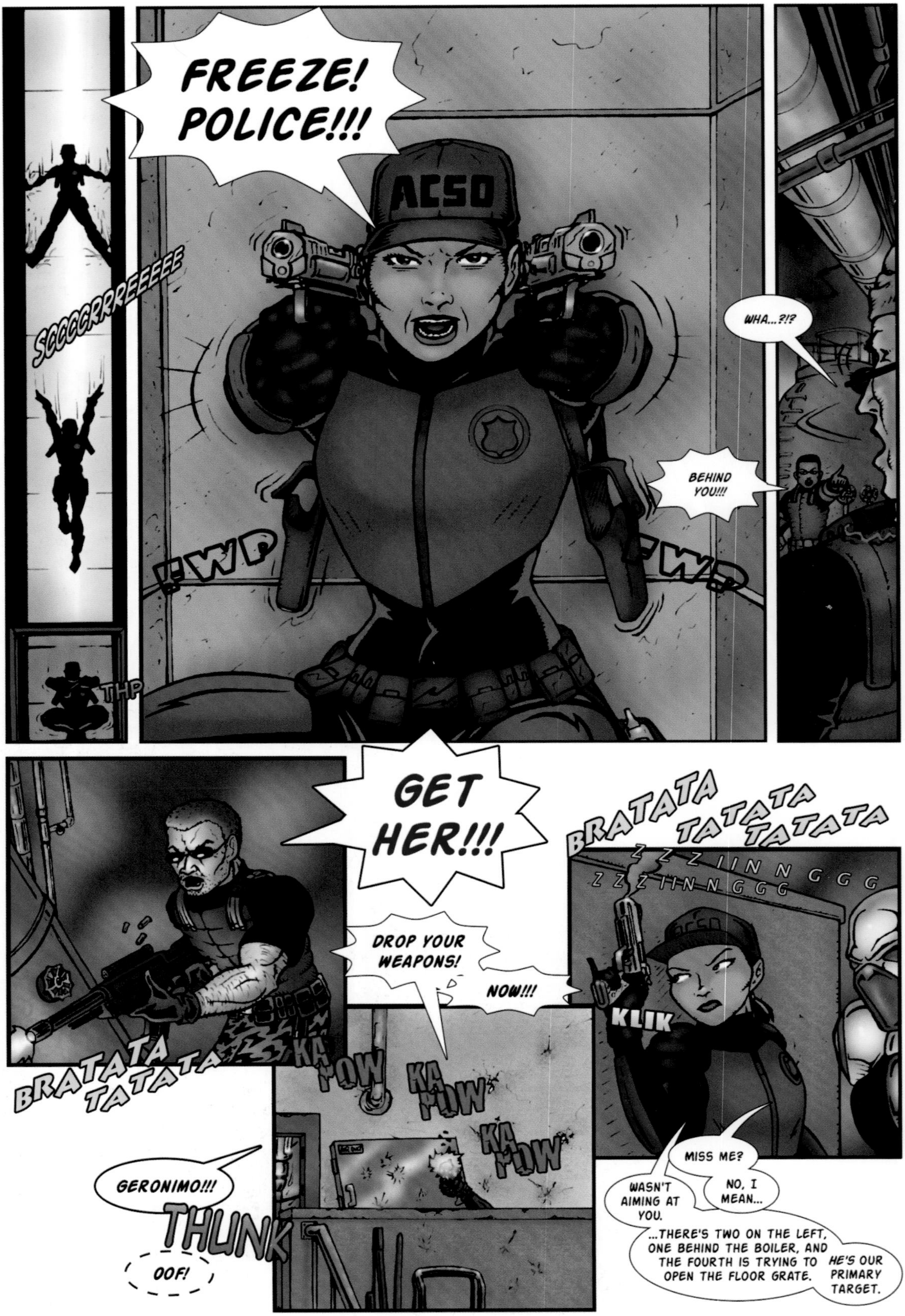
SCCCCRRREEEEEE
THP
FREEZE! POLICE!!!
FWP
FWP
WHA...?!?
BEHIND YOU!!!
GET HER!!!
BRATATA TATATA
DROP YOUR WEAPONS!
NOW!!!
BRATATA TATATA TATATA
ZZZIINNGGG
ZZZIINNGGG
KLIK
KA POW
KA POW
KA POW
GERONIMO!!!
THUNK
OOF!
MISS ME?
WASN'T AIMING AT YOU.
NO, I MEAN...
...THERE'S TWO ON THE LEFT, ONE BEHIND THE BOILER, AND THE FOURTH IS TRYING TO OPEN THE FLOOR GRATE.
HE'S OUR PRIMARY TARGET.

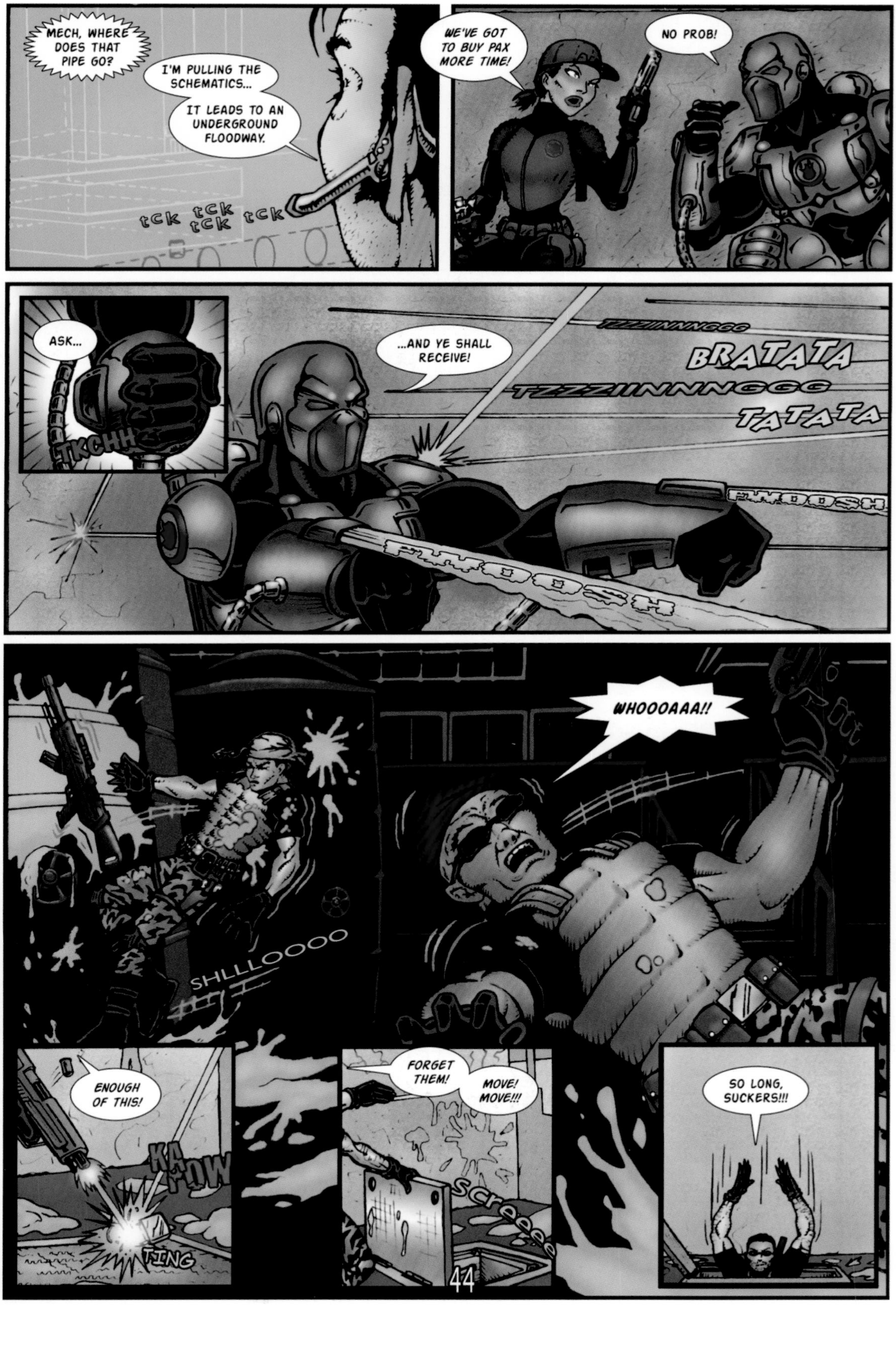
MECH, WHERE DOES THAT PIPE GO?
I'M PULLING THE SCHEMATICS...
IT LEADS TO AN UNDERGROUND FLOODWAY.
tck tck tck tck
WE'VE GOT TO BUY PAX MORE TIME!
NO PROB!
ASK...
TKCHH
...AND YE SHALL RECEIVE!
TZZZIINNNGGG
BRATATA
TZZZIINNNGGG
TATATA
FWOOSH
FWOOSH
WHOOOAAA!!
SHLLLOOOO
ENOUGH OF THIS!
KA-POW
TING
FORGET THEM!
MOVE! MOVE!!!
screeee
SO LONG, SUCKERS!!!

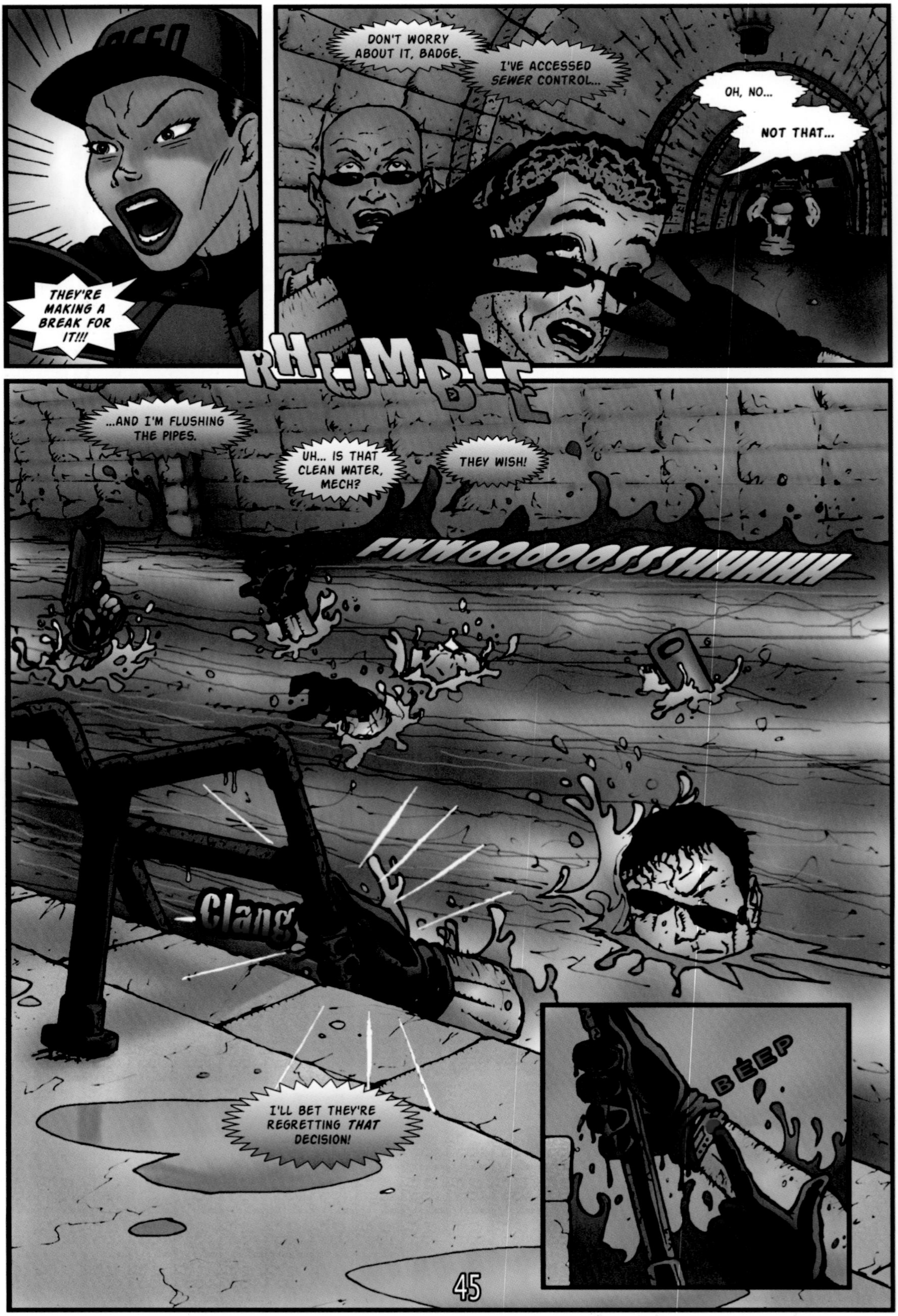
THEY'RE MAKING A BREAK FOR IT!!!
DON'T WORRY ABOUT IT, BADGE.
I'VE ACCESSED SEWER CONTROL...
OH, NO...
NOT THAT...
RHUMBLE
...AND I'M FLUSHING THE PIPES.
UH... IS THAT CLEAN WATER, MECH?
THEY WISH!
FWWOOOOOOSSSHHHHHH
Clang
I'LL BET THEY'RE REGRETTING THAT DECISION!
BEEP

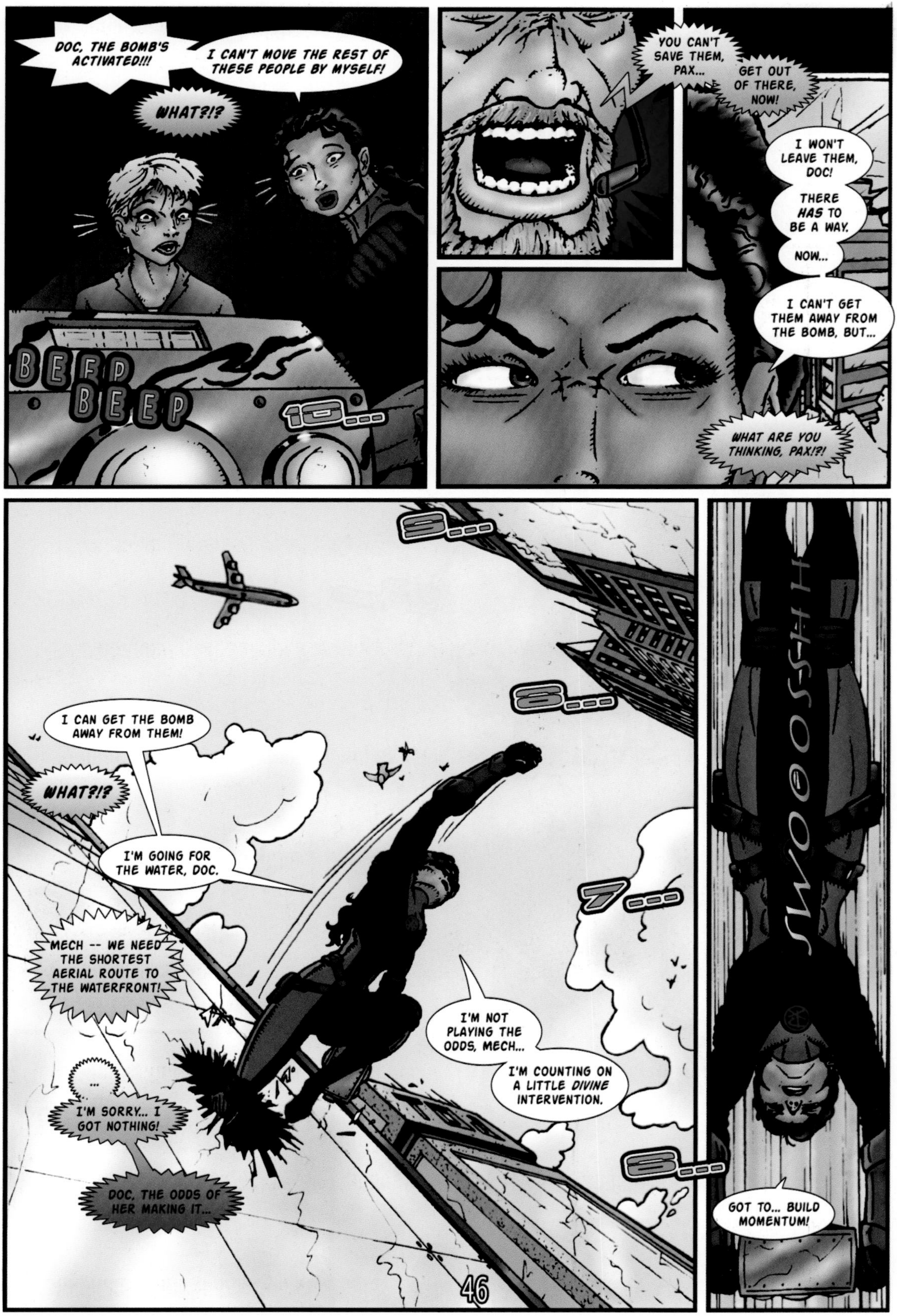
DOC, THE BOMB'S ACTIVATED!!!
I CAN'T MOVE THE REST OF THESE PEOPLE BY MYSELF!
WHAT?!?
BEEP BEEP
10...
YOU CAN'T SAVE THEM, PAX...
GET OUT OF THERE, NOW!
I WON'T LEAVE THEM, DOC!
THERE *HAS* TO BE A WAY.
NOW...
I CAN'T GET THEM AWAY FROM THE BOMB, BUT...
WHAT ARE YOU THINKING, PAX!?!
9...
8...
I CAN GET THE BOMB AWAY FROM THEM!
WHAT?!?
I'M GOING FOR THE WATER, DOC.
7...
MECH -- WE NEED THE SHORTEST AERIAL ROUTE TO THE WATERFRONT!
...
I'M SORRY... I GOT NOTHING!
DOC, THE ODDS OF HER MAKING IT...
I'M NOT PLAYING THE ODDS, MECH...
I'M COUNTING ON A LITTLE *DIVINE* INTERVENTION.
6...
SWOOOSSHH
GOT TO... BUILD MOMENTUM!

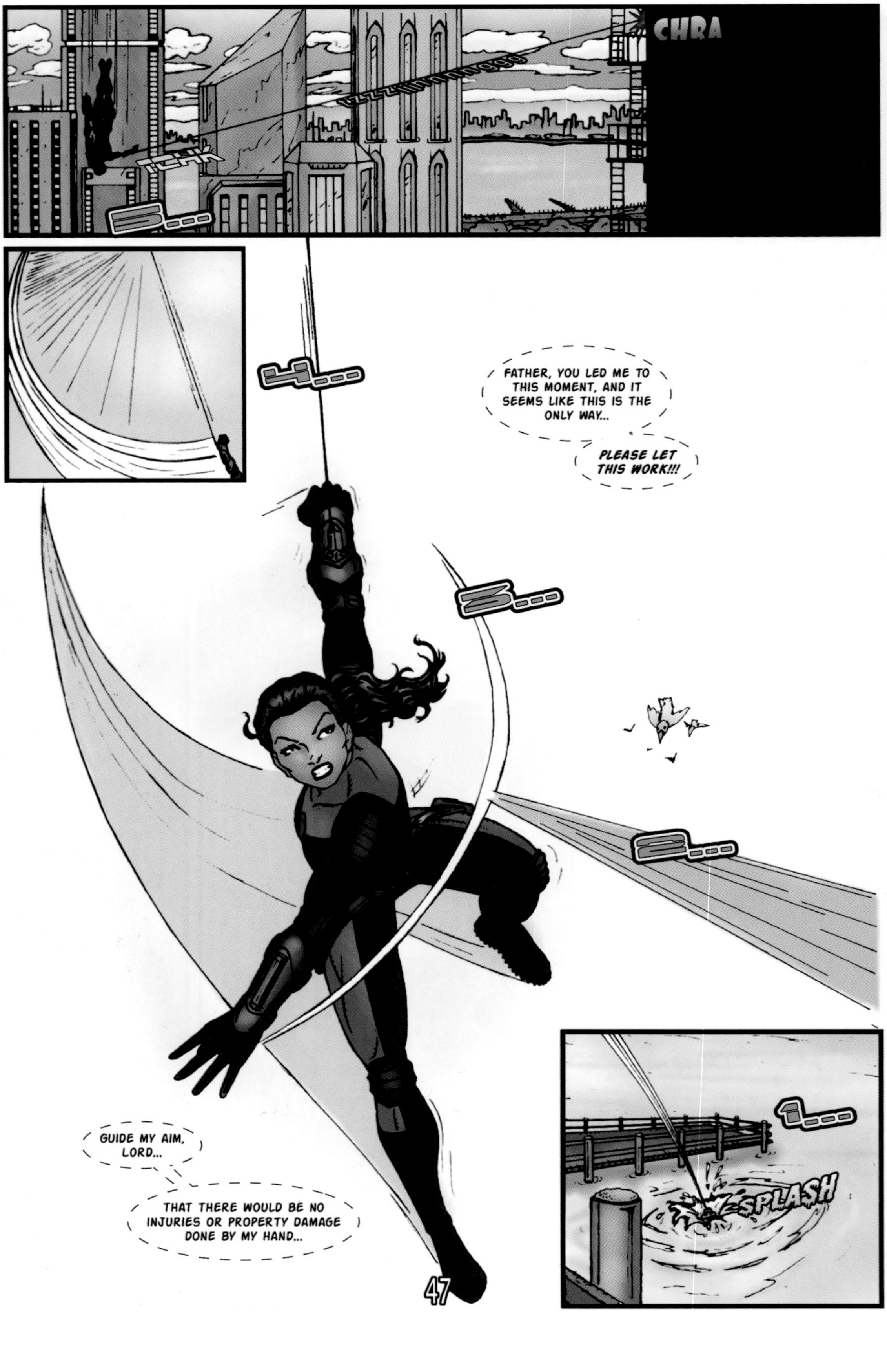
CHRA
5...
4...
FATHER, YOU LED ME TO THIS MOMENT, AND IT SEEMS LIKE THIS IS THE ONLY WAY...
PLEASE LET THIS WORK!!!
3...
2...
GUIDE MY AIM, LORD...
THAT THERE WOULD BE NO INJURIES OR PROPERTY DAMAGE DONE BY MY HAND...
1...
SPLASH

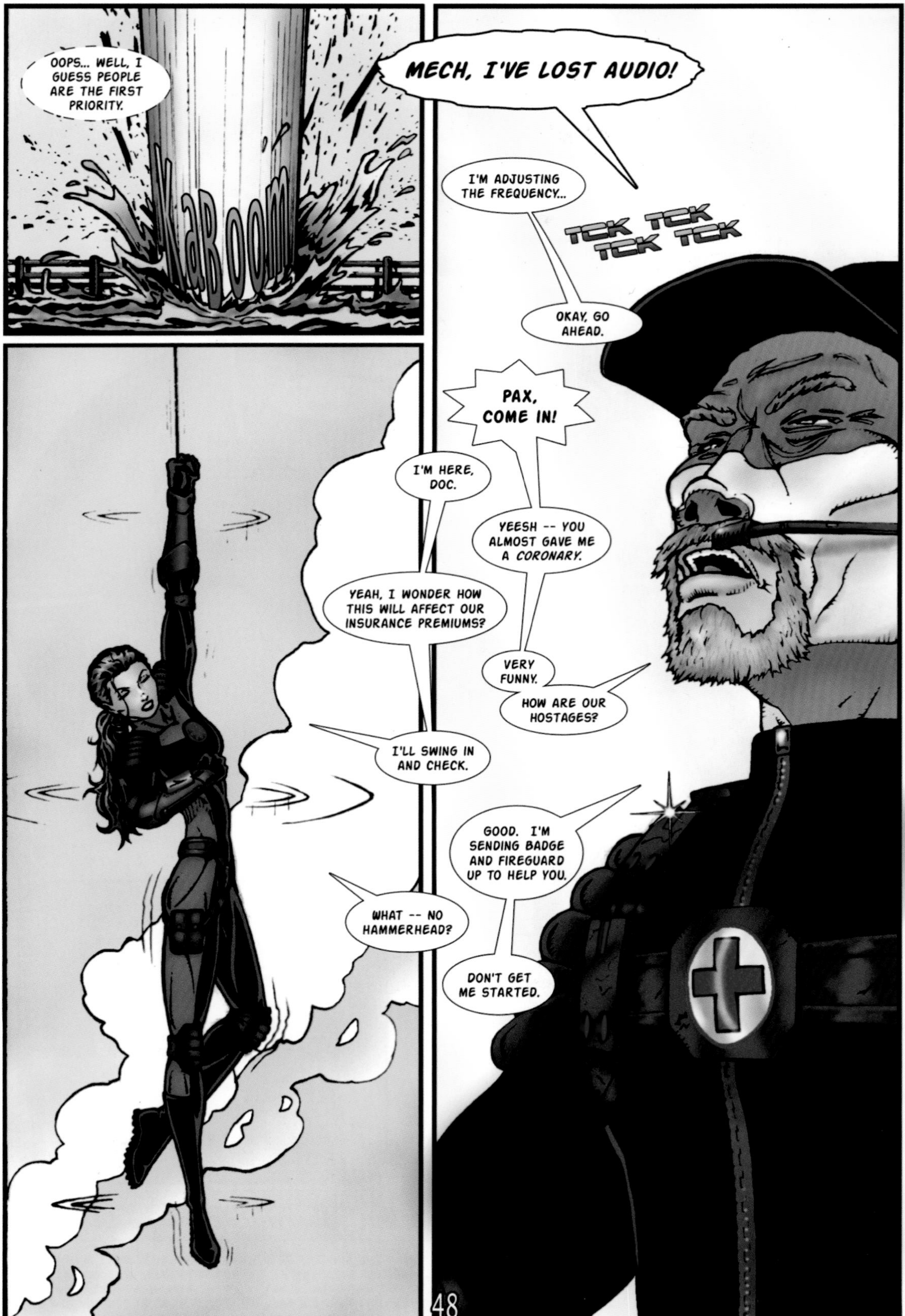
OOPS... WELL, I GUESS PEOPLE ARE THE FIRST PRIORITY.
KaBoom
MECH, I'VE LOST AUDIO!
I'M ADJUSTING THE FREQUENCY...
TCK TCK TCK TCK
OKAY, GO AHEAD.
PAX, COME IN!
I'M HERE, DOC.
YEESH -- YOU ALMOST GAVE ME A *CORONARY.*
YEAH, I WONDER HOW THIS WILL AFFECT OUR INSURANCE PREMIUMS?
VERY FUNNY.
HOW ARE OUR HOSTAGES?
I'LL SWING IN AND CHECK.
GOOD. I'M SENDING BADGE AND FIREGUARD UP TO HELP YOU.
WHAT -- NO HAMMERHEAD?
DON'T GET ME STARTED.

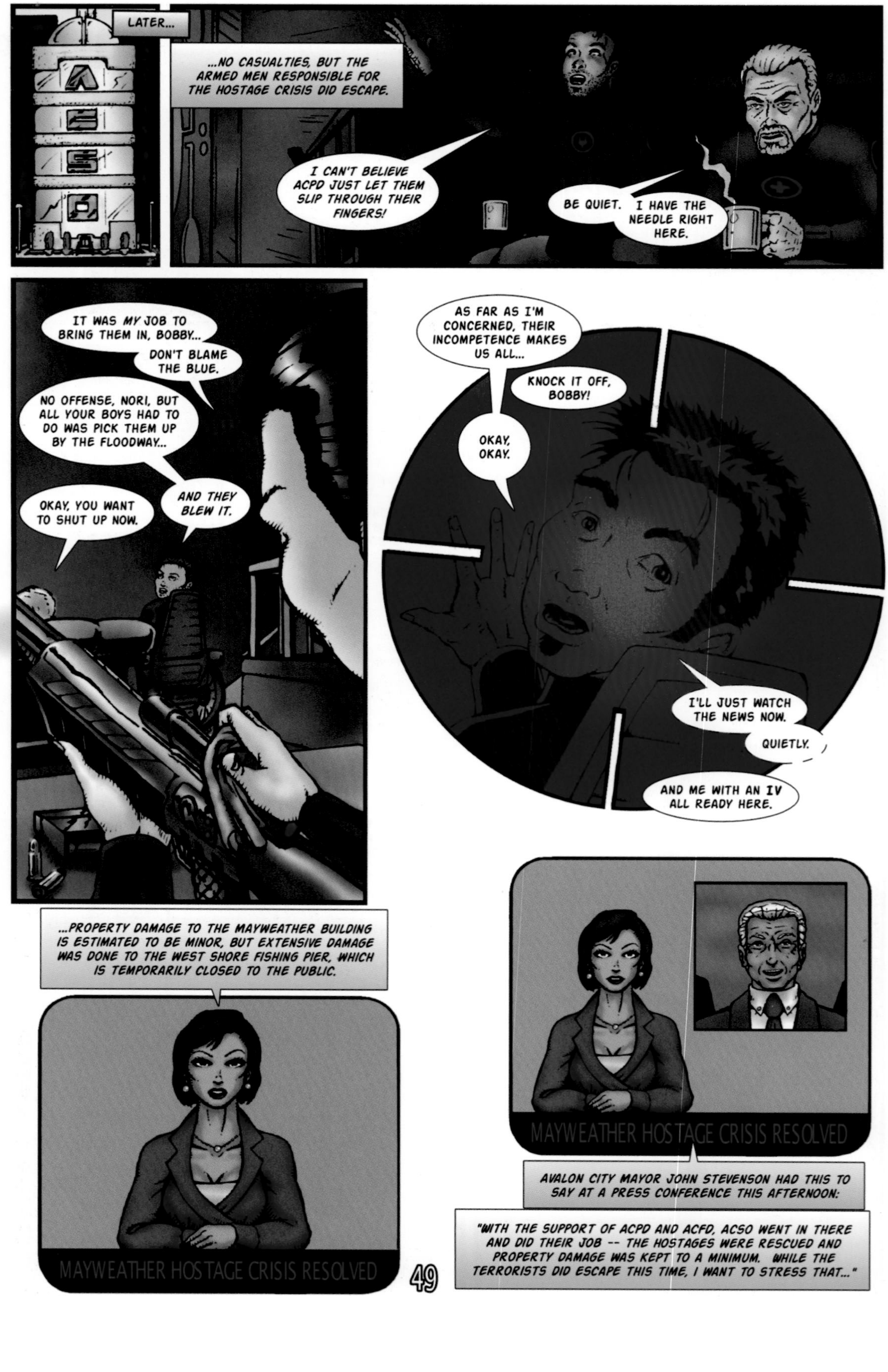
LATER...
...NO CASUALTIES, BUT THE ARMED MEN RESPONSIBLE FOR THE HOSTAGE CRISIS DID ESCAPE.
I CAN'T BELIEVE ACPD JUST LET THEM SLIP THROUGH THEIR FINGERS!
BE QUIET.
I HAVE THE NEEDLE RIGHT HERE.
IT WAS MY JOB TO BRING THEM IN, BOBBY...
DON'T BLAME THE BLUE.
NO OFFENSE, NORI, BUT ALL YOUR BOYS HAD TO DO WAS PICK THEM UP BY THE FLOODWAY...
AND THEY BLEW IT.
OKAY, YOU WANT TO SHUT UP NOW.
AS FAR AS I'M CONCERNED, THEIR INCOMPETENCE MAKES US ALL...
KNOCK IT OFF, BOBBY!
OKAY, OKAY.
I'LL JUST WATCH THE NEWS NOW.
QUIETLY.
AND ME WITH AN IV ALL READY HERE.
...PROPERTY DAMAGE TO THE MAYWEATHER BUILDING IS ESTIMATED TO BE MINOR, BUT EXTENSIVE DAMAGE WAS DONE TO THE WEST SHORE FISHING PIER, WHICH IS TEMPORARILY CLOSED TO THE PUBLIC.
MAYWEATHER HOSTAGE CRISIS RESOLVED
MAYWEATHER HOSTAGE CRISIS RESOLVED
AVALON CITY MAYOR JOHN STEVENSON HAD THIS TO SAY AT A PRESS CONFERENCE THIS AFTERNOON:
"WITH THE SUPPORT OF ACPD AND ACFD, ACSO WENT IN THERE AND DID THEIR JOB -- THE HOSTAGES WERE RESCUED AND PROPERTY DAMAGE WAS KEPT TO A MINIMUM. WHILE THE TERRORISTS DID ESCAPE THIS TIME, I WANT TO STRESS THAT..."

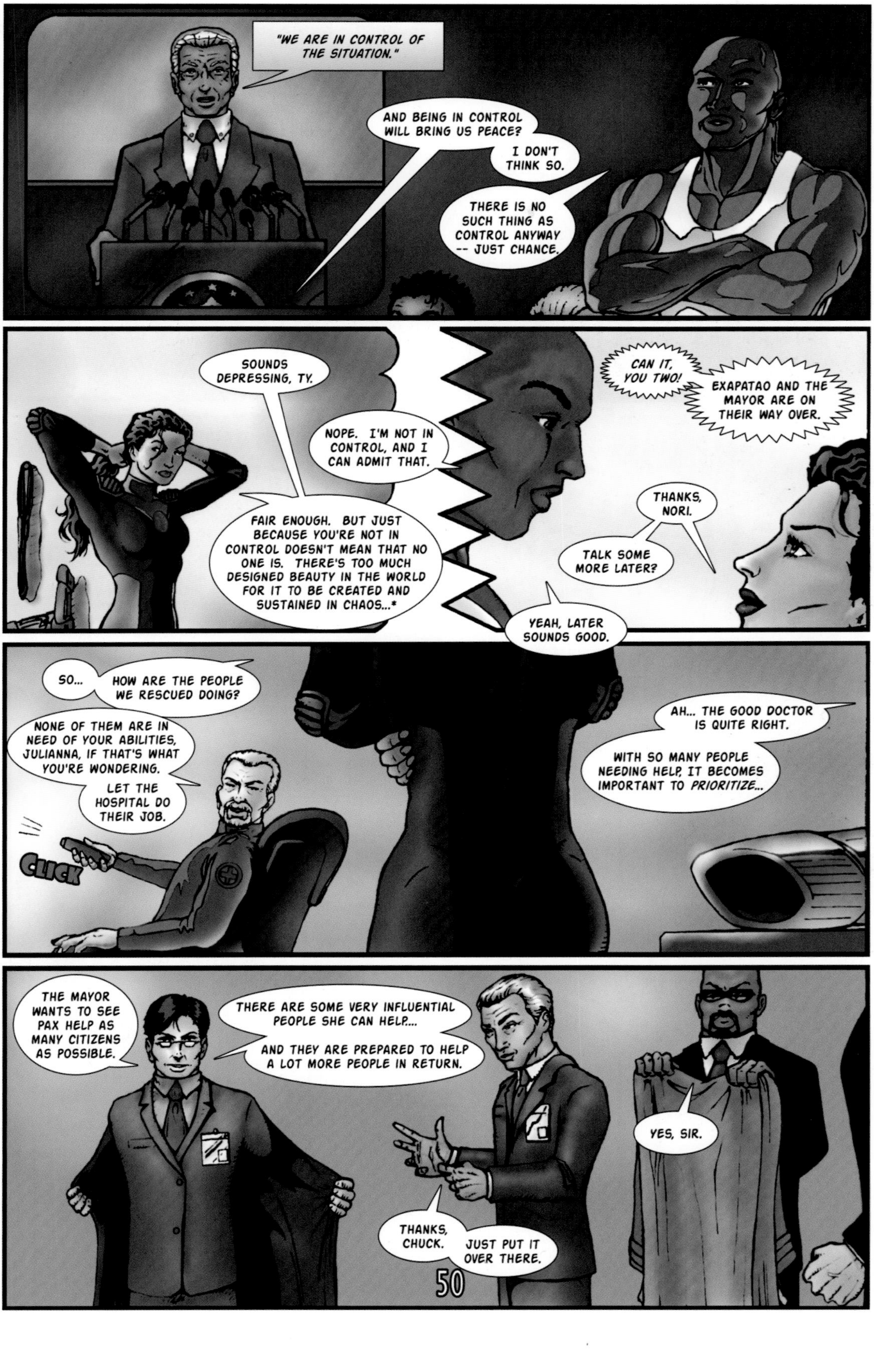
"WE ARE IN CONTROL OF THE SITUATION."
AND BEING IN CONTROL WILL BRING US PEACE?
I DON'T THINK SO.
THERE IS NO SUCH THING AS CONTROL ANYWAY -- JUST CHANCE.
SOUNDS DEPRESSING, TY.
NOPE. I'M NOT IN CONTROL, AND I CAN ADMIT THAT.
FAIR ENOUGH. BUT JUST BECAUSE YOU'RE NOT IN CONTROL DOESN'T MEAN THAT NO ONE IS. THERE'S TOO MUCH DESIGNED BEAUTY IN THE WORLD FOR IT TO BE CREATED AND SUSTAINED IN CHAOS...*
CAN IT, YOU TWO!
EXAPATAO AND THE MAYOR ARE ON THEIR WAY OVER.
THANKS, NORI.
TALK SOME MORE LATER?
YEAH, LATER SOUNDS GOOD.
SO...
HOW ARE THE PEOPLE WE RESCUED DOING?
NONE OF THEM ARE IN NEED OF YOUR ABILITIES, JULIANNA, IF THAT'S WHAT YOU'RE WONDERING.
LET THE HOSPITAL DO THEIR JOB.
CLICK
AH... THE GOOD DOCTOR IS QUITE RIGHT.
WITH SO MANY PEOPLE NEEDING HELP, IT BECOMES IMPORTANT TO *PRIORITIZE*...
THE MAYOR WANTS TO SEE PAX HELP AS MANY CITIZENS AS POSSIBLE.
THERE ARE SOME VERY INFLUENTIAL PEOPLE SHE CAN HELP....
AND THEY ARE PREPARED TO HELP A LOT MORE PEOPLE IN RETURN.
YES, SIR.
THANKS, CHUCK.
JUST PUT IT OVER THERE.

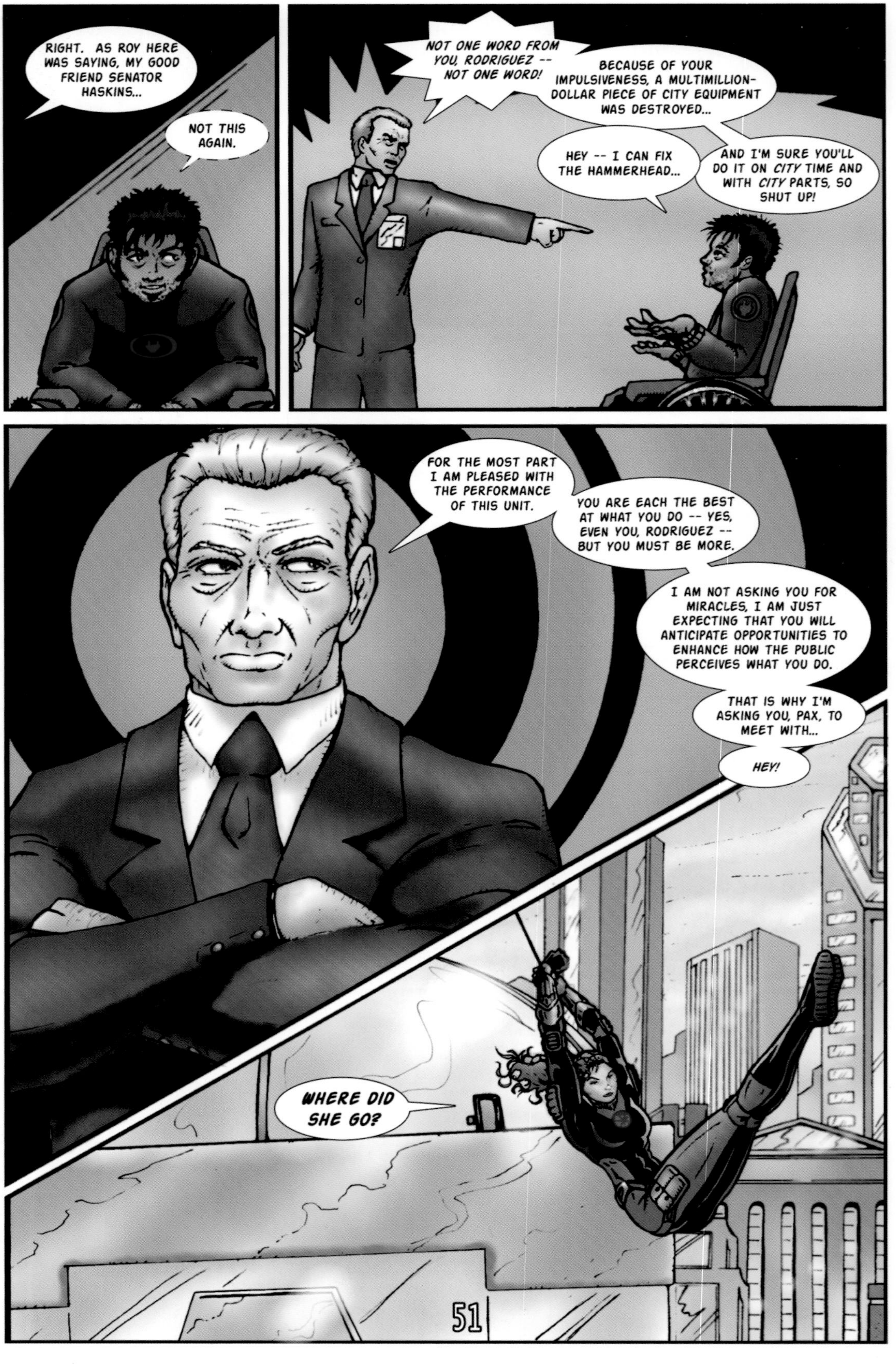
RIGHT. AS ROY HERE WAS SAYING, MY GOOD FRIEND SENATOR HASKINS...
NOT THIS AGAIN.
NOT ONE WORD FROM YOU, RODRIGUEZ -- NOT ONE WORD!
BECAUSE OF YOUR IMPULSIVENESS, A MULTIMILLION-DOLLAR PIECE OF CITY EQUIPMENT WAS DESTROYED...
HEY -- I CAN FIX THE HAMMERHEAD...
AND I'M SURE YOU'LL DO IT ON CITY TIME AND WITH CITY PARTS, SO SHUT UP!
FOR THE MOST PART I AM PLEASED WITH THE PERFORMANCE OF THIS UNIT.
YOU ARE EACH THE BEST AT WHAT YOU DO -- YES, EVEN YOU, RODRIGUEZ -- BUT YOU MUST BE MORE.
I AM NOT ASKING YOU FOR MIRACLES, I AM JUST EXPECTING THAT YOU WILL ANTICIPATE OPPORTUNITIES TO ENHANCE HOW THE PUBLIC PERCEIVES WHAT YOU DO.
THAT IS WHY I'M ASKING YOU, PAX, TO MEET WITH...
HEY!
WHERE DID SHE GO?

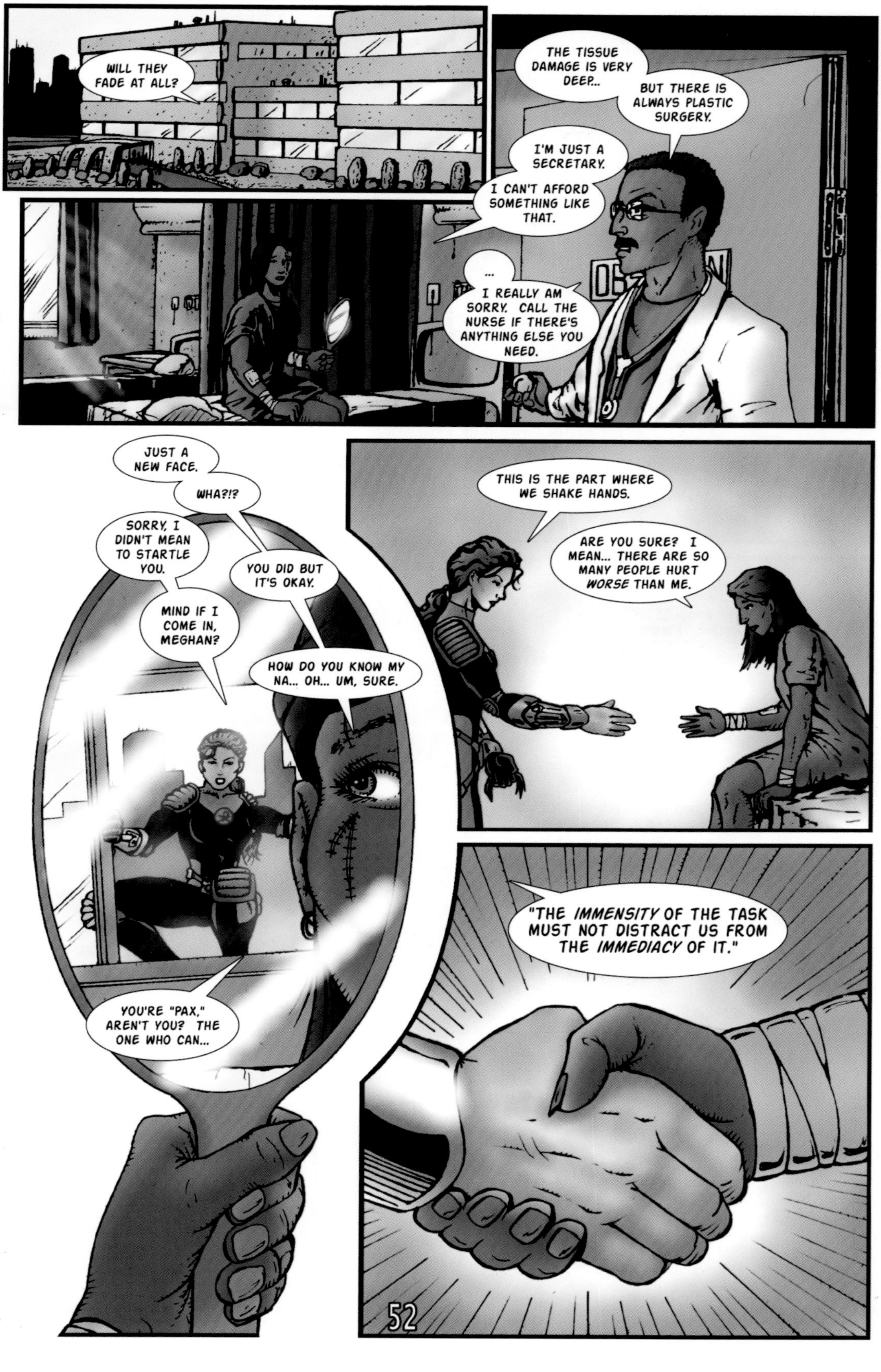
WILL THEY FADE AT ALL?
THE TISSUE DAMAGE IS VERY DEEP...
BUT THERE IS ALWAYS PLASTIC SURGERY.
I'M JUST A SECRETARY.
I CAN'T AFFORD SOMETHING LIKE THAT.
...
I REALLY AM SORRY. CALL THE NURSE IF THERE'S ANYTHING ELSE YOU NEED.
JUST A NEW FACE.
WHA?!?
SORRY, I DIDN'T MEAN TO STARTLE YOU.
YOU DID BUT IT'S OKAY.
MIND IF I COME IN, MEGHAN?
HOW DO YOU KNOW MY NA... OH... UM, SURE.
YOU'RE "PAX," AREN'T YOU? THE ONE WHO CAN...
THIS IS THE PART WHERE WE SHAKE HANDS.
ARE YOU SURE? I MEAN... THERE ARE SO MANY PEOPLE HURT *WORSE* THAN ME.
"THE *IMMENSITY* OF THE TASK MUST NOT DISTRACT US FROM THE *IMMEDIACY* OF IT."

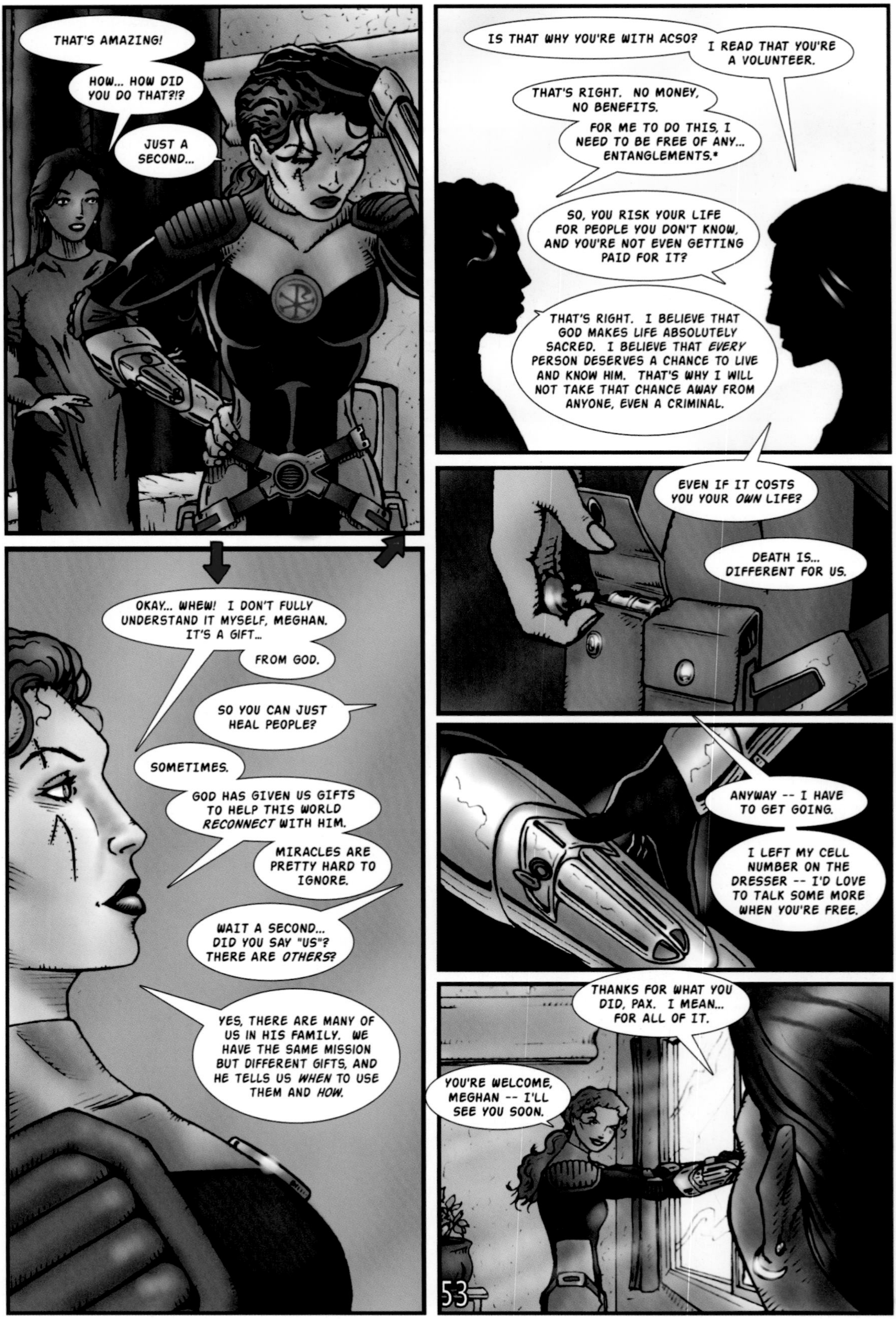
THAT'S AMAZING!
HOW... HOW DID YOU DO THAT?!?
JUST A SECOND...
OKAY... WHEW! I DON'T FULLY UNDERSTAND IT MYSELF, MEGHAN. IT'S A GIFT...
FROM GOD.
SO YOU CAN JUST HEAL PEOPLE?
SOMETIMES.
GOD HAS GIVEN US GIFTS TO HELP THIS WORLD *RECONNECT* WITH HIM.
MIRACLES ARE PRETTY HARD TO IGNORE.
WAIT A SECOND... DID YOU SAY "US"? THERE ARE *OTHERS*?
YES, THERE ARE MANY OF US IN HIS FAMILY. WE HAVE THE SAME MISSION BUT DIFFERENT GIFTS, AND HE TELLS US *WHEN* TO USE THEM AND *HOW*.
IS THAT WHY YOU'RE WITH ACSO?
I READ THAT YOU'RE A VOLUNTEER.
THAT'S RIGHT. NO MONEY, NO BENEFITS.
FOR ME TO DO THIS, I NEED TO BE FREE OF ANY... ENTANGLEMENTS.*
SO, YOU RISK YOUR LIFE FOR PEOPLE YOU DON'T KNOW, AND YOU'RE NOT EVEN GETTING PAID FOR IT?
THAT'S RIGHT. I BELIEVE THAT GOD MAKES LIFE ABSOLUTELY SACRED. I BELIEVE THAT *EVERY* PERSON DESERVES A CHANCE TO LIVE AND KNOW HIM. THAT'S WHY I WILL NOT TAKE THAT CHANCE AWAY FROM ANYONE, EVEN A CRIMINAL.
EVEN IF IT COSTS YOU YOUR *OWN* LIFE?
DEATH IS... DIFFERENT FOR US.
ANYWAY -- I HAVE TO GET GOING.
I LEFT MY CELL NUMBER ON THE DRESSER -- I'D LOVE TO TALK SOME MORE WHEN YOU'RE FREE.
THANKS FOR WHAT YOU DID, PAX. I MEAN... FOR ALL OF IT.
YOU'RE WELCOME, MEGHAN -- I'LL SEE YOU SOON.

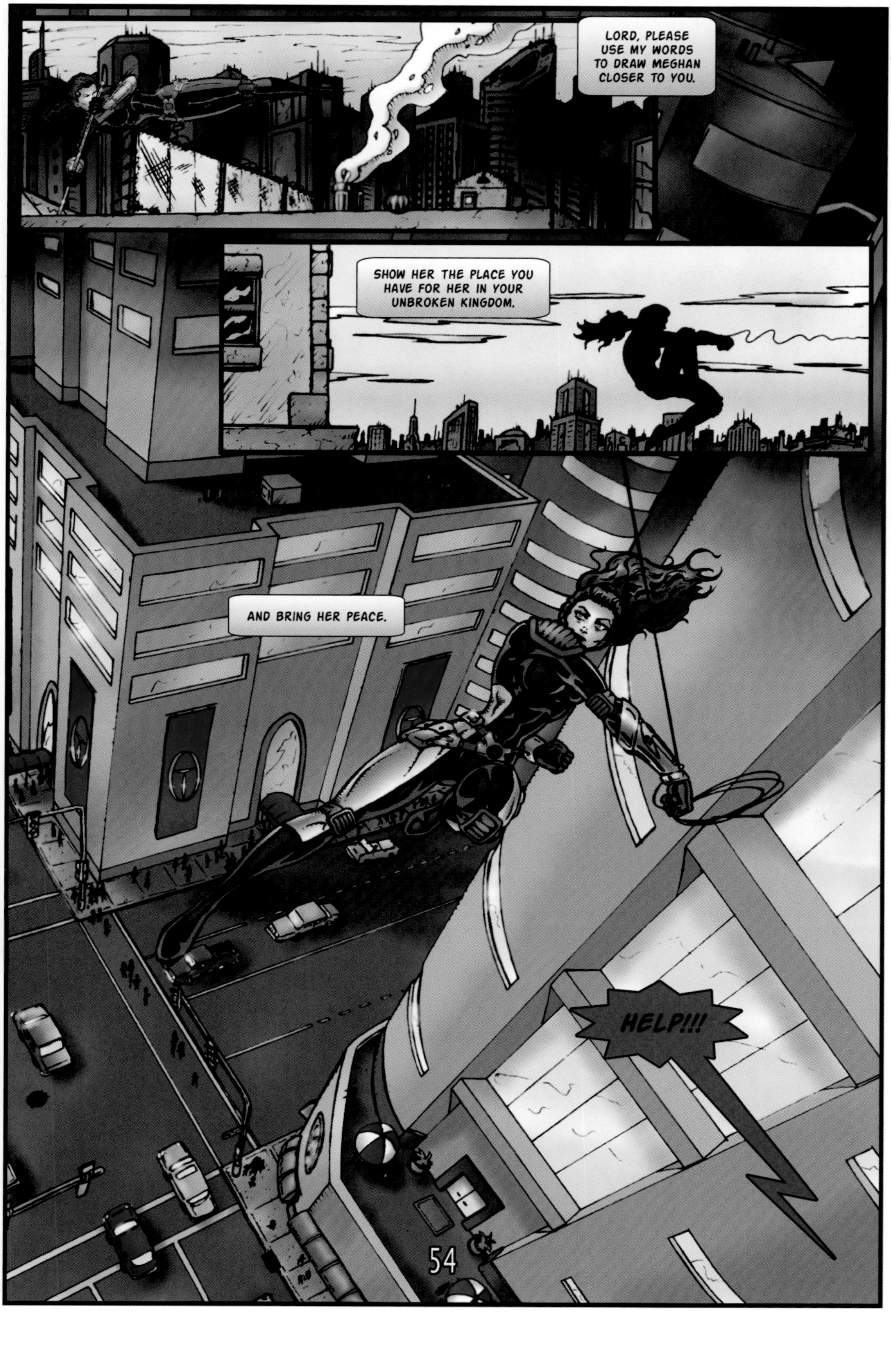
LORD, PLEASE USE MY WORDS TO DRAW MEGHAN CLOSER TO YOU.
SHOW HER THE PLACE YOU HAVE FOR HER IN YOUR UNBROKEN KINGDOM.
AND BRING HER PEACE.
HELP!!!

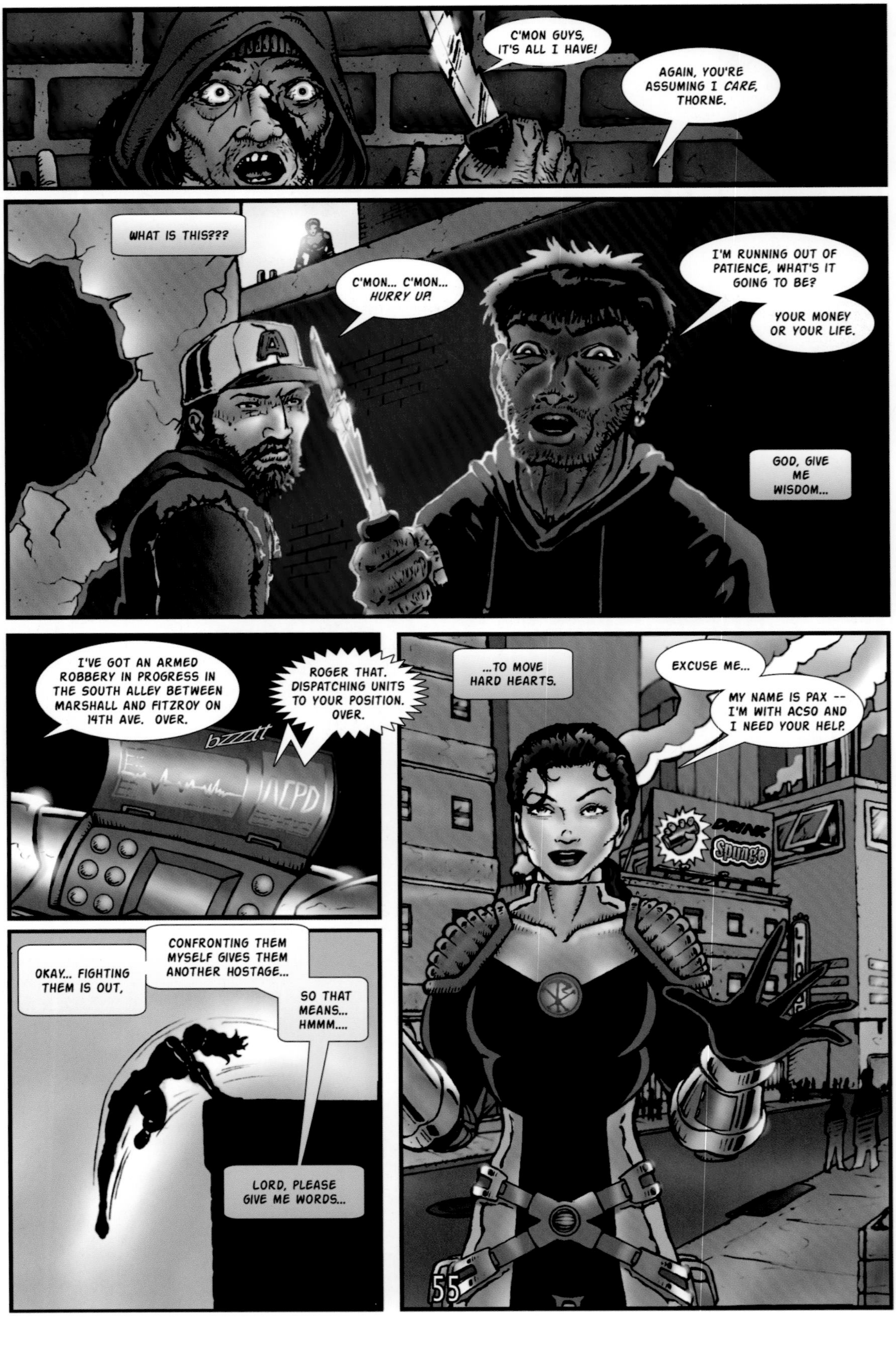

C'MON GUYS, IT'S ALL I HAVE!
AGAIN, YOU'RE ASSUMING I CARE, THORNE.
WHAT IS THIS???
C'MON... C'MON... HURRY UP!
I'M RUNNING OUT OF PATIENCE, WHAT'S IT GOING TO BE?
YOUR MONEY OR YOUR LIFE.
GOD, GIVE ME WISDOM...
I'VE GOT AN ARMED ROBBERY IN PROGRESS IN THE SOUTH ALLEY BETWEEN MARSHALL AND FITZROY ON 14TH AVE. OVER.
ROGER THAT. DISPATCHING UNITS TO YOUR POSITION. OVER.
bzzztt
ACPD
OKAY... FIGHTING THEM IS OUT,
CONFRONTING THEM MYSELF GIVES THEM ANOTHER HOSTAGE...
SO THAT MEANS... HMMM....
LORD, PLEASE GIVE ME WORDS...
...TO MOVE HARD HEARTS.
EXCUSE ME...
MY NAME IS PAX -- I'M WITH ACSO AND I NEED YOUR HELP.
DRINK
Spunge

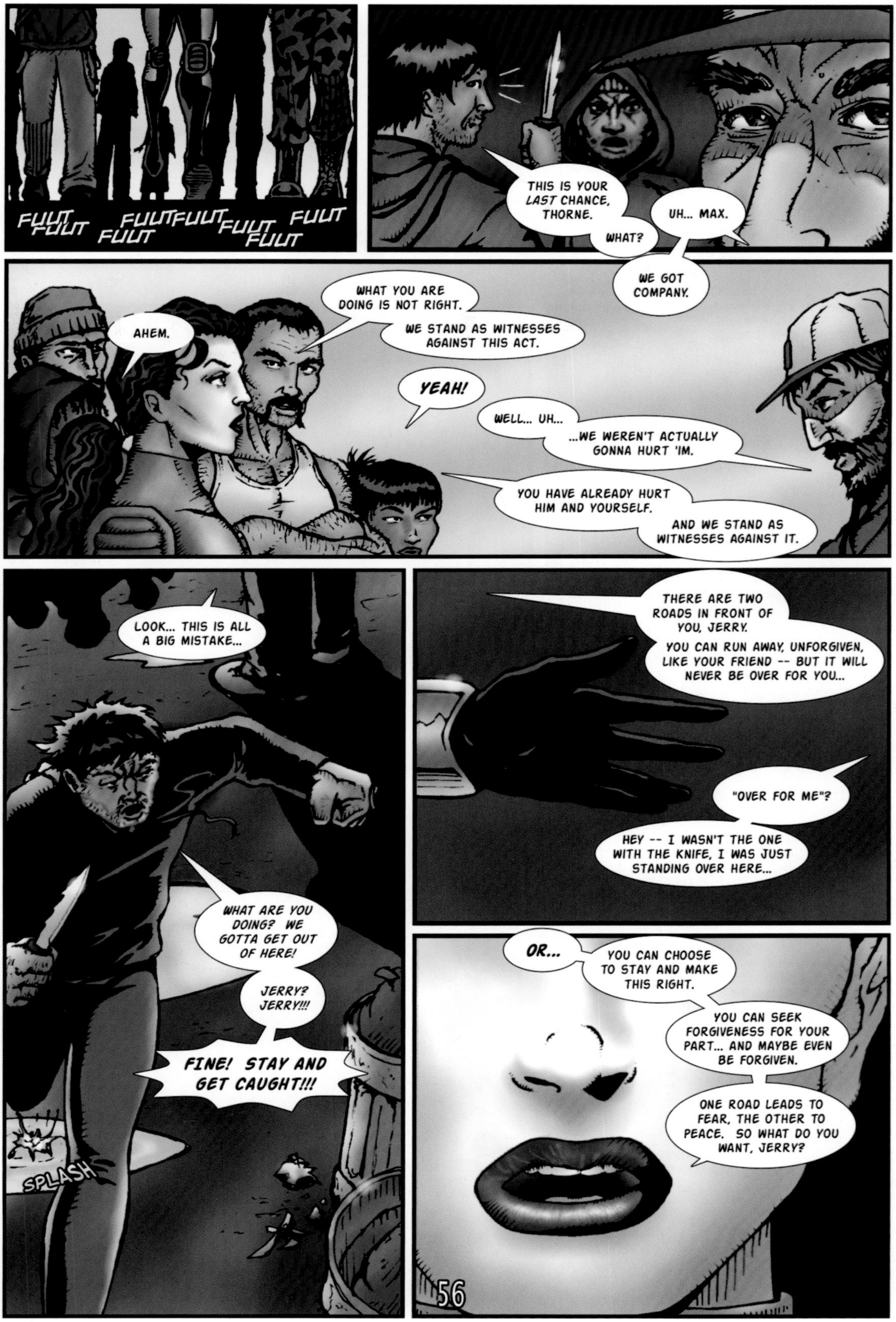
FUUT FUUT FUUT FUUT FUUT FUUT FUUT FUUT
THIS IS YOUR *LAST* CHANCE, THORNE.
WHAT?
UH... MAX.
WE GOT COMPANY.
AHEM.
WHAT YOU ARE DOING IS NOT RIGHT.
WE STAND AS WITNESSES AGAINST THIS ACT.
YEAH!
WELL... UH...
...WE WEREN'T ACTUALLY GONNA HURT 'IM.
YOU HAVE ALREADY HURT HIM AND YOURSELF.
AND WE STAND AS WITNESSES AGAINST IT.
LOOK... THIS IS ALL A BIG MISTAKE...
WHAT ARE YOU DOING? WE GOTTA GET OUT OF HERE!
JERRY? JERRY!!!
FINE! STAY AND GET CAUGHT!!!
SPLASH
THERE ARE TWO ROADS IN FRONT OF YOU, JERRY.
YOU CAN RUN AWAY, UNFORGIVEN, LIKE YOUR FRIEND -- BUT IT WILL NEVER BE OVER FOR YOU...
"OVER FOR ME"?
HEY -- I WASN'T THE ONE WITH THE KNIFE, I WAS JUST STANDING OVER HERE...
OR...
YOU CAN CHOOSE TO STAY AND MAKE THIS RIGHT.
YOU CAN SEEK FORGIVENESS FOR YOUR PART... AND MAYBE EVEN BE FORGIVEN.
ONE ROAD LEADS TO FEAR, THE OTHER TO PEACE. SO WHAT DO YOU WANT, JERRY?

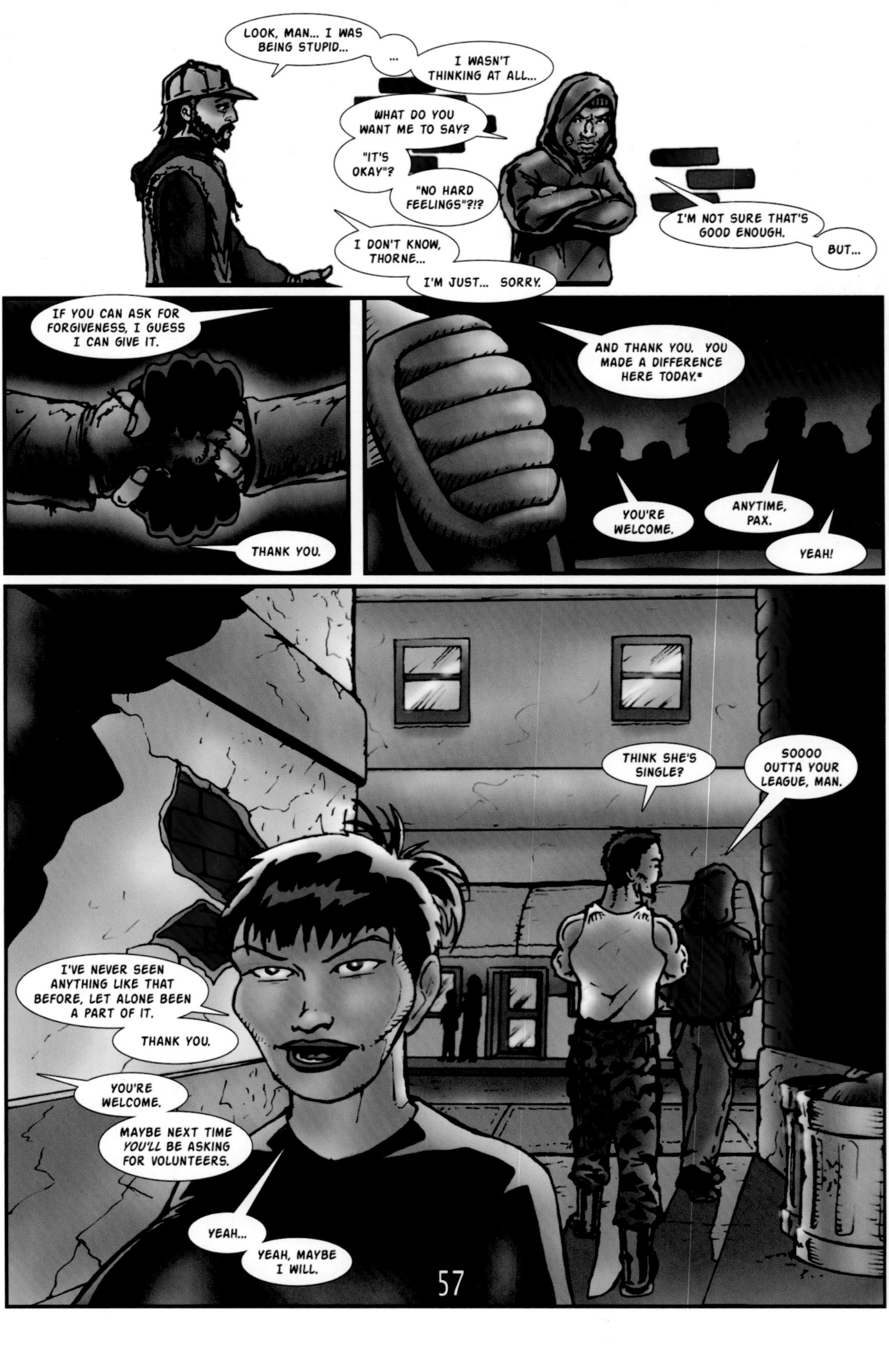

LOOK, MAN... I WAS BEING STUPID...
...
I WASN'T THINKING AT ALL...
WHAT DO YOU WANT ME TO SAY?
"IT'S OKAY"?
"NO HARD FEELINGS"?!?
I DON'T KNOW, THORNE...
I'M JUST... SORRY.
I'M NOT SURE THAT'S GOOD ENOUGH.
BUT...
IF YOU CAN ASK FOR FORGIVENESS, I GUESS I CAN GIVE IT.
THANK YOU.
AND THANK YOU. YOU MADE A DIFFERENCE HERE TODAY.*
YOU'RE WELCOME.
ANYTIME, PAX.
YEAH!
THINK SHE'S SINGLE?
SOOOO OUTTA YOUR LEAGUE, MAN.
I'VE NEVER SEEN ANYTHING LIKE THAT BEFORE, LET ALONE BEEN A PART OF IT.
THANK YOU.
YOU'RE WELCOME.
MAYBE NEXT TIME *YOU'LL* BE ASKING FOR VOLUNTEERS.
YEAH...
YEAH, MAYBE I WILL.

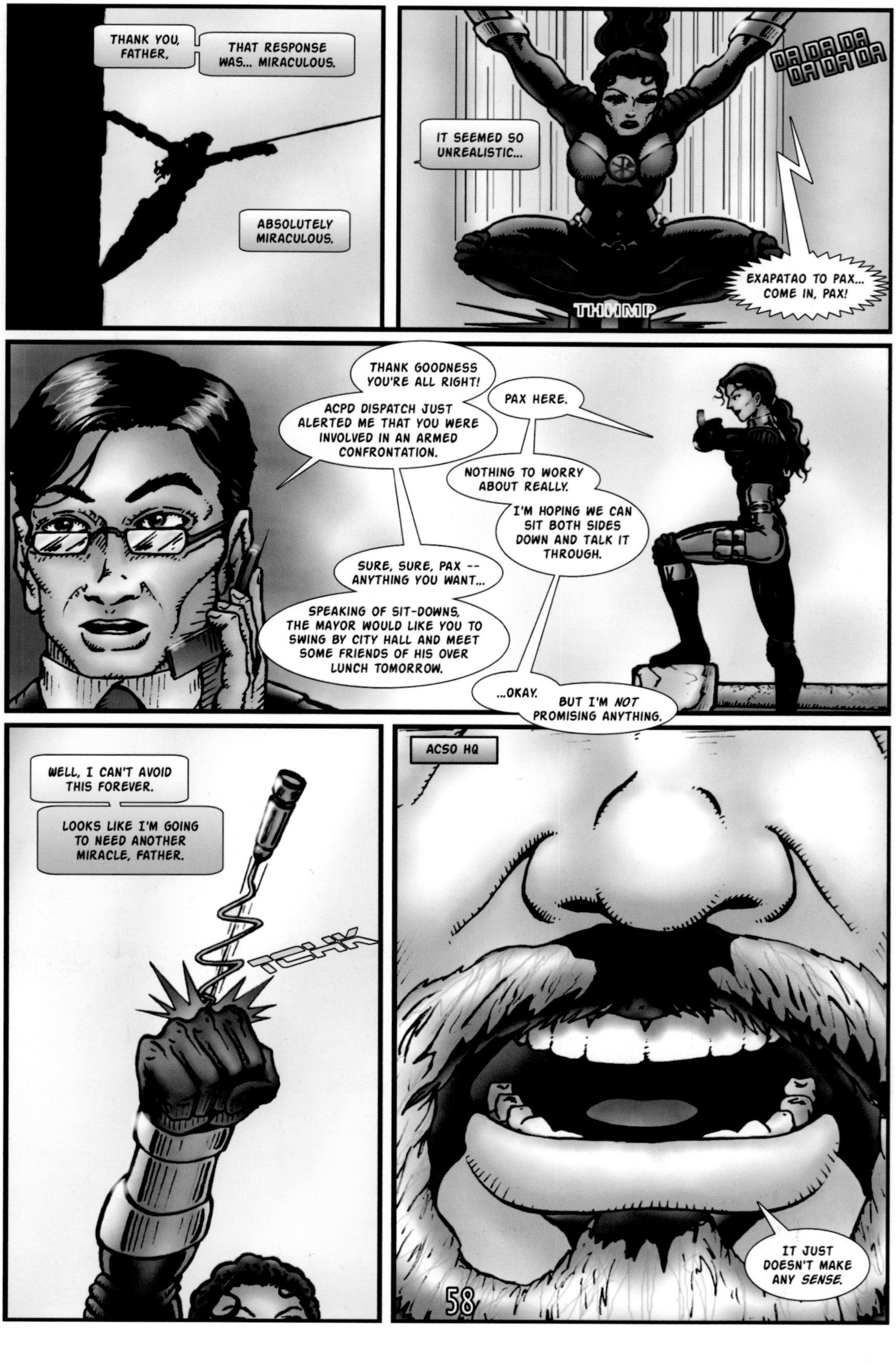
THANK YOU, FATHER.
THAT RESPONSE WAS... MIRACULOUS.
ABSOLUTELY MIRACULOUS.
DA DA DA DA DA DA
IT SEEMED SO UNREALISTIC...
EXAPATAO TO PAX... COME IN, PAX!
THMMP
THANK GOODNESS YOU'RE ALL RIGHT!
ACPD DISPATCH JUST ALERTED ME THAT YOU WERE INVOLVED IN AN ARMED CONFRONTATION.
PAX HERE.
NOTHING TO WORRY ABOUT REALLY.
I'M HOPING WE CAN SIT BOTH SIDES DOWN AND TALK IT THROUGH.
SURE, SURE, PAX -- ANYTHING YOU WANT...
SPEAKING OF SIT-DOWNS, THE MAYOR WOULD LIKE YOU TO SWING BY CITY HALL AND MEET SOME FRIENDS OF HIS OVER LUNCH TOMORROW.
...OKAY.
BUT I'M *NOT* PROMISING ANYTHING.
WELL, I CAN'T AVOID THIS FOREVER.
LOOKS LIKE I'M GOING TO NEED ANOTHER MIRACLE, FATHER.
TCHK
ACSO HQ
IT JUST DOESN'T MAKE ANY *SENSE*.

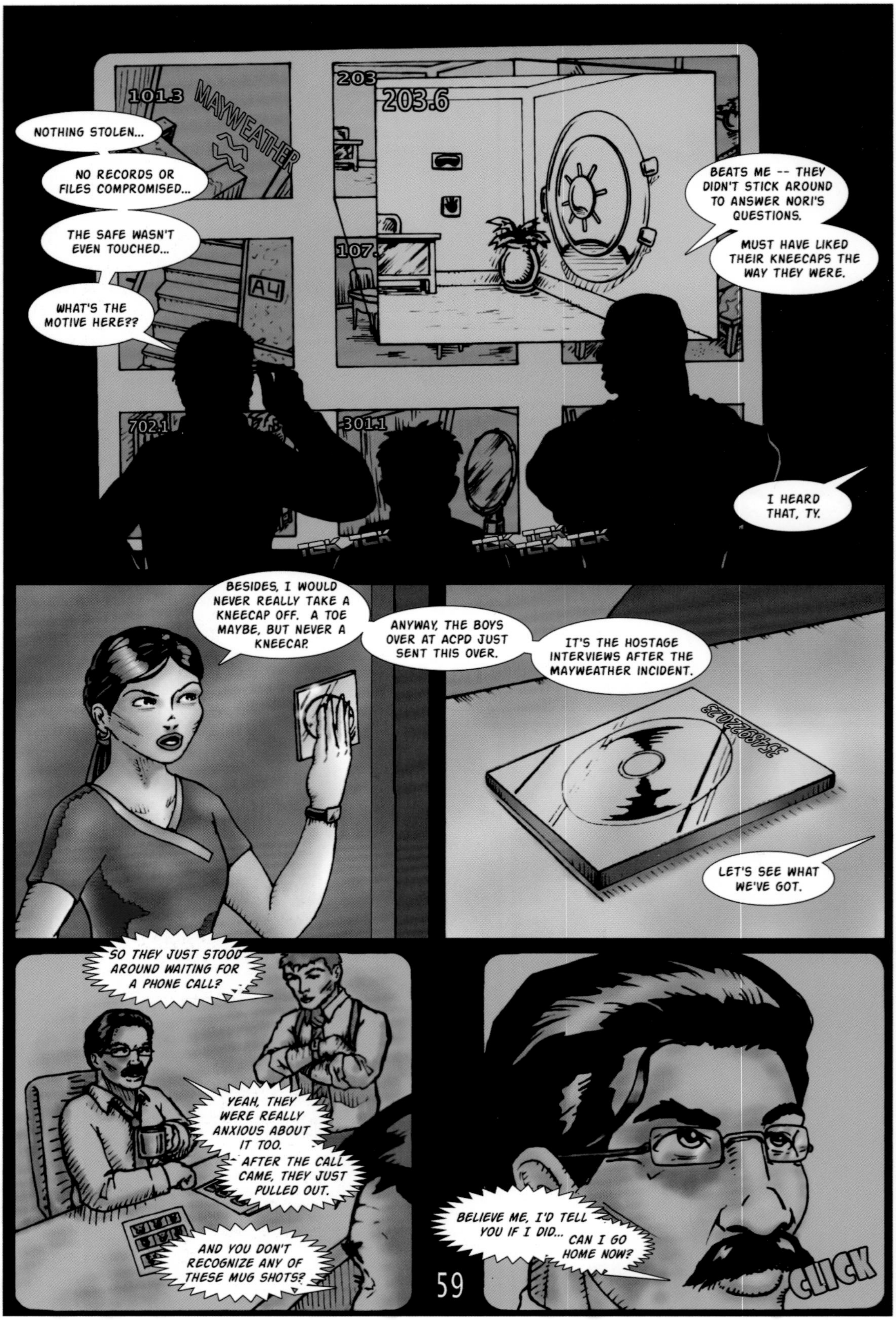
101.3
MAYWEATHER
203
203.6
NOTHING STOLEN...
NO RECORDS OR FILES COMPROMISED...
THE SAFE WASN'T EVEN TOUCHED...
WHAT'S THE MOTIVE HERE??
BEATS ME -- THEY DIDN'T STICK AROUND TO ANSWER NORI'S QUESTIONS.
MUST HAVE LIKED THEIR KNEECAPS THE WAY THEY WERE.
A4
702.1
301.1
I HEARD THAT, TY.
BESIDES, I WOULD NEVER REALLY TAKE A KNEECAP OFF. A TOE MAYBE, BUT NEVER A KNEECAP.
ANYWAY, THE BOYS OVER AT ACPD JUST SENT THIS OVER.
IT'S THE HOSTAGE INTERVIEWS AFTER THE MAYWEATHER INCIDENT.
LET'S SEE WHAT WE'VE GOT.
SO THEY JUST STOOD AROUND WAITING FOR A PHONE CALL?
YEAH, THEY WERE REALLY ANXIOUS ABOUT IT TOO.
AFTER THE CALL CAME, THEY JUST PULLED OUT.
AND YOU DON'T RECOGNIZE ANY OF THESE MUG SHOTS?
BELIEVE ME, I'D TELL YOU IF I DID... CAN I GO HOME NOW?
CLICK

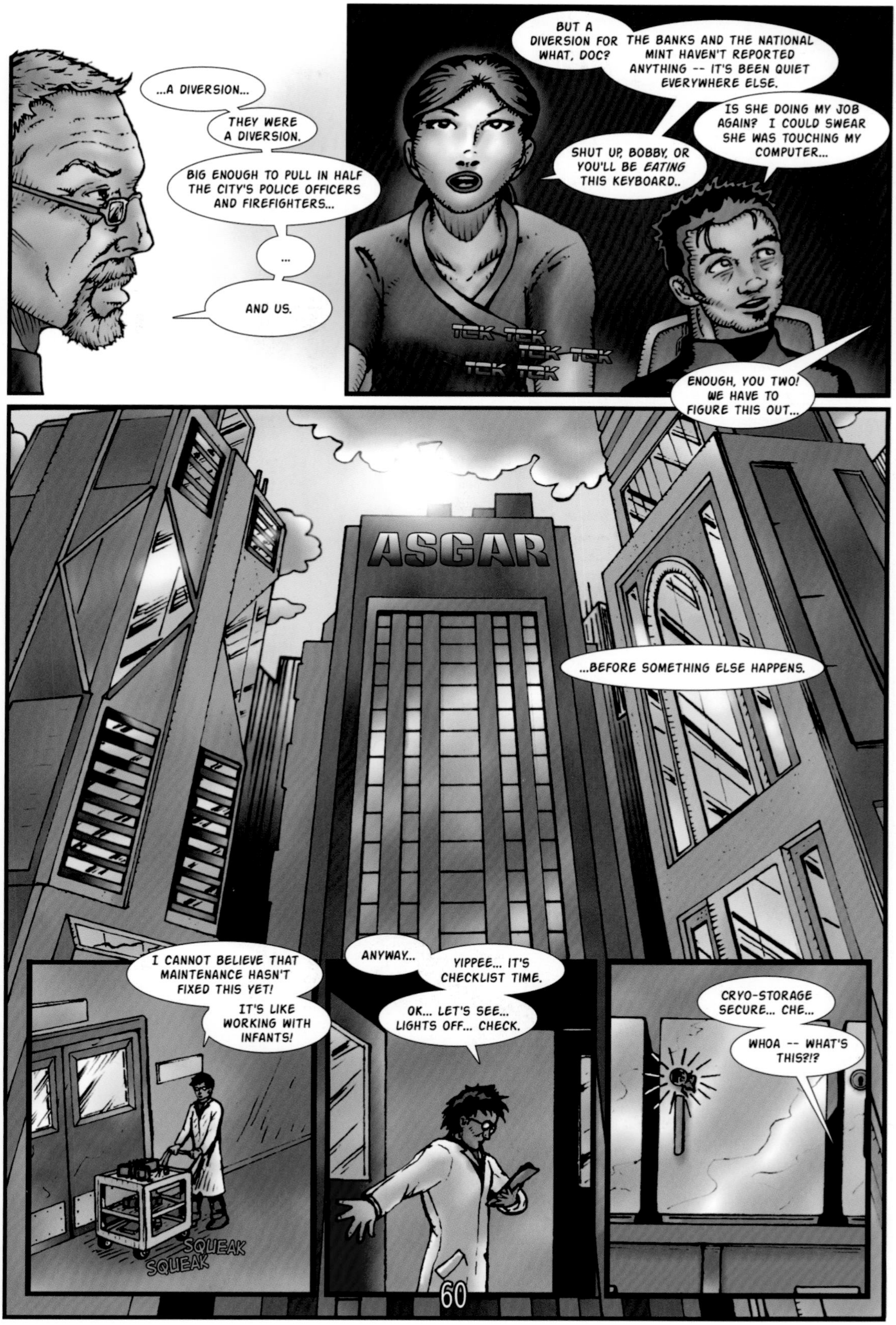
...A DIVERSION...
THEY WERE A DIVERSION.
BIG ENOUGH TO PULL IN HALF THE CITY'S POLICE OFFICERS AND FIREFIGHTERS...
...
AND US.
BUT A DIVERSION FOR WHAT, DOC?
THE BANKS AND THE NATIONAL MINT HAVEN'T REPORTED ANYTHING -- IT'S BEEN QUIET EVERYWHERE ELSE.
IS SHE DOING MY JOB AGAIN? I COULD SWEAR SHE WAS TOUCHING MY COMPUTER...
SHUT UP, BOBBY, OR YOU'LL BE *EATING* THIS KEYBOARD..
TCK TCK TCK TCK TCK TCK
ENOUGH, YOU TWO! WE HAVE TO FIGURE THIS OUT...
ASGAR
...BEFORE SOMETHING ELSE HAPPENS.
I CANNOT BELIEVE THAT MAINTENANCE HASN'T FIXED THIS YET!
IT'S LIKE WORKING WITH INFANTS!
SQUEAK SQUEAK
ANYWAY...
YIPPEE... IT'S CHECKLIST TIME.
OK... LET'S SEE... LIGHTS OFF... CHECK.
CRYO-STORAGE SECURE... CHE...
WHOA -- WHAT'S THIS?!?

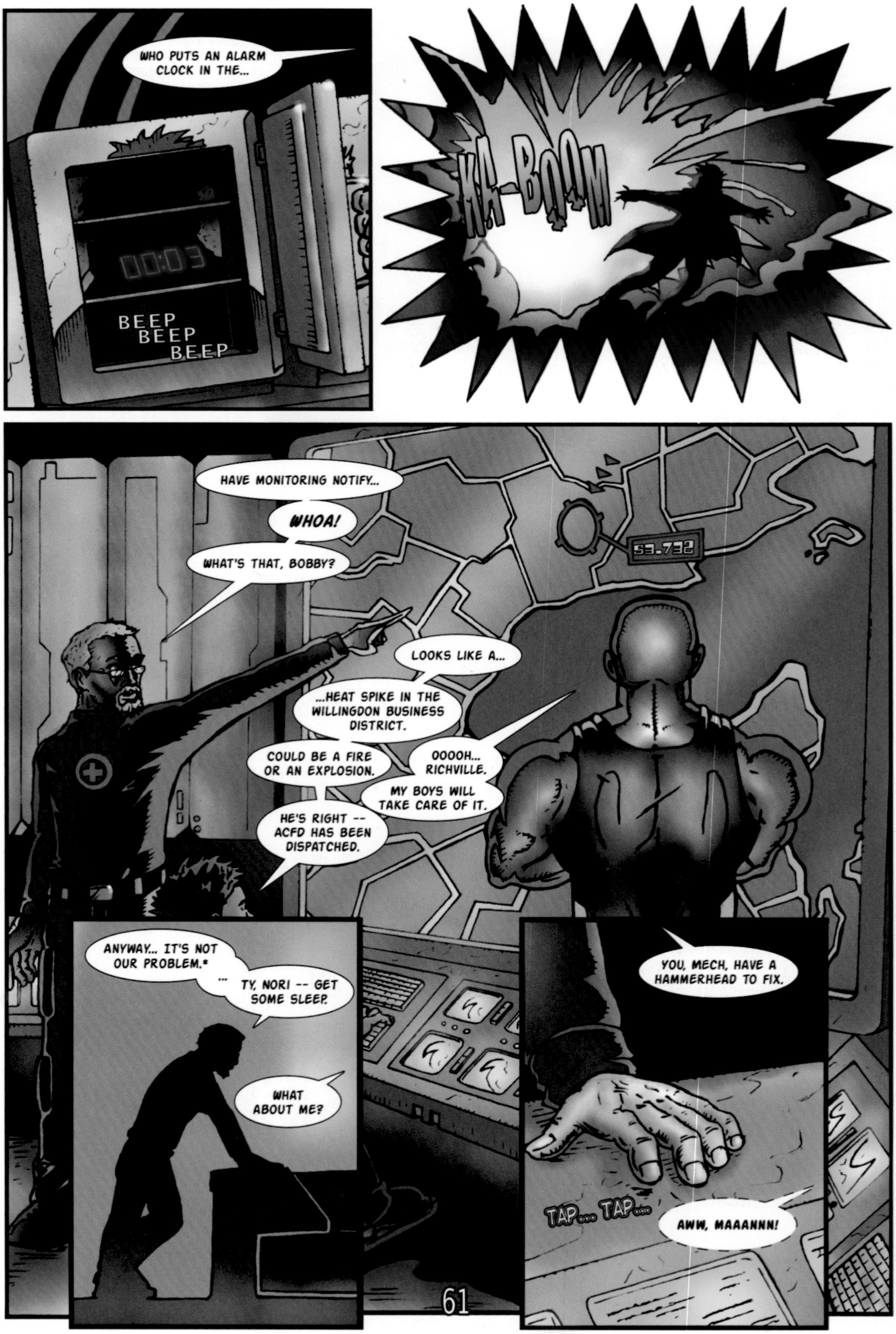
WHO PUTS AN ALARM CLOCK IN THE...
00:03
BEEP BEEP BEEP
KA-BOOM
HAVE MONITORING NOTIFY...
WHOA!
WHAT'S THAT, BOBBY?
53.732
LOOKS LIKE A...
...HEAT SPIKE IN THE WILLINGDON BUSINESS DISTRICT.
COULD BE A FIRE OR AN EXPLOSION.
OOOOH... RICHVILLE.
MY BOYS WILL TAKE CARE OF IT.
HE'S RIGHT -- ACFD HAS BEEN DISPATCHED.
ANYWAY... IT'S NOT OUR PROBLEM.*
... TY, NORI -- GET SOME SLEEP.
WHAT ABOUT ME?
YOU, MECH, HAVE A HAMMERHEAD TO FIX.
TAP... TAP...
AWW, MAAANNN!

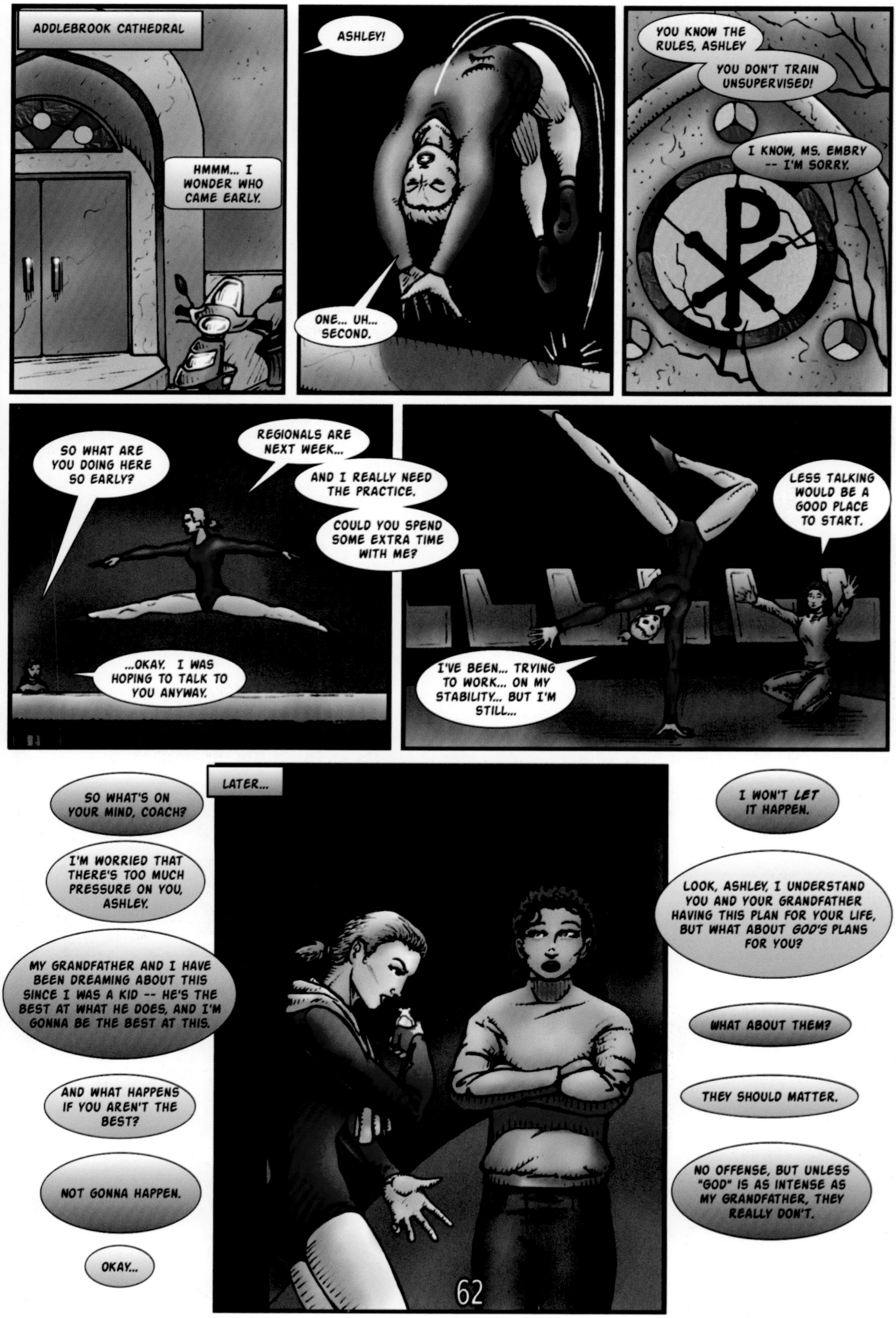

ADDLEBROOK CATHEDRAL
HMMM... I WONDER WHO CAME EARLY.
ASHLEY!
ONE... UH... SECOND.
YOU KNOW THE RULES, ASHLEY
YOU DON'T TRAIN UNSUPERVISED!
I KNOW, MS. EMBRY -- I'M SORRY.
SO WHAT ARE YOU DOING HERE SO EARLY?
REGIONALS ARE NEXT WEEK...
AND I REALLY NEED THE PRACTICE.
COULD YOU SPEND SOME EXTRA TIME WITH ME?
...OKAY. I WAS HOPING TO TALK TO YOU ANYWAY.
I'VE BEEN... TRYING TO WORK... ON MY STABILITY... BUT I'M STILL...
LESS TALKING WOULD BE A GOOD PLACE TO START.
LATER...
SO WHAT'S ON YOUR MIND, COACH?
I'M WORRIED THAT THERE'S TOO MUCH PRESSURE ON YOU, ASHLEY.
MY GRANDFATHER AND I HAVE BEEN DREAMING ABOUT THIS SINCE I WAS A KID -- HE'S THE BEST AT WHAT HE DOES, AND I'M GONNA BE THE BEST AT THIS.
AND WHAT HAPPENS IF YOU AREN'T THE BEST?
NOT GONNA HAPPEN.
OKAY...
I WON'T *LET* IT HAPPEN.
LOOK, ASHLEY, I UNDERSTAND YOU AND YOUR GRANDFATHER HAVING THIS PLAN FOR YOUR LIFE, BUT WHAT ABOUT *GOD'S* PLANS FOR YOU?
WHAT ABOUT THEM?
THEY SHOULD MATTER.
NO OFFENSE, BUT UNLESS "GOD" IS AS INTENSE AS MY GRANDFATHER, THEY REALLY DON'T.

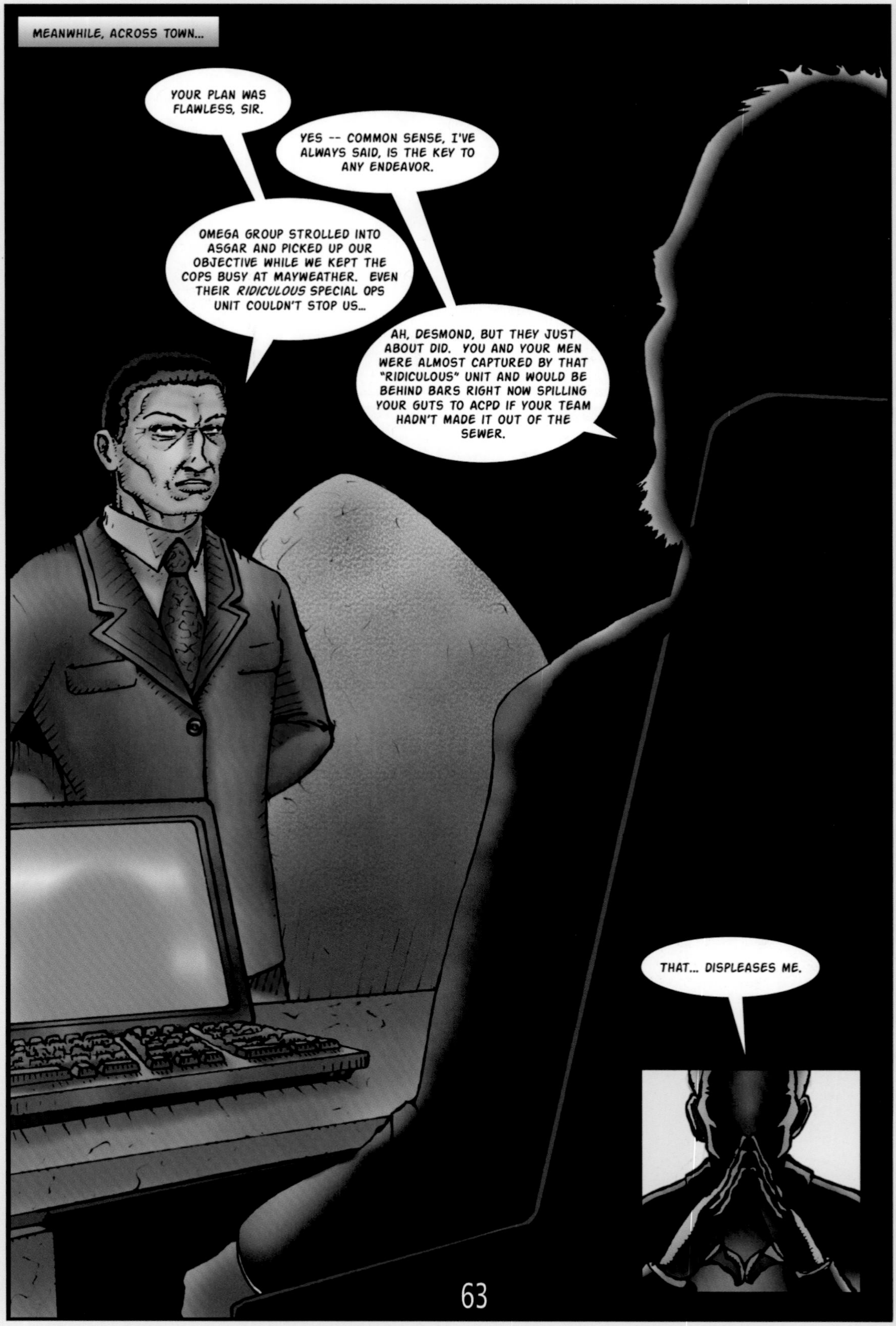
MEANWHILE, ACROSS TOWN...
YOUR PLAN WAS FLAWLESS, SIR.
YES -- COMMON SENSE, I'VE ALWAYS SAID, IS THE KEY TO ANY ENDEAVOR.
OMEGA GROUP STROLLED INTO ASGAR AND PICKED UP OUR OBJECTIVE WHILE WE KEPT THE COPS BUSY AT MAYWEATHER. EVEN THEIR *RIDICULOUS* SPECIAL OPS UNIT COULDN'T STOP US...
AH, DESMOND, BUT THEY JUST ABOUT DID. YOU AND YOUR MEN WERE ALMOST CAPTURED BY THAT "RIDICULOUS" UNIT AND WOULD BE BEHIND BARS RIGHT NOW SPILLING YOUR GUTS TO ACPD IF YOUR TEAM HADN'T MADE IT OUT OF THE SEWER.
THAT... DISPLEASES ME.

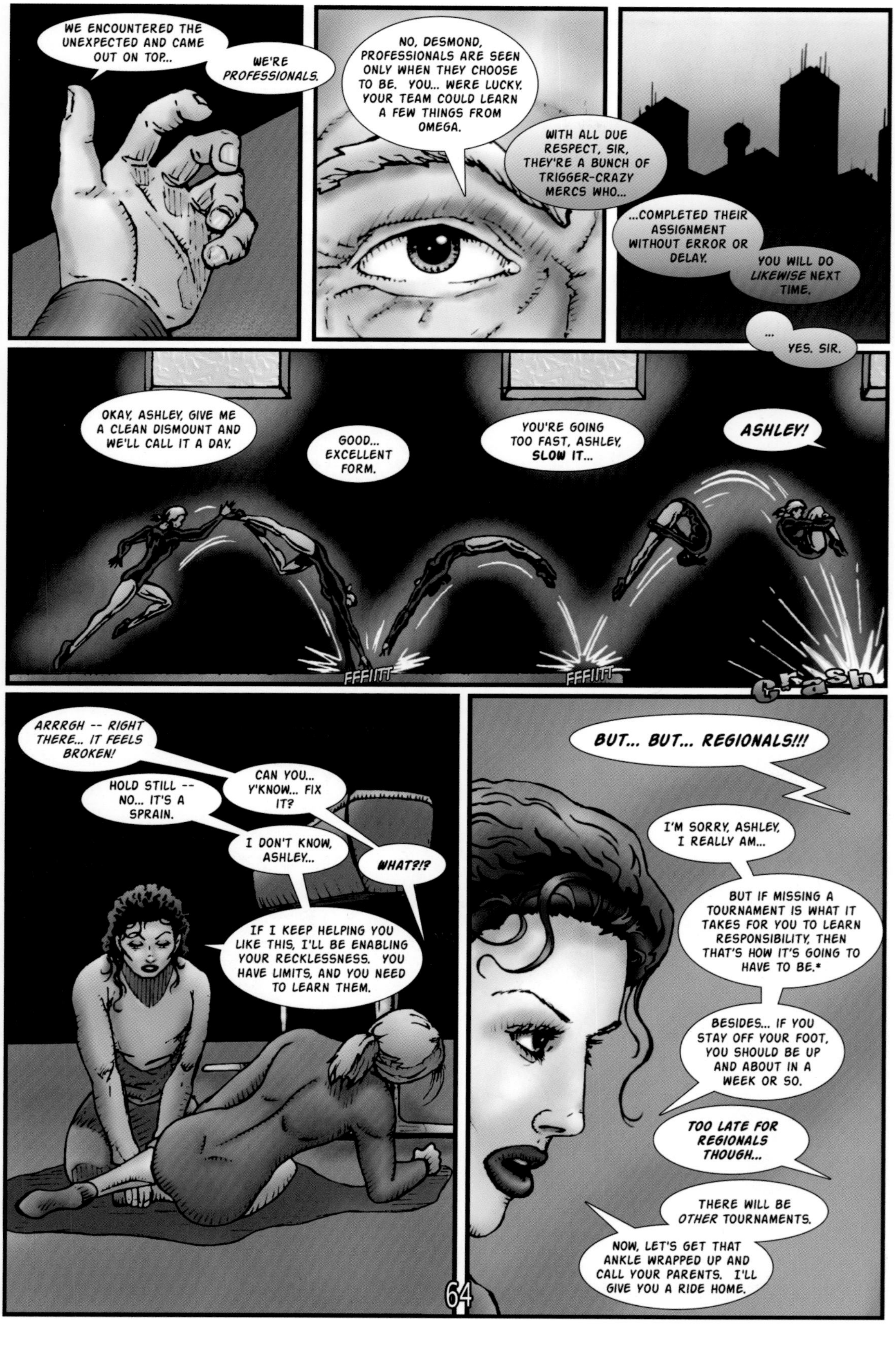
WE ENCOUNTERED THE UNEXPECTED AND CAME OUT ON TOP...
WE'RE *PROFESSIONALS.*
NO, DESMOND, PROFESSIONALS ARE SEEN ONLY WHEN THEY CHOOSE TO BE. YOU... WERE LUCKY. YOUR TEAM COULD LEARN A FEW THINGS FROM OMEGA.
WITH ALL DUE RESPECT, SIR, THEY'RE A BUNCH OF TRIGGER-CRAZY MERCS WHO...
...COMPLETED THEIR ASSIGNMENT WITHOUT ERROR OR DELAY.
YOU WILL DO *LIKEWISE* NEXT TIME.
... YES, SIR.
OKAY, ASHLEY, GIVE ME A CLEAN DISMOUNT AND WE'LL CALL IT A DAY.
GOOD... EXCELLENT FORM.
YOU'RE GOING TOO FAST, ASHLEY, **SLOW** IT...
ASHLEY!
FFFIIITT
FFFIIITT
CRASH
ARRRGH -- RIGHT THERE... IT FEELS BROKEN!
HOLD STILL -- NO... IT'S A SPRAIN.
CAN YOU... Y'KNOW... FIX IT?
I DON'T KNOW, ASHLEY...
WHAT?!?
IF I KEEP HELPING YOU LIKE THIS, I'LL BE ENABLING YOUR RECKLESSNESS. YOU HAVE LIMITS, AND YOU NEED TO LEARN THEM.
BUT... BUT... REGIONALS!!!
I'M SORRY, ASHLEY, I REALLY AM...
BUT IF MISSING A TOURNAMENT IS WHAT IT TAKES FOR YOU TO LEARN RESPONSIBILITY, THEN THAT'S HOW IT'S GOING TO HAVE TO BE.*
BESIDES... IF YOU STAY OFF YOUR FOOT, YOU SHOULD BE UP AND ABOUT IN A WEEK OR SO.
TOO LATE FOR REGIONALS THOUGH...
THERE WILL BE *OTHER* TOURNAMENTS.
NOW, LET'S GET THAT ANKLE WRAPPED UP AND CALL YOUR PARENTS. I'LL GIVE YOU A RIDE HOME.

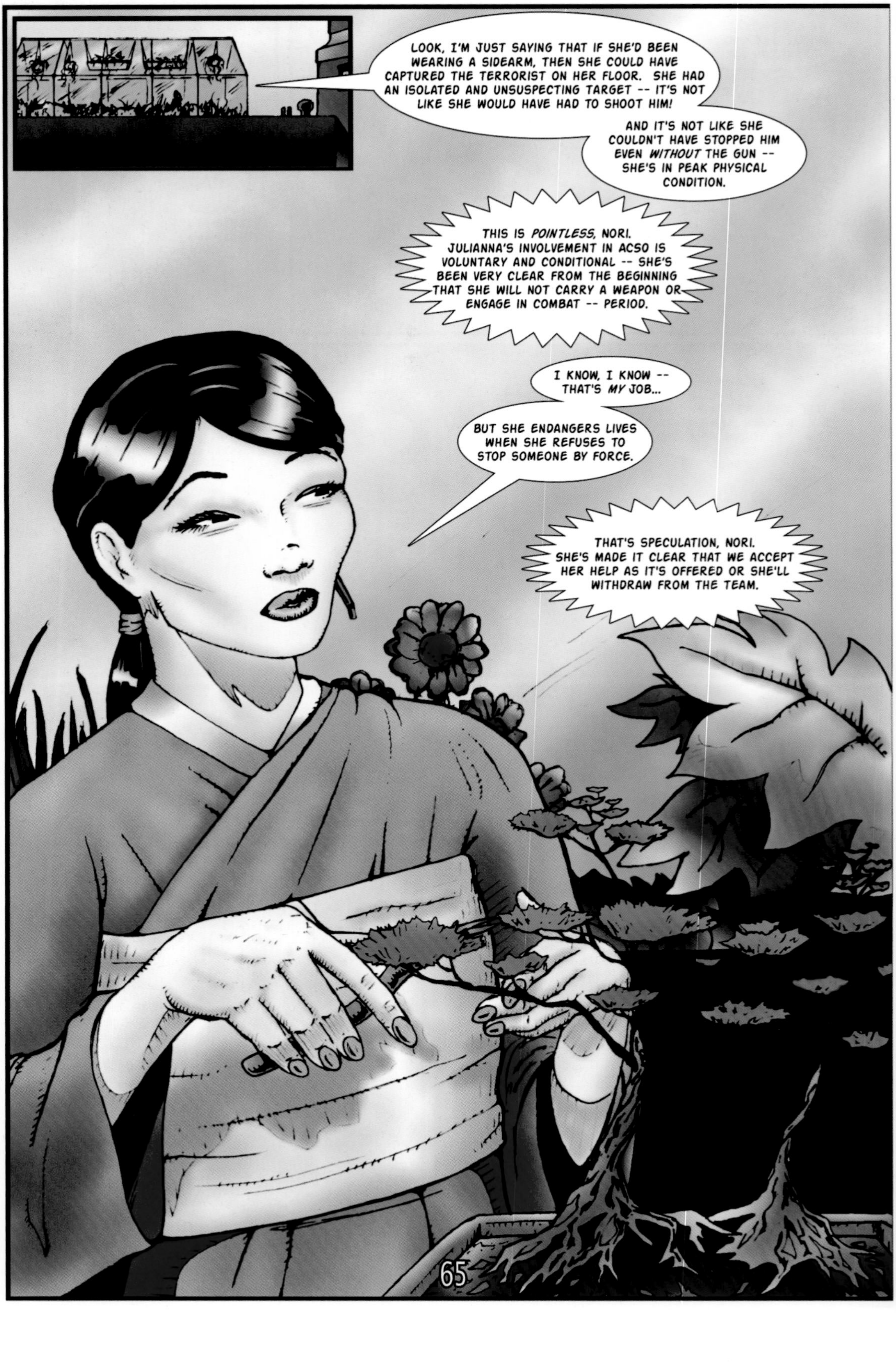
LOOK, I'M JUST SAYING THAT IF SHE'D BEEN WEARING A SIDEARM, THEN SHE COULD HAVE CAPTURED THE TERRORIST ON HER FLOOR. SHE HAD AN ISOLATED AND UNSUSPECTING TARGET -- IT'S NOT LIKE SHE WOULD HAVE HAD TO SHOOT HIM!
AND IT'S NOT LIKE SHE COULDN'T HAVE STOPPED HIM EVEN *WITHOUT* THE GUN -- SHE'S IN PEAK PHYSICAL CONDITION.
THIS IS *POINTLESS*, NORI. JULIANNA'S INVOLVEMENT IN ACSO IS VOLUNTARY AND CONDITIONAL -- SHE'S BEEN VERY CLEAR FROM THE BEGINNING THAT SHE WILL NOT CARRY A WEAPON OR ENGAGE IN COMBAT -- PERIOD.
I KNOW, I KNOW -- THAT'S *MY* JOB...
BUT SHE ENDANGERS LIVES WHEN SHE REFUSES TO STOP SOMEONE BY FORCE.
THAT'S SPECULATION, NORI. SHE'S MADE IT CLEAR THAT WE ACCEPT HER HELP AS IT'S OFFERED OR SHE'LL WITHDRAW FROM THE TEAM.

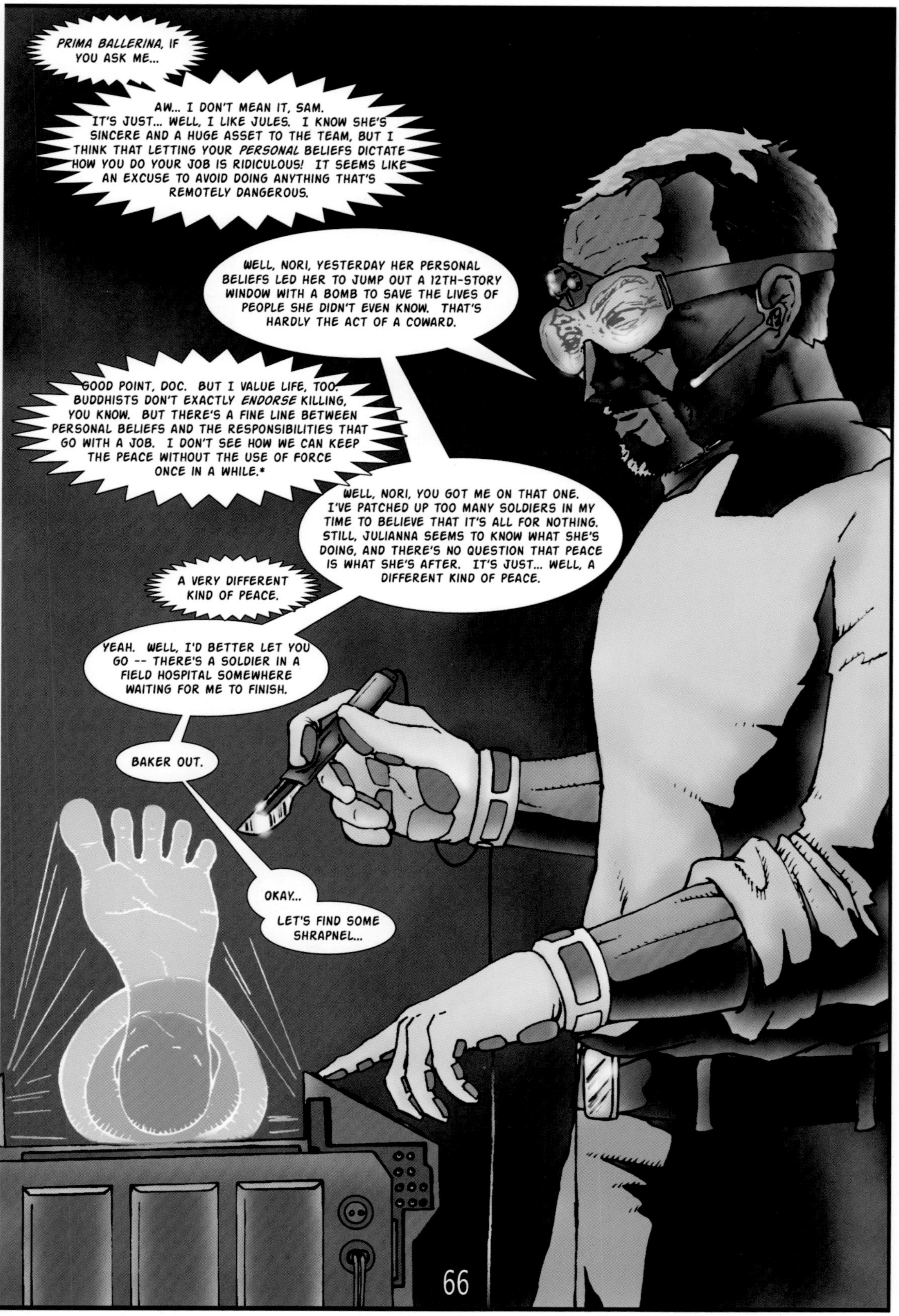
PRIMA BALLERINA, IF YOU ASK ME...
AW... I DON'T MEAN IT, SAM. IT'S JUST... WELL, I LIKE JULES. I KNOW SHE'S SINCERE AND A HUGE ASSET TO THE TEAM, BUT I THINK THAT LETTING YOUR PERSONAL BELIEFS DICTATE HOW YOU DO YOUR JOB IS RIDICULOUS! IT SEEMS LIKE AN EXCUSE TO AVOID DOING ANYTHING THAT'S REMOTELY DANGEROUS.
WELL, NORI, YESTERDAY HER PERSONAL BELIEFS LED HER TO JUMP OUT A 12TH-STORY WINDOW WITH A BOMB TO SAVE THE LIVES OF PEOPLE SHE DIDN'T EVEN KNOW. THAT'S HARDLY THE ACT OF A COWARD.
GOOD POINT, DOC. BUT I VALUE LIFE, TOO. BUDDHISTS DON'T EXACTLY ENDORSE KILLING, YOU KNOW. BUT THERE'S A FINE LINE BETWEEN PERSONAL BELIEFS AND THE RESPONSIBILITIES THAT GO WITH A JOB. I DON'T SEE HOW WE CAN KEEP THE PEACE WITHOUT THE USE OF FORCE ONCE IN A WHILE.*
WELL, NORI, YOU GOT ME ON THAT ONE. I'VE PATCHED UP TOO MANY SOLDIERS IN MY TIME TO BELIEVE THAT IT'S ALL FOR NOTHING. STILL, JULIANNA SEEMS TO KNOW WHAT SHE'S DOING, AND THERE'S NO QUESTION THAT PEACE IS WHAT SHE'S AFTER. IT'S JUST... WELL, A DIFFERENT KIND OF PEACE.
A VERY DIFFERENT KIND OF PEACE.
YEAH. WELL, I'D BETTER LET YOU GO -- THERE'S A SOLDIER IN A FIELD HOSPITAL SOMEWHERE WAITING FOR ME TO FINISH.
BAKER OUT.
OKAY...
LET'S FIND SOME SHRAPNEL...

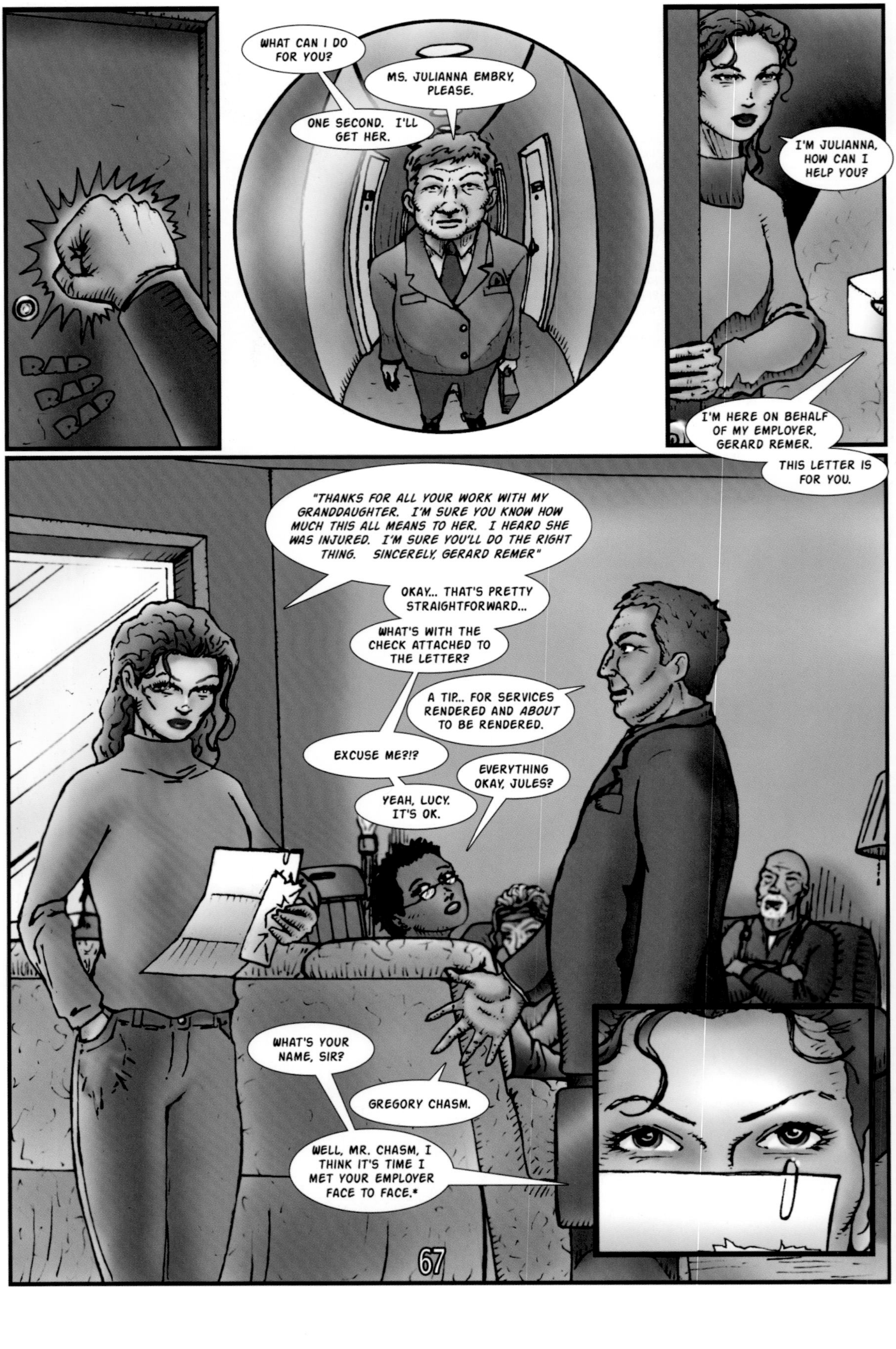
RAP
RAP
RAP
WHAT CAN I DO FOR YOU?
MS. JULIANNA EMBRY, PLEASE.
ONE SECOND. I'LL GET HER.
I'M JULIANNA, HOW CAN I HELP YOU?
I'M HERE ON BEHALF OF MY EMPLOYER, GERARD REMER.
THIS LETTER IS FOR YOU.
"THANKS FOR ALL YOUR WORK WITH MY GRANDDAUGHTER. I'M SURE YOU KNOW HOW MUCH THIS ALL MEANS TO HER. I HEARD SHE WAS INJURED. I'M SURE YOU'LL DO THE RIGHT THING. SINCERELY, GERARD REMER"
OKAY... THAT'S PRETTY STRAIGHTFORWARD...
WHAT'S WITH THE CHECK ATTACHED TO THE LETTER?
A TIP... FOR SERVICES RENDERED AND ABOUT TO BE RENDERED.
EXCUSE ME?!?
EVERYTHING OKAY, JULES?
YEAH, LUCY. IT'S OK.
WHAT'S YOUR NAME, SIR?
GREGORY CHASM.
WELL, MR. CHASM, I THINK IT'S TIME I MET YOUR EMPLOYER FACE TO FACE.*

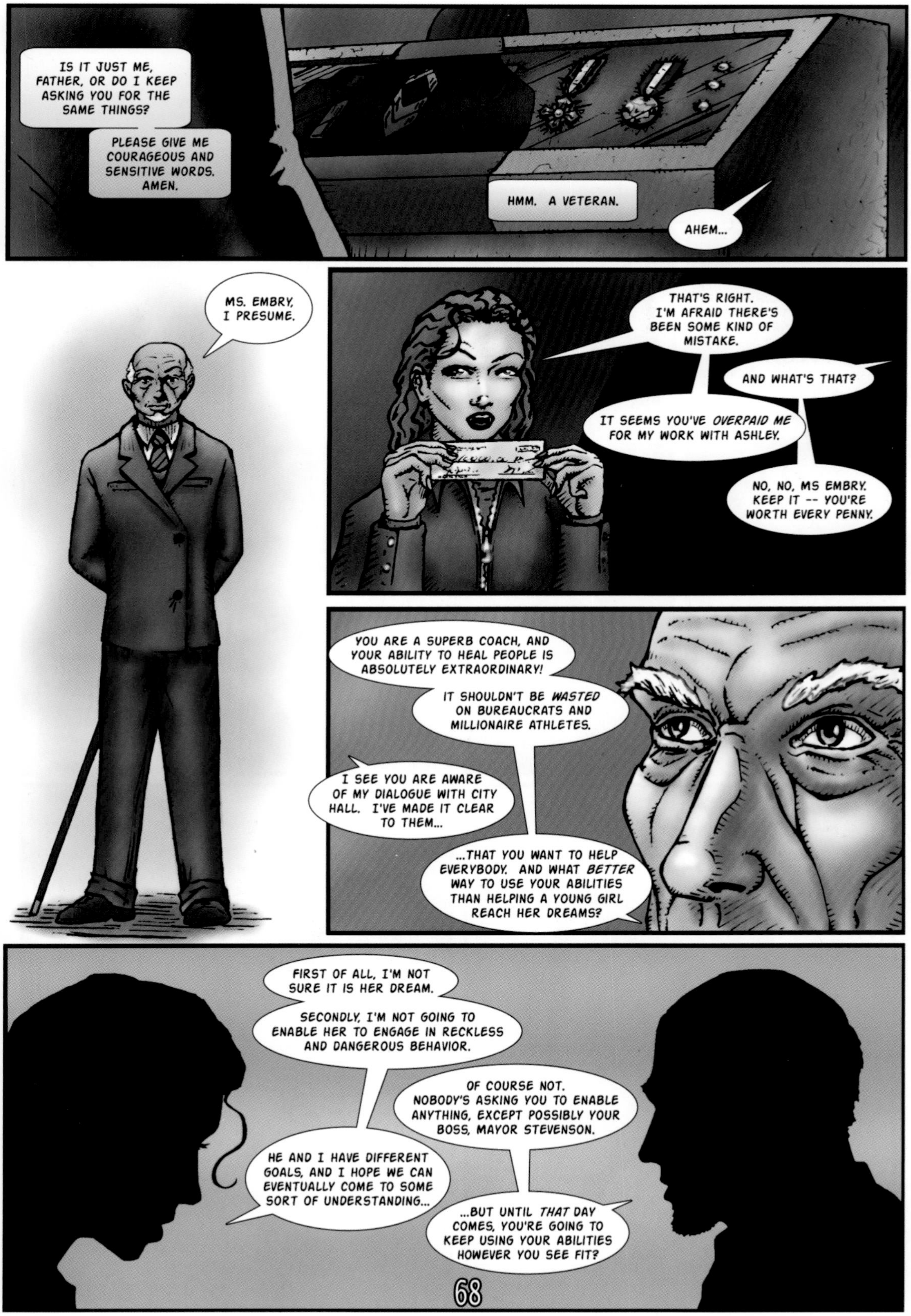
IS IT JUST ME, FATHER, OR DO I KEEP ASKING YOU FOR THE SAME THINGS?
PLEASE GIVE ME COURAGEOUS AND SENSITIVE WORDS. AMEN.
HMM. A VETERAN.
AHEM...
MS. EMBRY, I PRESUME.
THAT'S RIGHT. I'M AFRAID THERE'S BEEN SOME KIND OF MISTAKE.
AND WHAT'S THAT?
IT SEEMS YOU'VE OVERPAID ME FOR MY WORK WITH ASHLEY.
NO, NO, MS EMBRY. KEEP IT -- YOU'RE WORTH EVERY PENNY.
YOU ARE A SUPERB COACH, AND YOUR ABILITY TO HEAL PEOPLE IS ABSOLUTELY EXTRAORDINARY!
IT SHOULDN'T BE WASTED ON BUREAUCRATS AND MILLIONAIRE ATHLETES.
I SEE YOU ARE AWARE OF MY DIALOGUE WITH CITY HALL. I'VE MADE IT CLEAR TO THEM...
...THAT YOU WANT TO HELP EVERYBODY. AND WHAT BETTER WAY TO USE YOUR ABILITIES THAN HELPING A YOUNG GIRL REACH HER DREAMS?
FIRST OF ALL, I'M NOT SURE IT IS HER DREAM.
SECONDLY, I'M NOT GOING TO ENABLE HER TO ENGAGE IN RECKLESS AND DANGEROUS BEHAVIOR.
OF COURSE NOT. NOBODY'S ASKING YOU TO ENABLE ANYTHING, EXCEPT POSSIBLY YOUR BOSS, MAYOR STEVENSON.
HE AND I HAVE DIFFERENT GOALS, AND I HOPE WE CAN EVENTUALLY COME TO SOME SORT OF UNDERSTANDING...
...BUT UNTIL THAT DAY COMES, YOU'RE GOING TO KEEP USING YOUR ABILITIES HOWEVER YOU SEE FIT?

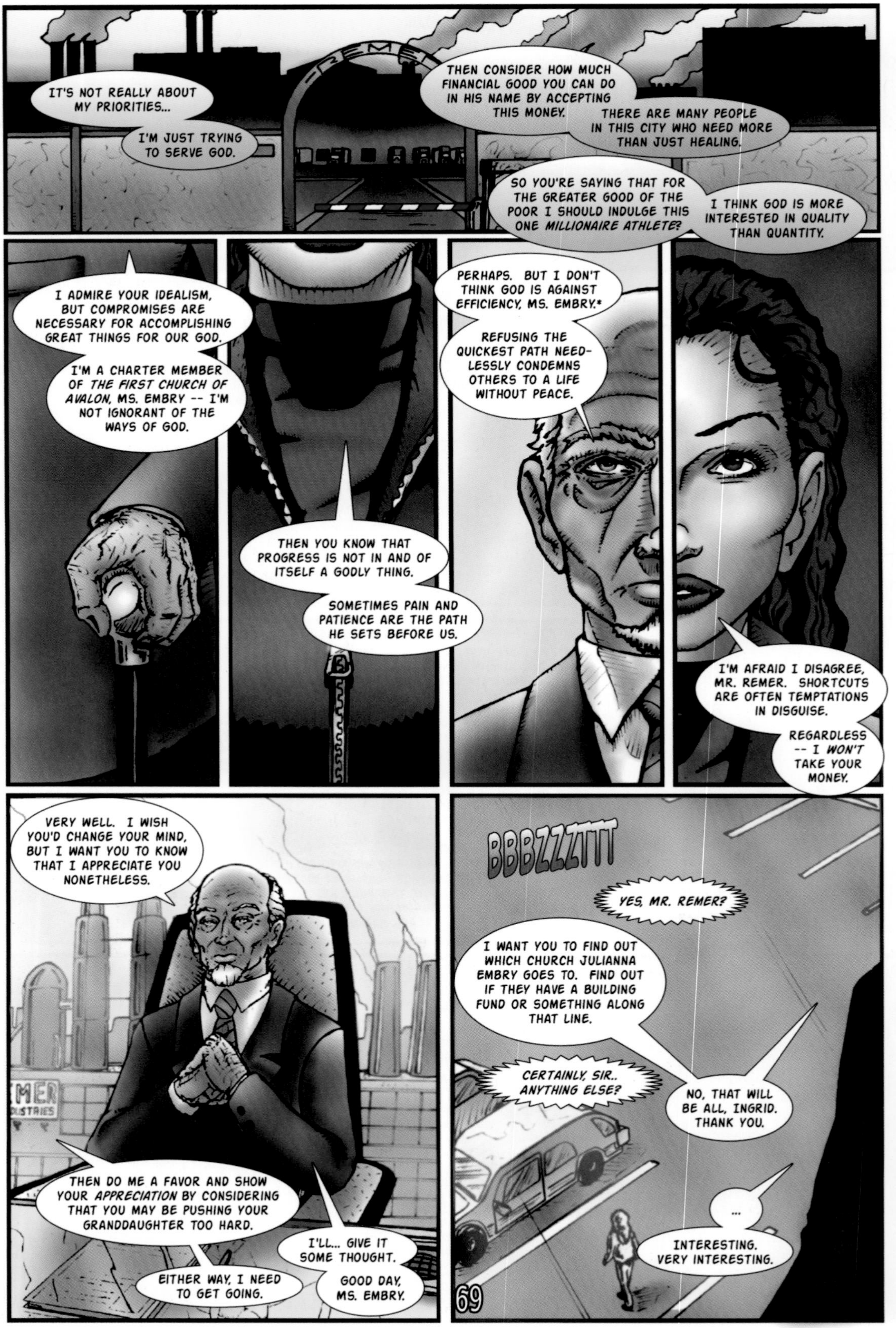
IT'S NOT REALLY ABOUT MY PRIORITIES...
I'M JUST TRYING TO SERVE GOD.
THEN CONSIDER HOW MUCH FINANCIAL GOOD YOU CAN DO IN HIS NAME BY ACCEPTING THIS MONEY.
THERE ARE MANY PEOPLE IN THIS CITY WHO NEED MORE THAN JUST HEALING.
SO YOU'RE SAYING THAT FOR THE GREATER GOOD OF THE POOR I SHOULD INDULGE THIS ONE *MILLIONAIRE ATHLETE*?
I THINK GOD IS MORE INTERESTED IN QUALITY THAN QUANTITY.
I ADMIRE YOUR IDEALISM, BUT COMPROMISES ARE NECESSARY FOR ACCOMPLISHING GREAT THINGS FOR OUR GOD.
I'M A CHARTER MEMBER OF *THE FIRST CHURCH OF AVALON*, MS. EMBRY -- I'M NOT IGNORANT OF THE WAYS OF GOD.
THEN YOU KNOW THAT PROGRESS IS NOT IN AND OF ITSELF A GODLY THING.
SOMETIMES PAIN AND PATIENCE ARE THE PATH HE SETS BEFORE US.
PERHAPS. BUT I DON'T THINK GOD IS AGAINST EFFICIENCY, MS. EMBRY.*
REFUSING THE QUICKEST PATH NEEDLESSLY CONDEMNS OTHERS TO A LIFE WITHOUT PEACE.
I'M AFRAID I DISAGREE, MR. REMER. SHORTCUTS ARE OFTEN TEMPTATIONS IN DISGUISE.
REGARDLESS -- I *WON'T* TAKE YOUR MONEY.
VERY WELL. I WISH YOU'D CHANGE YOUR MIND, BUT I WANT YOU TO KNOW THAT I APPRECIATE YOU NONETHELESS.
THEN DO ME A FAVOR AND SHOW YOUR *APPRECIATION* BY CONSIDERING THAT YOU MAY BE PUSHING YOUR GRANDDAUGHTER TOO HARD.
EITHER WAY, I NEED TO GET GOING.
I'LL... GIVE IT SOME THOUGHT.
GOOD DAY, MS. EMBRY.
BBBZZZTTT
YES, MR. REMER?
I WANT YOU TO FIND OUT WHICH CHURCH JULIANNA EMBRY GOES TO. FIND OUT IF THEY HAVE A BUILDING FUND OR SOMETHING ALONG THAT LINE.
CERTAINLY, SIR.. ANYTHING ELSE?
NO, THAT WILL BE ALL, INGRID. THANK YOU.
...
INTERESTING. VERY INTERESTING.

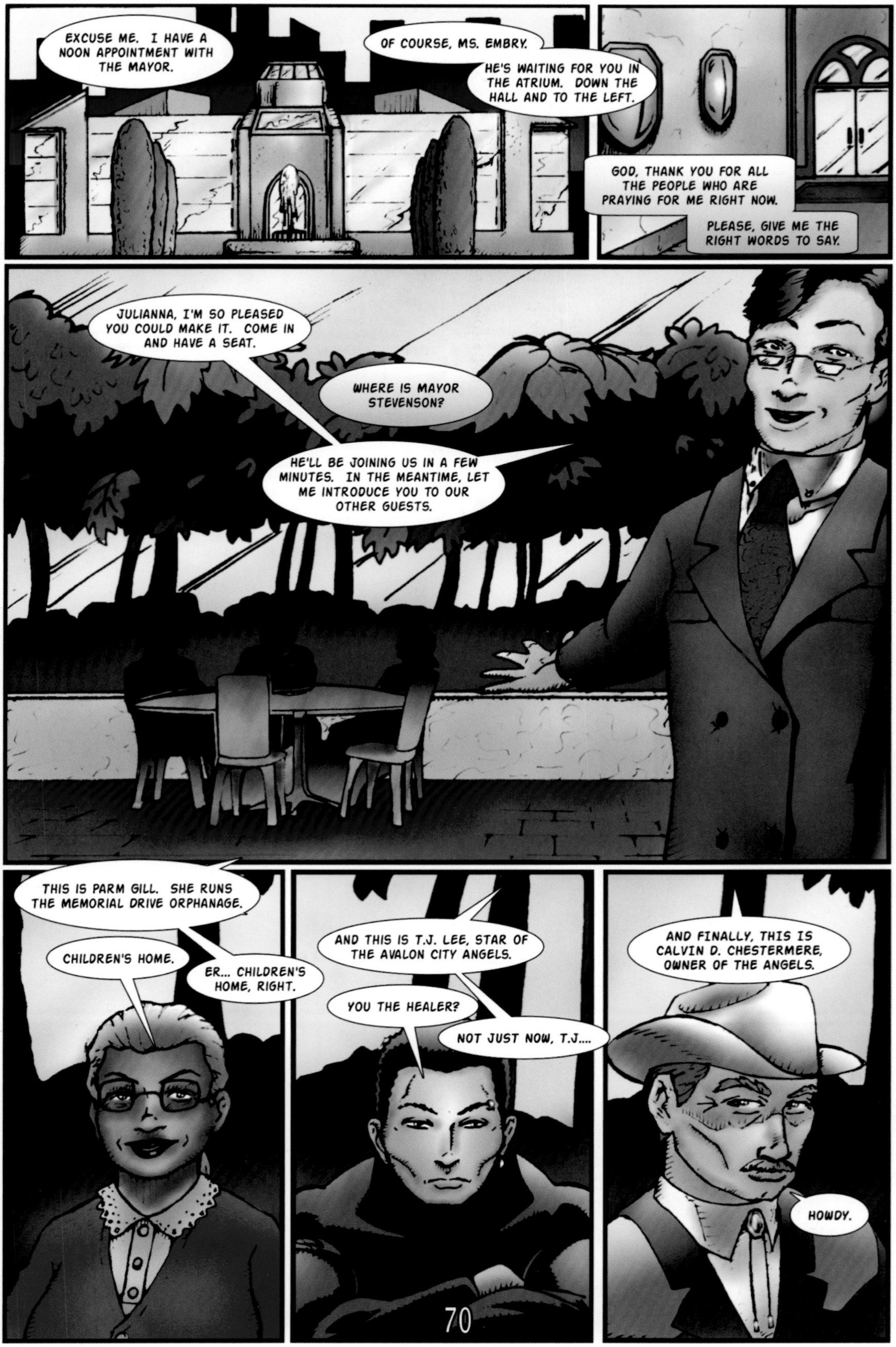
EXCUSE ME. I HAVE A NOON APPOINTMENT WITH THE MAYOR.
OF COURSE, MS. EMBRY.
HE'S WAITING FOR YOU IN THE ATRIUM. DOWN THE HALL AND TO THE LEFT.
GOD, THANK YOU FOR ALL THE PEOPLE WHO ARE PRAYING FOR ME RIGHT NOW.
PLEASE, GIVE ME THE RIGHT WORDS TO SAY.
JULIANNA, I'M SO PLEASED YOU COULD MAKE IT. COME IN AND HAVE A SEAT.
WHERE IS MAYOR STEVENSON?
HE'LL BE JOINING US IN A FEW MINUTES. IN THE MEANTIME, LET ME INTRODUCE YOU TO OUR OTHER GUESTS.
THIS IS PARM GILL. SHE RUNS THE MEMORIAL DRIVE ORPHANAGE.
CHILDREN'S HOME.
ER... CHILDREN'S HOME, RIGHT.
AND THIS IS T.J. LEE, STAR OF THE AVALON CITY ANGELS.
YOU THE HEALER?
NOT JUST NOW, T.J....
AND FINALLY, THIS IS CALVIN D. CHESTERMERE, OWNER OF THE ANGELS.
HOWDY.

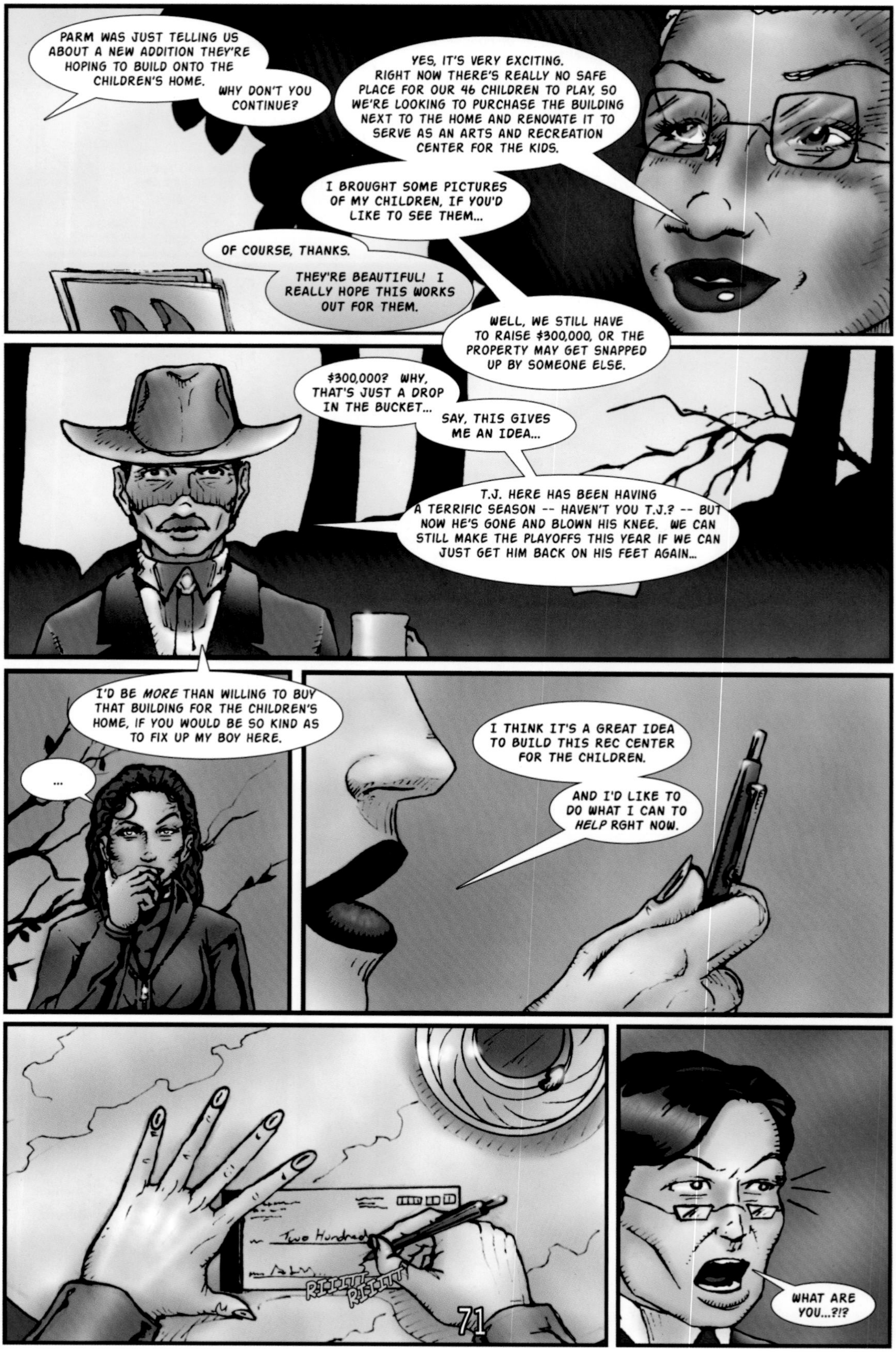
PARM WAS JUST TELLING US ABOUT A NEW ADDITION THEY'RE HOPING TO BUILD ONTO THE CHILDREN'S HOME.
WHY DON'T YOU CONTINUE?
YES, IT'S VERY EXCITING. RIGHT NOW THERE'S REALLY NO SAFE PLACE FOR OUR 46 CHILDREN TO PLAY, SO WE'RE LOOKING TO PURCHASE THE BUILDING NEXT TO THE HOME AND RENOVATE IT TO SERVE AS AN ARTS AND RECREATION CENTER FOR THE KIDS.
I BROUGHT SOME PICTURES OF MY CHILDREN, IF YOU'D LIKE TO SEE THEM...
OF COURSE, THANKS.
THEY'RE BEAUTIFUL! I REALLY HOPE THIS WORKS OUT FOR THEM.
WELL, WE STILL HAVE TO RAISE $300,000, OR THE PROPERTY MAY GET SNAPPED UP BY SOMEONE ELSE.
$300,000? WHY, THAT'S JUST A DROP IN THE BUCKET...
SAY, THIS GIVES ME AN IDEA...
T.J. HERE HAS BEEN HAVING A TERRIFIC SEASON -- HAVEN'T YOU T.J.? -- BUT NOW HE'S GONE AND BLOWN HIS KNEE. WE CAN STILL MAKE THE PLAYOFFS THIS YEAR IF WE CAN JUST GET HIM BACK ON HIS FEET AGAIN...
I'D BE *MORE* THAN WILLING TO BUY THAT BUILDING FOR THE CHILDREN'S HOME, IF YOU WOULD BE SO KIND AS TO FIX UP MY BOY HERE.
...
I THINK IT'S A GREAT IDEA TO BUILD THIS REC CENTER FOR THE CHILDREN.
AND I'D LIKE TO DO WHAT I CAN TO *HELP* RGHT NOW.
Two Hundred
WHAT ARE YOU...?!?

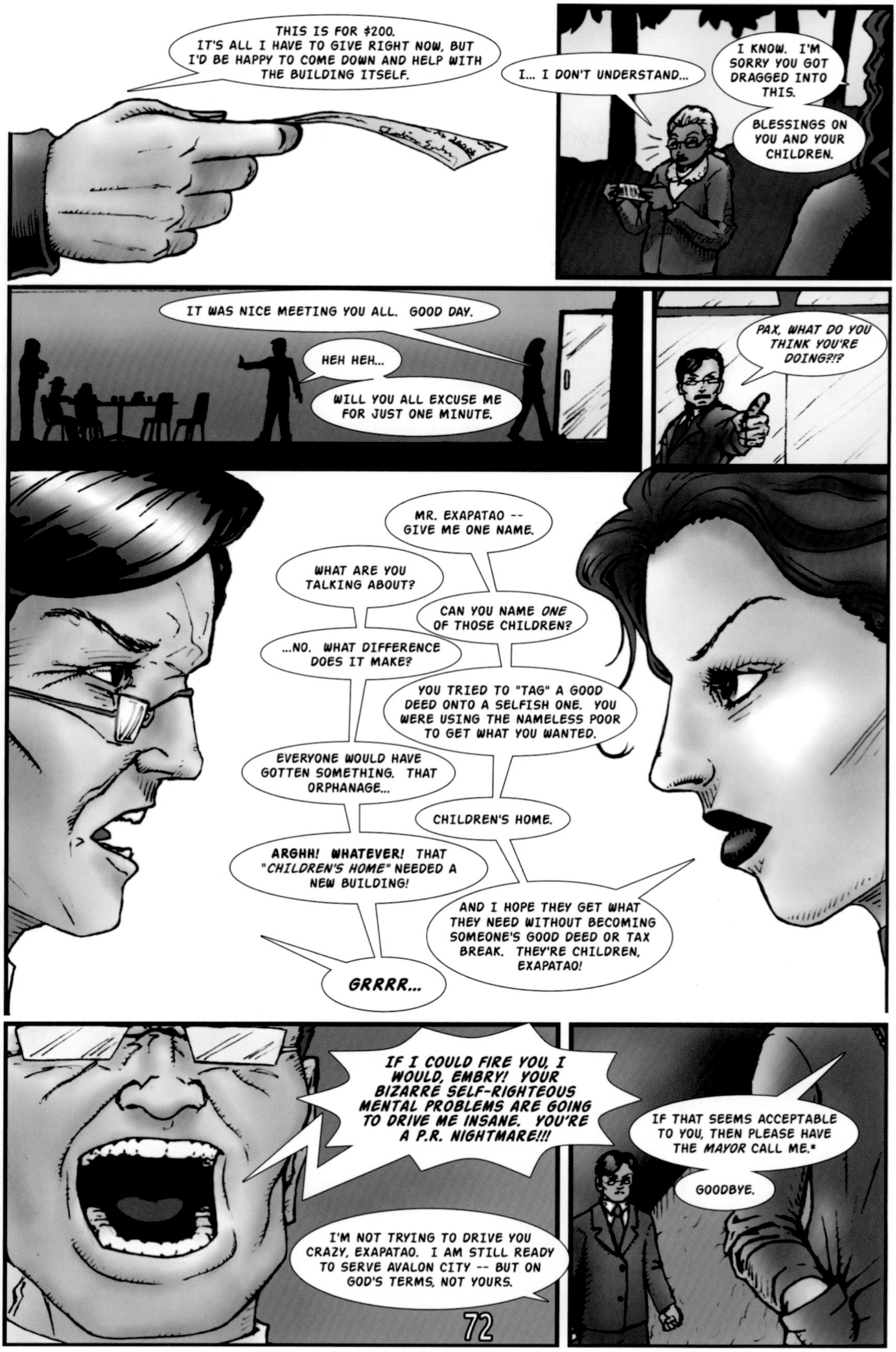
THIS IS FOR $200.
IT'S ALL I HAVE TO GIVE RIGHT NOW, BUT I'D BE HAPPY TO COME DOWN AND HELP WITH THE BUILDING ITSELF.
I... I DON'T UNDERSTAND...
I KNOW. I'M SORRY YOU GOT DRAGGED INTO THIS.
BLESSINGS ON YOU AND YOUR CHILDREN.
IT WAS NICE MEETING YOU ALL. GOOD DAY.
HEH HEH...
WILL YOU ALL EXCUSE ME FOR JUST ONE MINUTE.
PAX, WHAT DO YOU THINK YOU'RE DOING?!?
MR. EXAPATAO -- GIVE ME ONE NAME.
WHAT ARE YOU TALKING ABOUT?
CAN YOU NAME *ONE* OF THOSE CHILDREN?
...NO. WHAT DIFFERENCE DOES IT MAKE?
YOU TRIED TO "TAG" A GOOD DEED ONTO A SELFISH ONE. YOU WERE USING THE NAMELESS POOR TO GET WHAT YOU WANTED.
EVERYONE WOULD HAVE GOTTEN SOMETHING. THAT ORPHANAGE...
CHILDREN'S HOME.
ARGHH! WHATEVER! THAT "*CHILDREN'S HOME*" NEEDED A NEW BUILDING!
AND I HOPE THEY GET WHAT THEY NEED WITHOUT BECOMING SOMEONE'S GOOD DEED OR TAX BREAK. THEY'RE CHILDREN, EXAPATAO!
GRRRR...
IF I COULD FIRE YOU, I WOULD, EMBRY! YOUR BIZARRE SELF-RIGHTEOUS MENTAL PROBLEMS ARE GOING TO DRIVE ME INSANE. YOU'RE A P.R. NIGHTMARE!!!
I'M NOT TRYING TO DRIVE YOU CRAZY, EXAPATAO. I AM STILL READY TO SERVE AVALON CITY -- BUT ON GOD'S TERMS, NOT YOURS.
IF THAT SEEMS ACCEPTABLE TO YOU, THEN PLEASE HAVE THE *MAYOR* CALL ME.*
GOODBYE.

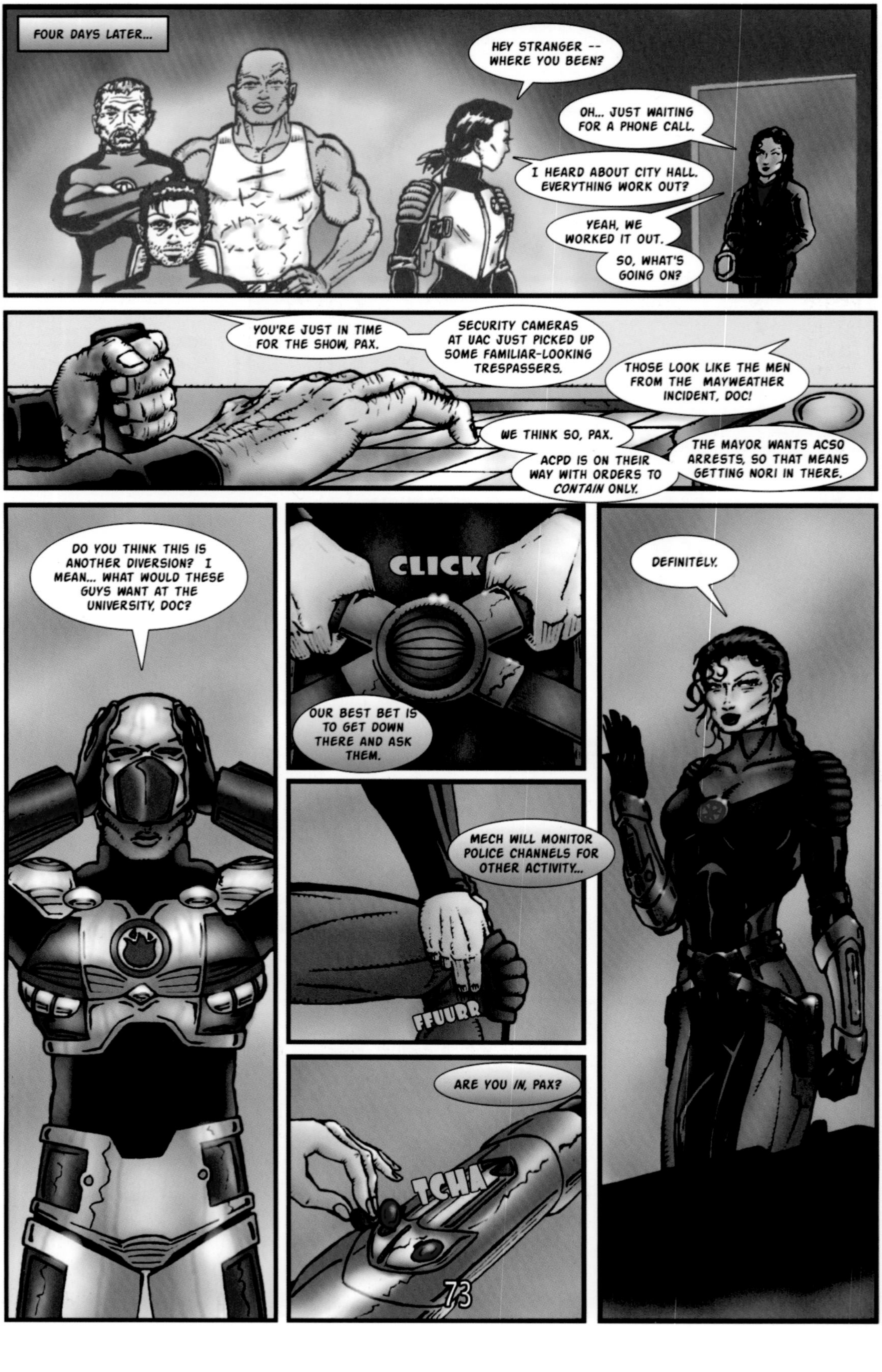
FOUR DAYS LATER...
HEY STRANGER -- WHERE YOU BEEN?
OH... JUST WAITING FOR A PHONE CALL.
I HEARD ABOUT CITY HALL. EVERYTHING WORK OUT?
YEAH, WE WORKED IT OUT.
SO, WHAT'S GOING ON?
YOU'RE JUST IN TIME FOR THE SHOW, PAX.
SECURITY CAMERAS AT UAC JUST PICKED UP SOME FAMILIAR-LOOKING TRESPASSERS.
THOSE LOOK LIKE THE MEN FROM THE MAYWEATHER INCIDENT, DOC!
WE THINK SO, PAX.
ACPD IS ON THEIR WAY WITH ORDERS TO *CONTAIN* ONLY.
THE MAYOR WANTS ACSO ARRESTS, SO THAT MEANS GETTING NORI IN THERE.
DO YOU THINK THIS IS ANOTHER DIVERSION? I MEAN... WHAT WOULD THESE GUYS WANT AT THE UNIVERSITY, DOC?
CLICK
OUR BEST BET IS TO GET DOWN THERE AND ASK THEM.
DEFINITELY.
MECH WILL MONITOR POLICE CHANNELS FOR OTHER ACTIVITY...
FFUURR
ARE YOU *IN*, PAX?
TCHA

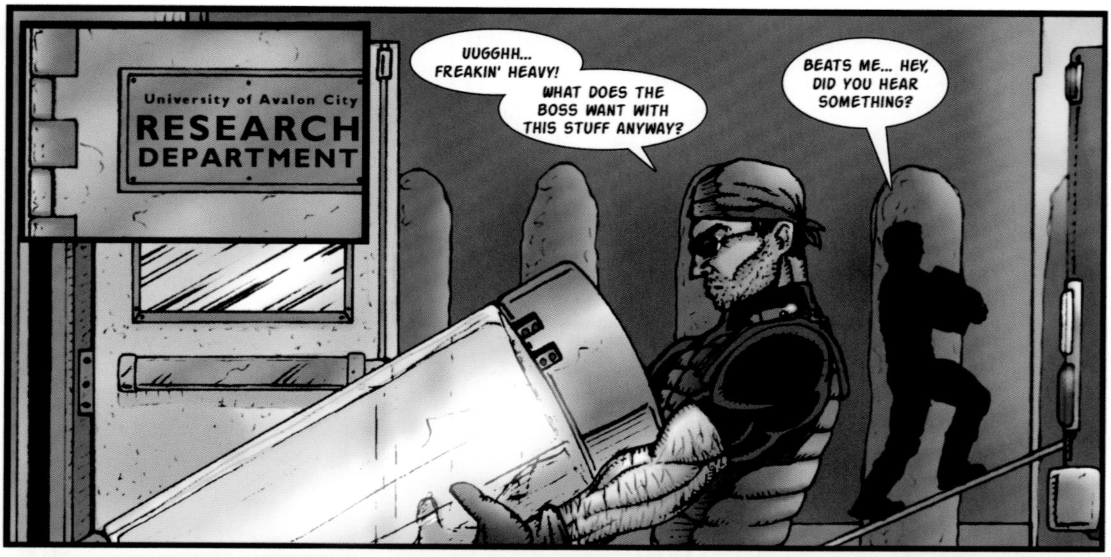
University of Avalon City
RESEARCH
DEPARTMENT
UUGGHH... FREAKIN' HEAVY!
WHAT DOES THE BOSS WANT WITH THIS STUFF ANYWAY?
BEATS ME... HEY, DID YOU HEAR SOMETHING?

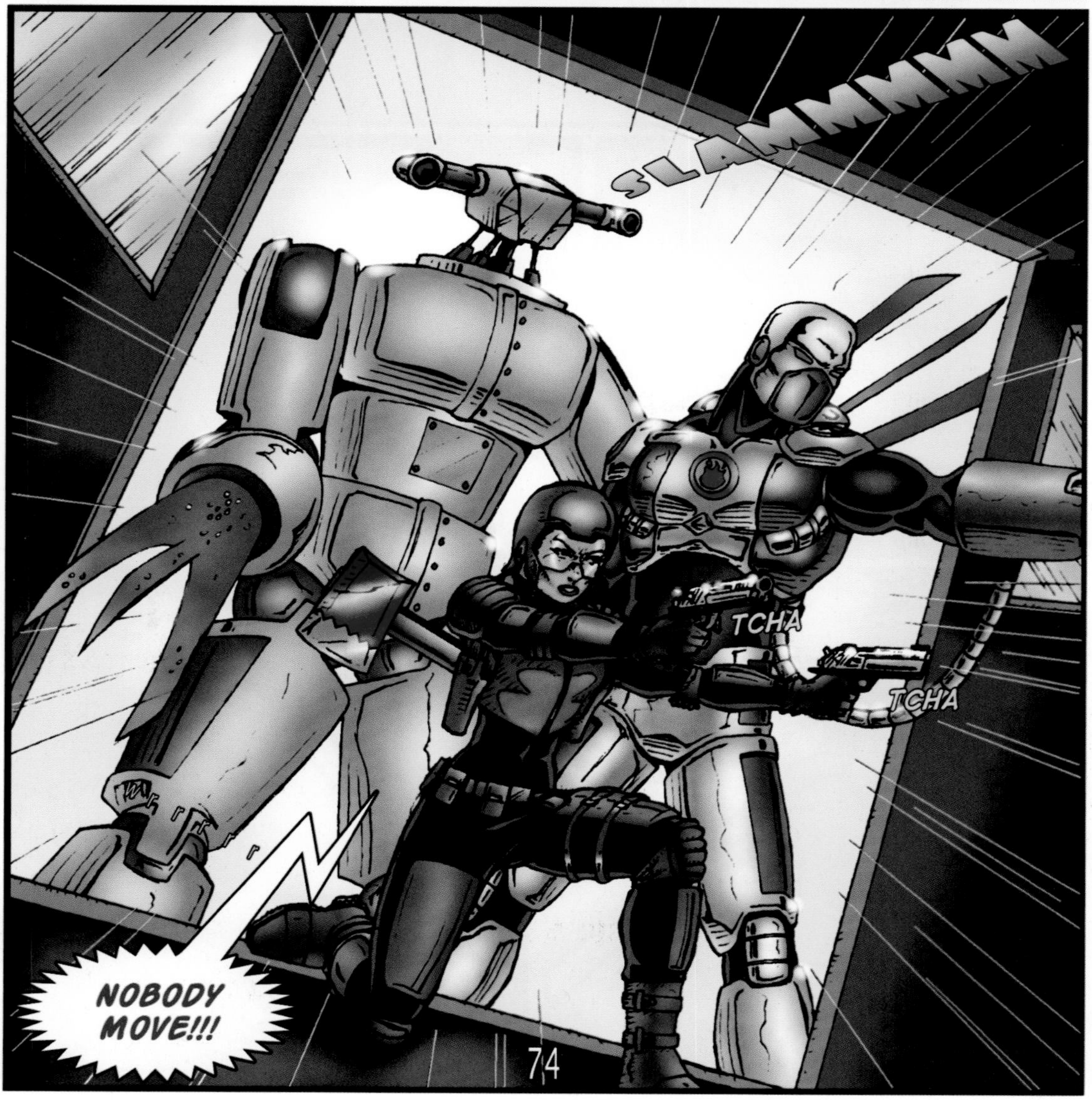
SLAMMMMM
TCHA
TCHA
NOBODY MOVE!!!

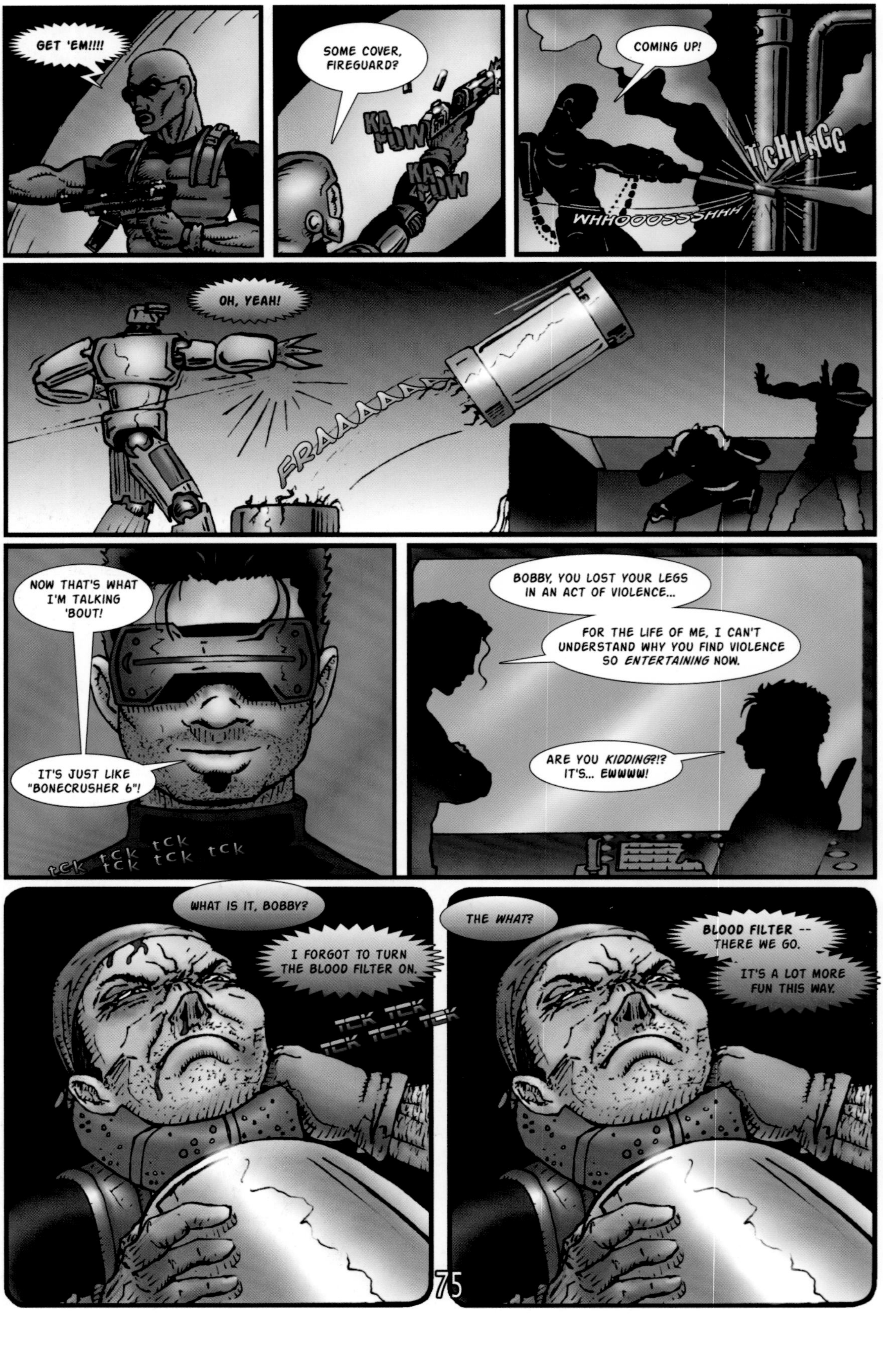
GET 'EM!!!!
SOME COVER, FIREGUARD?
KA POW
KA POW
COMING UP!
TCHIINGG
WHHOOOSSSHHH
OH, YEAH!
FRAAAAAS
NOW THAT'S WHAT I'M TALKING 'BOUT!
IT'S JUST LIKE "BONECRUSHER 6"!
tck tck tck tck tck tck
BOBBY, YOU LOST YOUR LEGS IN AN ACT OF VIOLENCE...
FOR THE LIFE OF ME, I CAN'T UNDERSTAND WHY YOU FIND VIOLENCE SO *ENTERTAINING* NOW.
ARE YOU *KIDDING?!?* IT'S... EWWWW!
WHAT IS IT, BOBBY?
I FORGOT TO TURN THE BLOOD FILTER ON.
TCK TCK TCK TCK TCK
THE *WHAT?*
BLOOD FILTER -- THERE WE GO.
IT'S A LOT MORE FUN THIS WAY.

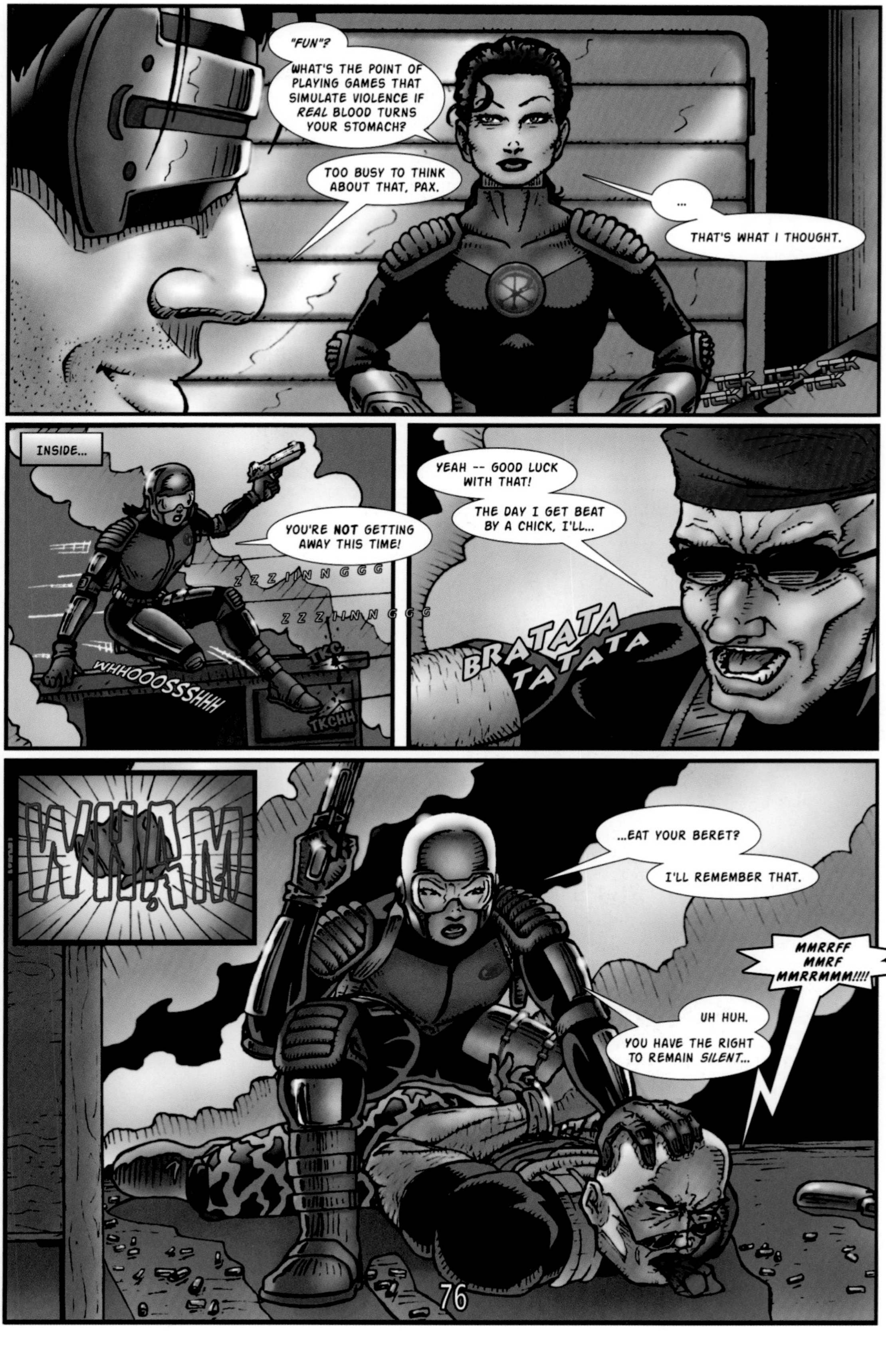
"FUN"?
WHAT'S THE POINT OF PLAYING GAMES THAT SIMULATE VIOLENCE IF *REAL* BLOOD TURNS YOUR STOMACH?
TOO BUSY TO THINK ABOUT THAT, PAX.
...
THAT'S WHAT I THOUGHT.
TCK TCK TCK TCK TCK TCK
INSIDE...
YOU'RE **NOT** GETTING AWAY THIS TIME!
ZZZIINNGGG
ZZZIINNGGG
WHHOOOSSSHHH
TKC
TKCHH
YEAH -- GOOD LUCK WITH THAT!
THE DAY I GET BEAT BY A CHICK, I'LL...
BRATATA TATATA
WHAM
...EAT YOUR BERET?
I'LL REMEMBER THAT.
MMRRFF MMRF MMRRMMM!!!!
UH HUH.
YOU HAVE THE RIGHT TO REMAIN *SILENT*...

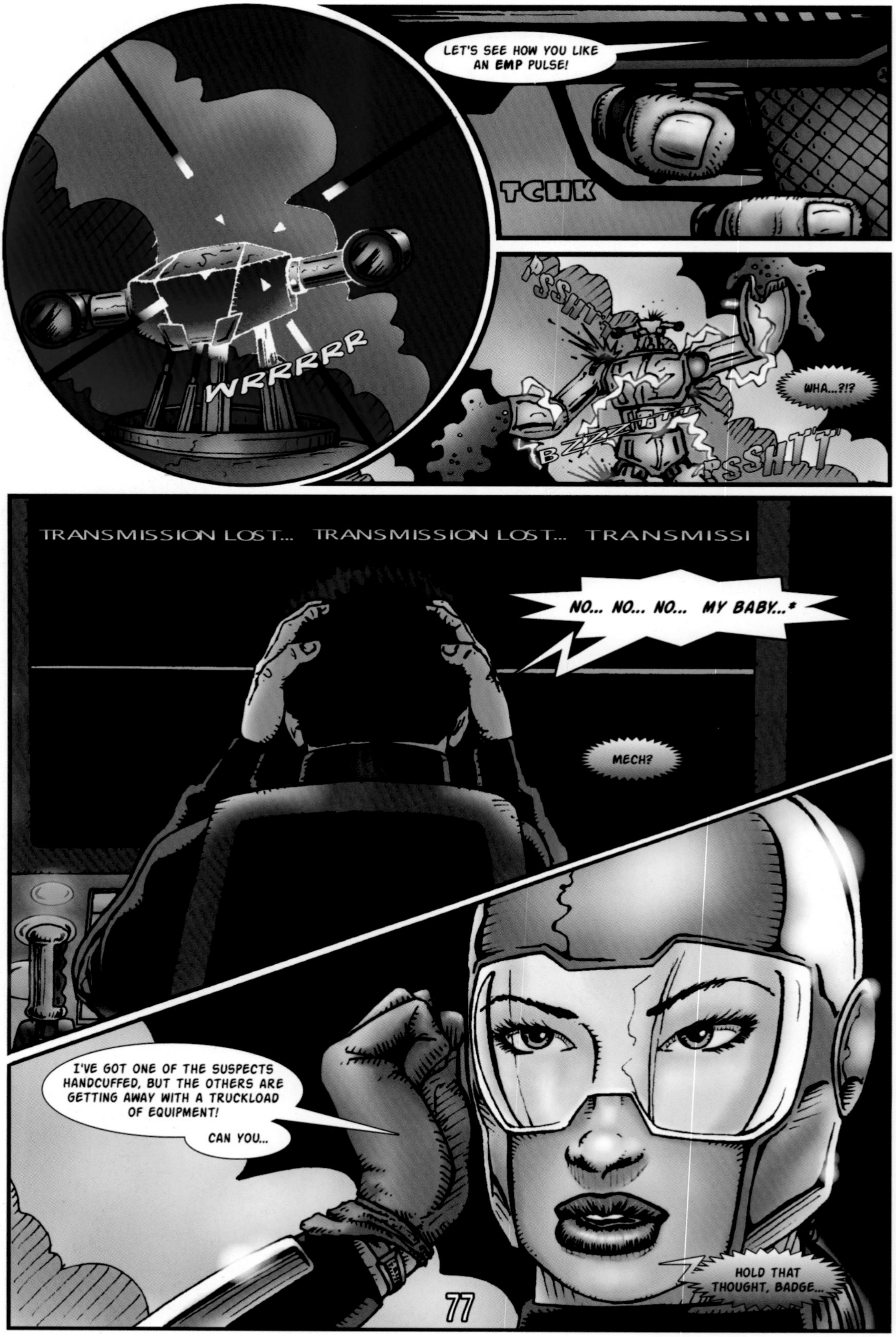
LET'S SEE HOW YOU LIKE AN EMP PULSE!
TCHK
WRRRRR
PSSHT'T
WHA...?!?
BZZZZZZ
PSSHT'T
TRANSMISSION LOST... TRANSMISSION LOST... TRANSMISSI
NO... NO... NO... MY BABY...*
MECH?
I'VE GOT ONE OF THE SUSPECTS HANDCUFFED, BUT THE OTHERS ARE GETTING AWAY WITH A TRUCKLOAD OF EQUIPMENT!
CAN YOU...
HOLD THAT THOUGHT, BADGE...

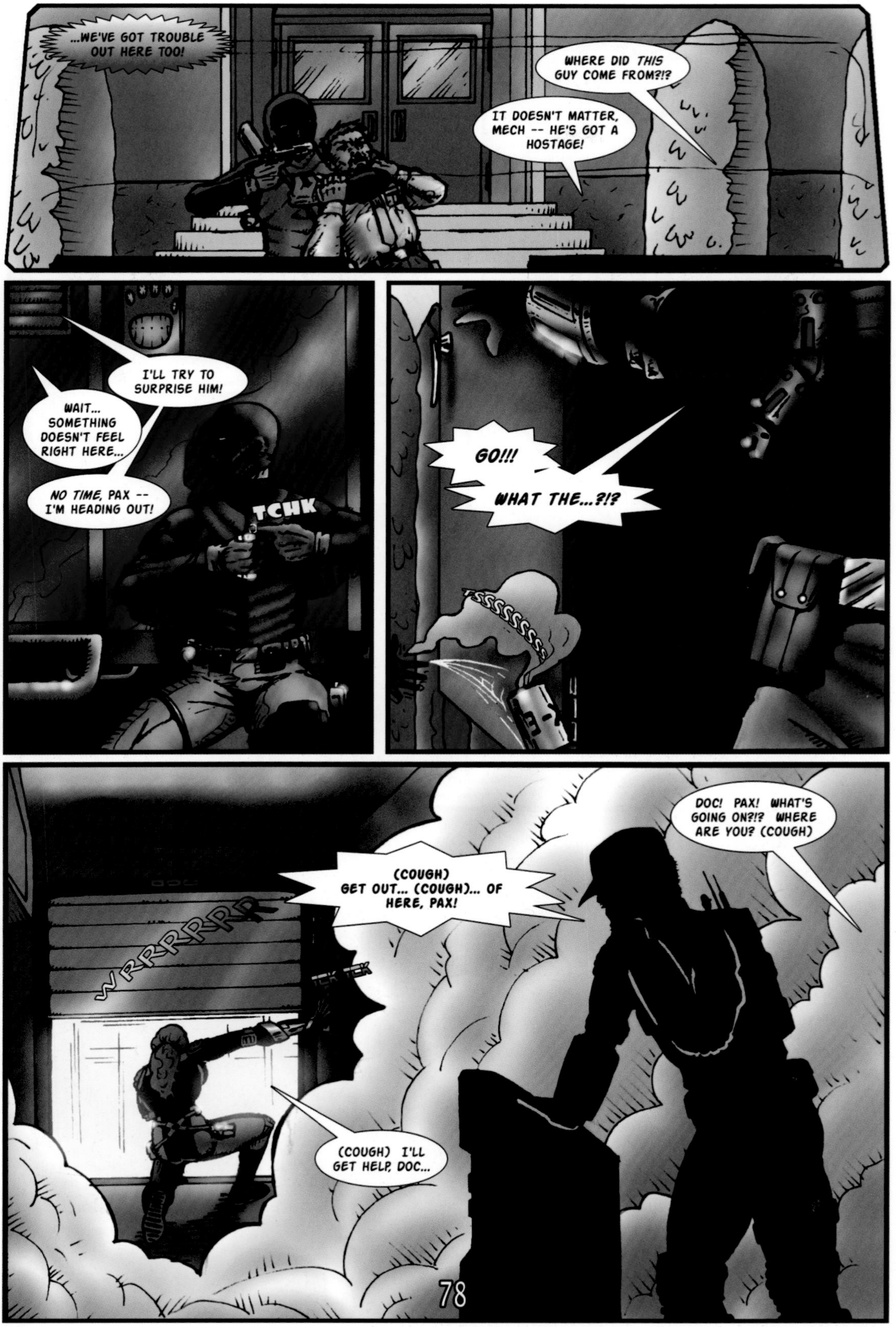
...WE'VE GOT TROUBLE OUT HERE TOO!
WHERE DID THIS GUY COME FROM?!?
IT DOESN'T MATTER, MECH -- HE'S GOT A HOSTAGE!
I'LL TRY TO SURPRISE HIM!
WAIT... SOMETHING DOESN'T FEEL RIGHT HERE...
NO TIME, PAX -- I'M HEADING OUT!
TCHK
GO!!!
WHAT THE...?!?
TSSSSSSSSS
DOC! PAX! WHAT'S GOING ON?!? WHERE ARE YOU? (COUGH)
(COUGH) GET OUT... (COUGH)... OF HERE, PAX!
WRRRRRR
TCK TCK
(COUGH) I'LL GET HELP, DOC...

CAN'T... FOCUS...
BAM
ZZZIIIPP
AHHH!!!
SHOUNNK
YES, SIR, I'VE GOT THE GIRL.
ALPHA IS ALSO CLEAR.
I'M CLEAR.
EXCELLENT!
RETURN IMMEDIATELY.
I'VE GOT MOVEMENT.
WE SHOULD GO.*

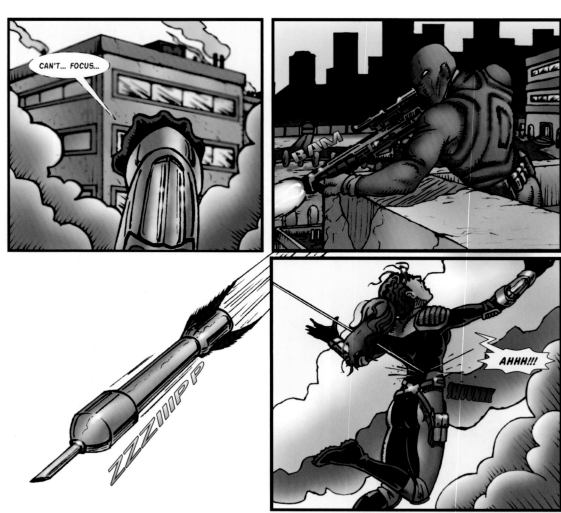

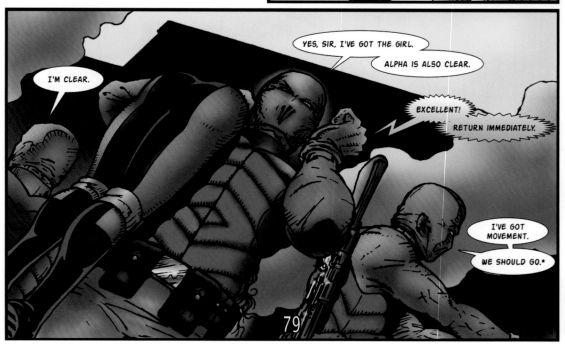

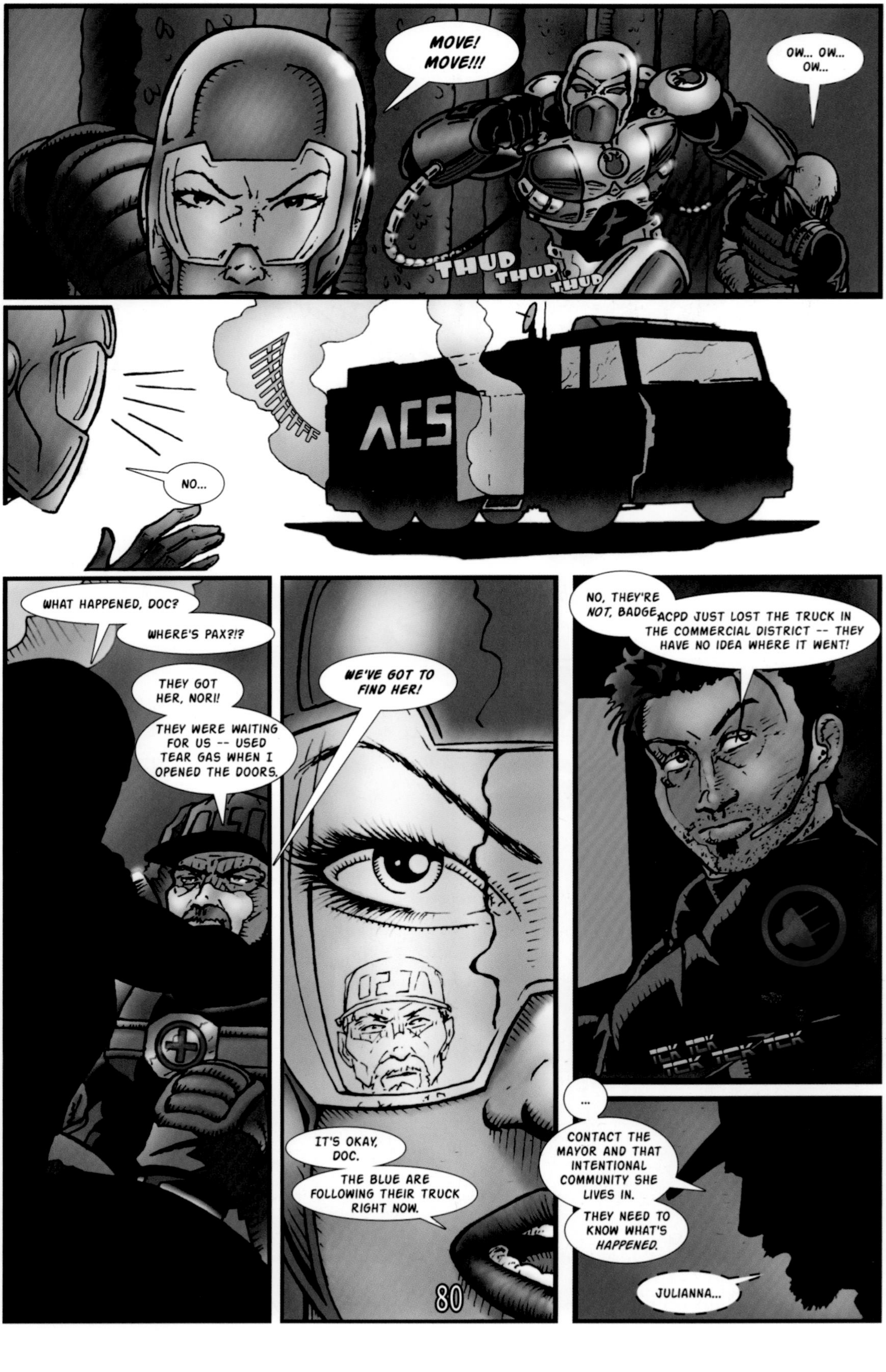
MOVE! MOVE!!!
OW... OW... OW...
THUD THUD THUD
FFFFFFFFFFF
ACS
NO...
WHAT HAPPENED, DOC?
WHERE'S PAX?!?
THEY GOT HER, NORI!
THEY WERE WAITING FOR US -- USED TEAR GAS WHEN I OPENED THE DOORS.
WE'VE GOT TO FIND HER!
NO, THEY'RE NOT, BADGE.
ACPD JUST LOST THE TRUCK IN THE COMMERCIAL DISTRICT -- THEY HAVE NO IDEA WHERE IT WENT!
TCK TCK TCK TCK TCK
IT'S OKAY, DOC.
THE BLUE ARE FOLLOWING THEIR TRUCK RIGHT NOW.
...
CONTACT THE MAYOR AND THAT INTENTIONAL COMMUNITY SHE LIVES IN.
THEY NEED TO KNOW WHAT'S HAPPENED.
JULIANNA...

THREE

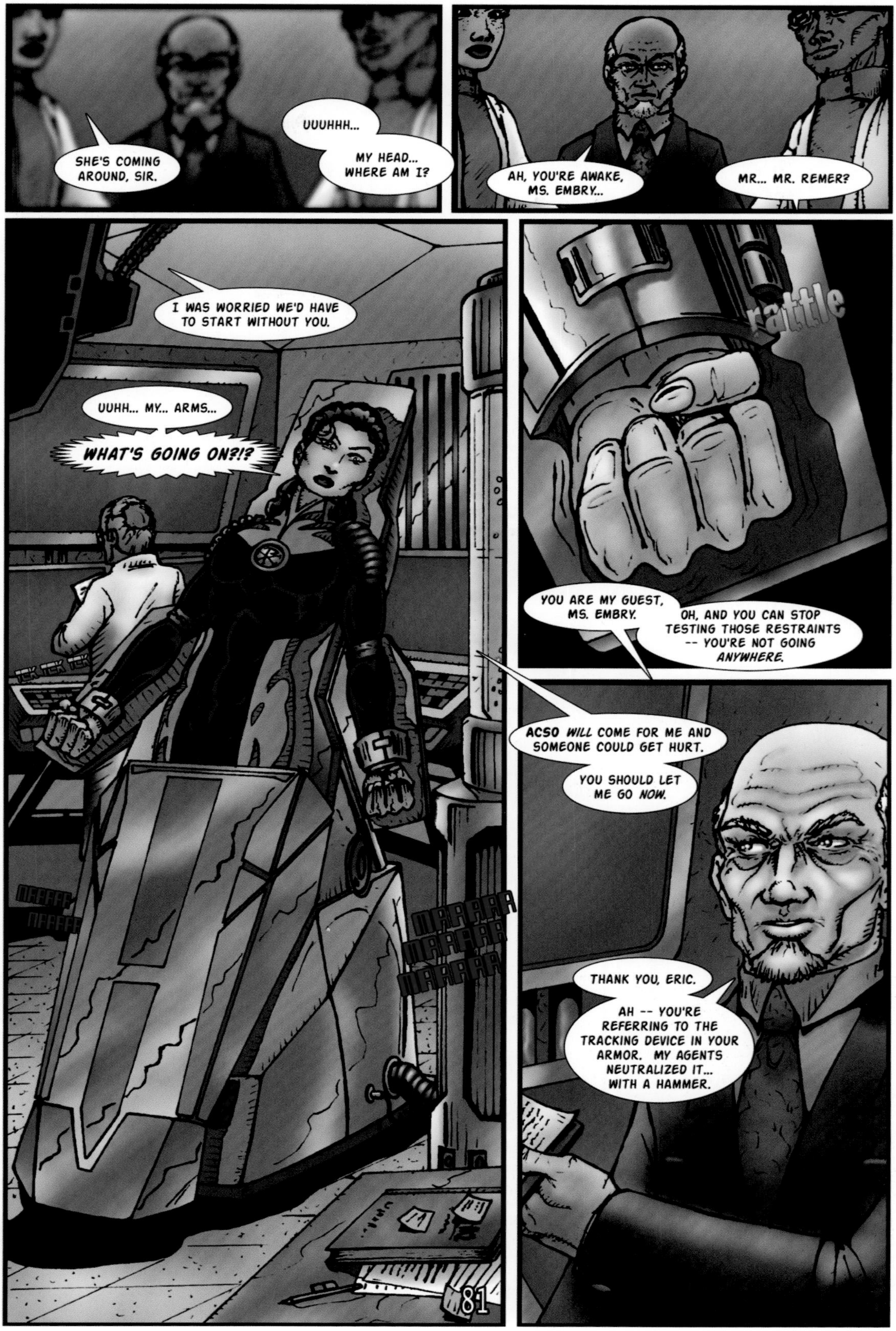
SHE'S COMING AROUND, SIR.
UUUHHH...
MY HEAD... WHERE AM I?
AH, YOU'RE AWAKE, MS. EMBRY...
MR... MR. REMER?
I WAS WORRIED WE'D HAVE TO START WITHOUT YOU.
UUHH... MY... ARMS...
WHAT'S GOING ON?!?
TEK TEK TEK
rattle
YOU ARE MY GUEST, MS. EMBRY.
OH, AND YOU CAN STOP TESTING THOSE RESTRAINTS -- YOU'RE NOT GOING ANYWHERE.
ACSO WILL COME FOR ME AND SOMEONE COULD GET HURT.
YOU SHOULD LET ME GO NOW.
THANK YOU, ERIC.
AH -- YOU'RE REFERRING TO THE TRACKING DEVICE IN YOUR ARMOR. MY AGENTS NEUTRALIZED IT... WITH A HAMMER.

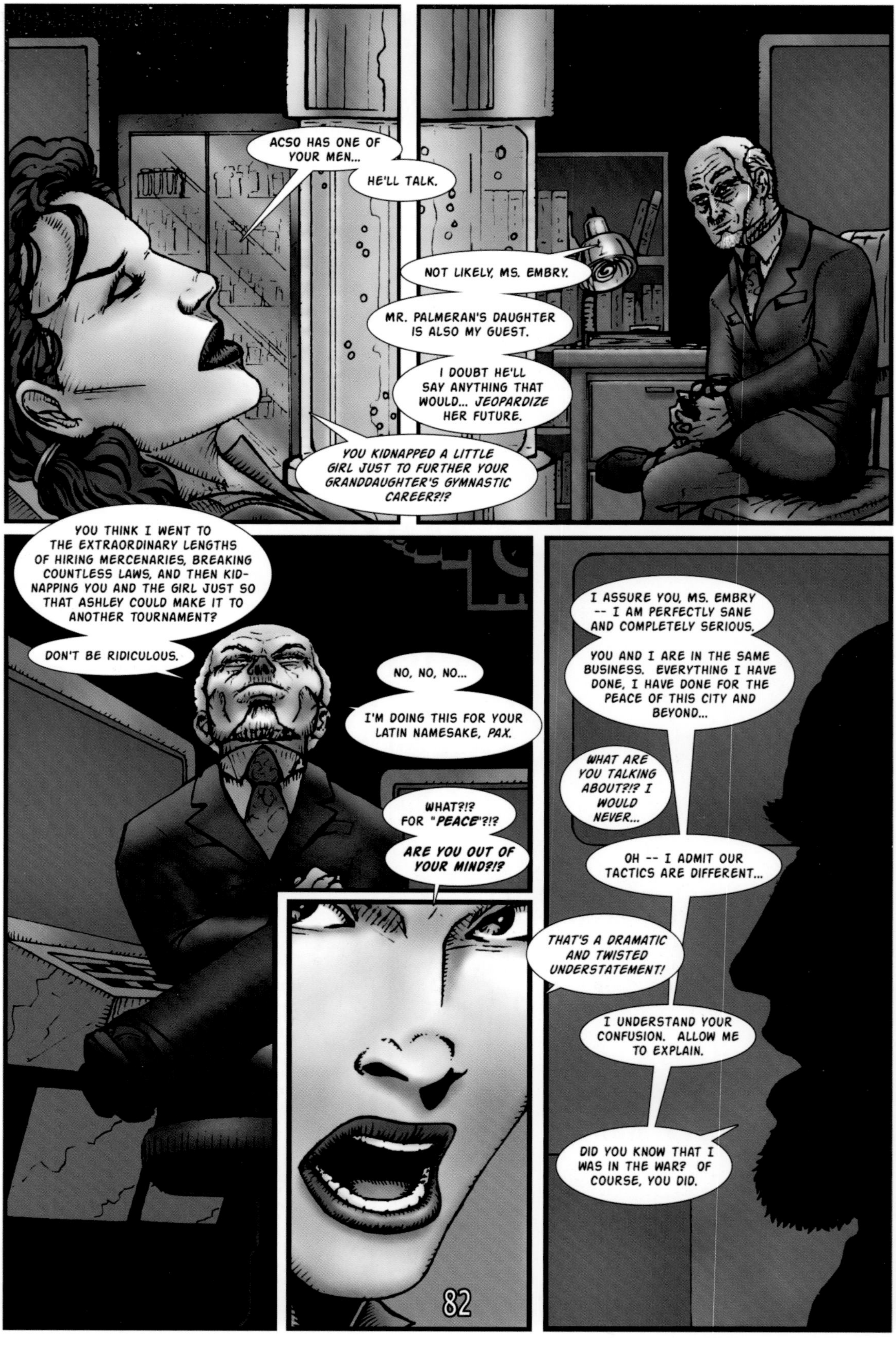
ACSO HAS ONE OF YOUR MEN...
HE'LL TALK.
NOT LIKELY, MS. EMBRY.
MR. PALMERAN'S DAUGHTER IS ALSO MY GUEST.
I DOUBT HE'LL SAY ANYTHING THAT WOULD... *JEOPARDIZE* HER FUTURE.
YOU KIDNAPPED A LITTLE GIRL JUST TO FURTHER YOUR GRANDDAUGHTER'S GYMNASTIC CAREER?!?
YOU THINK I WENT TO THE EXTRAORDINARY LENGTHS OF HIRING MERCENARIES, BREAKING COUNTLESS LAWS, AND THEN KIDNAPPING YOU AND THE GIRL JUST SO THAT ASHLEY COULD MAKE IT TO ANOTHER TOURNAMENT?
DON'T BE RIDICULOUS.
NO, NO, NO...
I'M DOING THIS FOR YOUR LATIN NAMESAKE, *PAX*.
WHAT?!? FOR "***PEACE***"?!?
ARE YOU OUT OF YOUR MIND?!?
I ASSURE YOU, MS. EMBRY -- I AM PERFECTLY SANE AND COMPLETELY SERIOUS.
YOU AND I ARE IN THE SAME BUSINESS. EVERYTHING I HAVE DONE, I HAVE DONE FOR THE PEACE OF THIS CITY AND BEYOND...
WHAT ARE YOU TALKING ABOUT?!? I WOULD NEVER...
OH -- I ADMIT OUR TACTICS ARE DIFFERENT...
THAT'S A DRAMATIC AND TWISTED UNDERSTATEMENT!
I UNDERSTAND YOUR CONFUSION. ALLOW ME TO EXPLAIN.
DID YOU KNOW THAT I WAS IN THE WAR? OF COURSE, YOU DID.

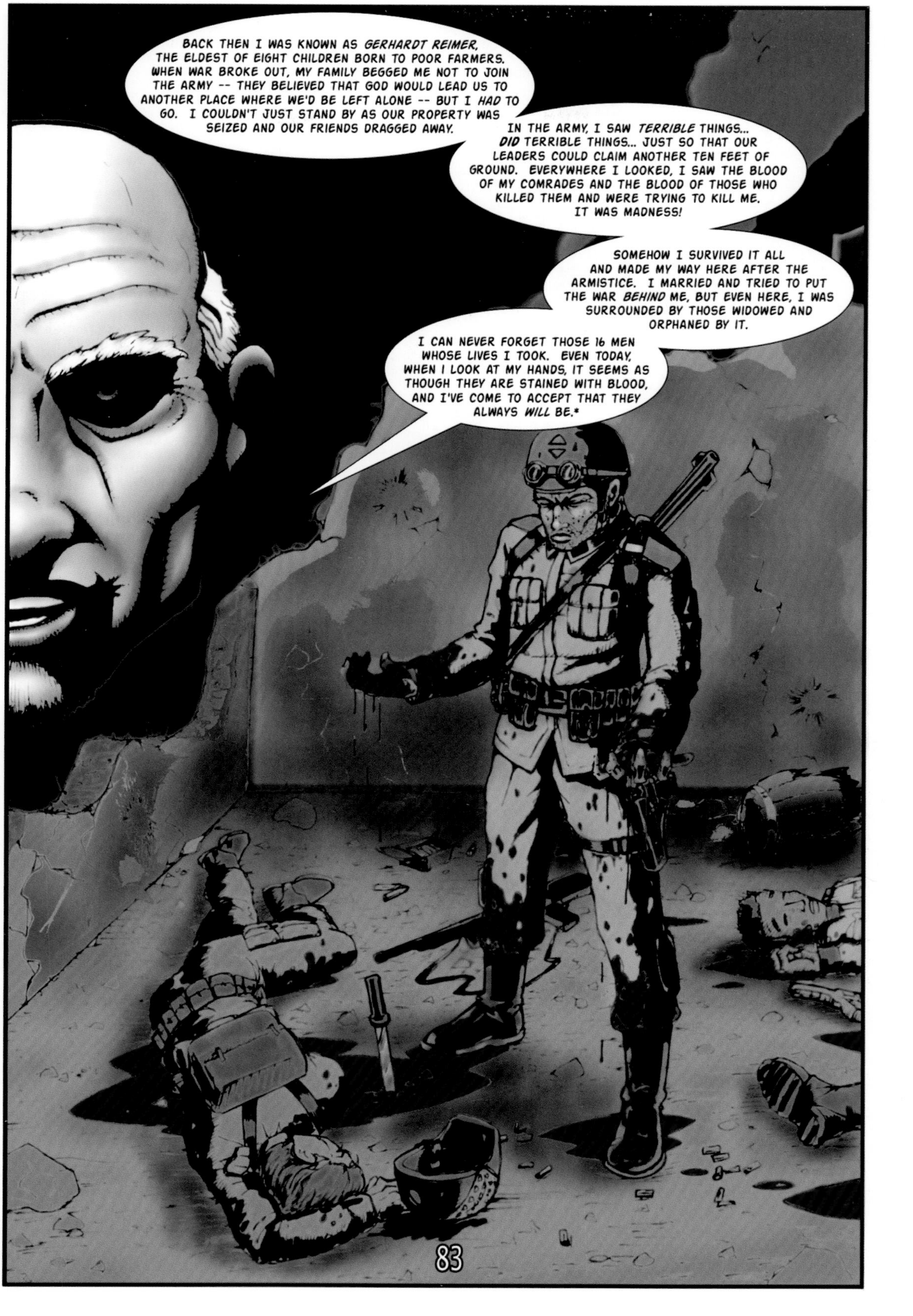
BACK THEN I WAS KNOWN AS GERHARDT REIMER, THE ELDEST OF EIGHT CHILDREN BORN TO POOR FARMERS. WHEN WAR BROKE OUT, MY FAMILY BEGGED ME NOT TO JOIN THE ARMY -- THEY BELIEVED THAT GOD WOULD LEAD US TO ANOTHER PLACE WHERE WE'D BE LEFT ALONE -- BUT I HAD TO GO. I COULDN'T JUST STAND BY AS OUR PROPERTY WAS SEIZED AND OUR FRIENDS DRAGGED AWAY.
IN THE ARMY, I SAW TERRIBLE THINGS... DID TERRIBLE THINGS... JUST SO THAT OUR LEADERS COULD CLAIM ANOTHER TEN FEET OF GROUND. EVERYWHERE I LOOKED, I SAW THE BLOOD OF MY COMRADES AND THE BLOOD OF THOSE WHO KILLED THEM AND WERE TRYING TO KILL ME. IT WAS MADNESS!
SOMEHOW I SURVIVED IT ALL AND MADE MY WAY HERE AFTER THE ARMISTICE. I MARRIED AND TRIED TO PUT THE WAR BEHIND ME, BUT EVEN HERE, I WAS SURROUNDED BY THOSE WIDOWED AND ORPHANED BY IT.
I CAN NEVER FORGET THOSE 16 MEN WHOSE LIVES I TOOK. EVEN TODAY, WHEN I LOOK AT MY HANDS, IT SEEMS AS THOUGH THEY ARE STAINED WITH BLOOD, AND I'VE COME TO ACCEPT THAT THEY ALWAYS WILL BE.*

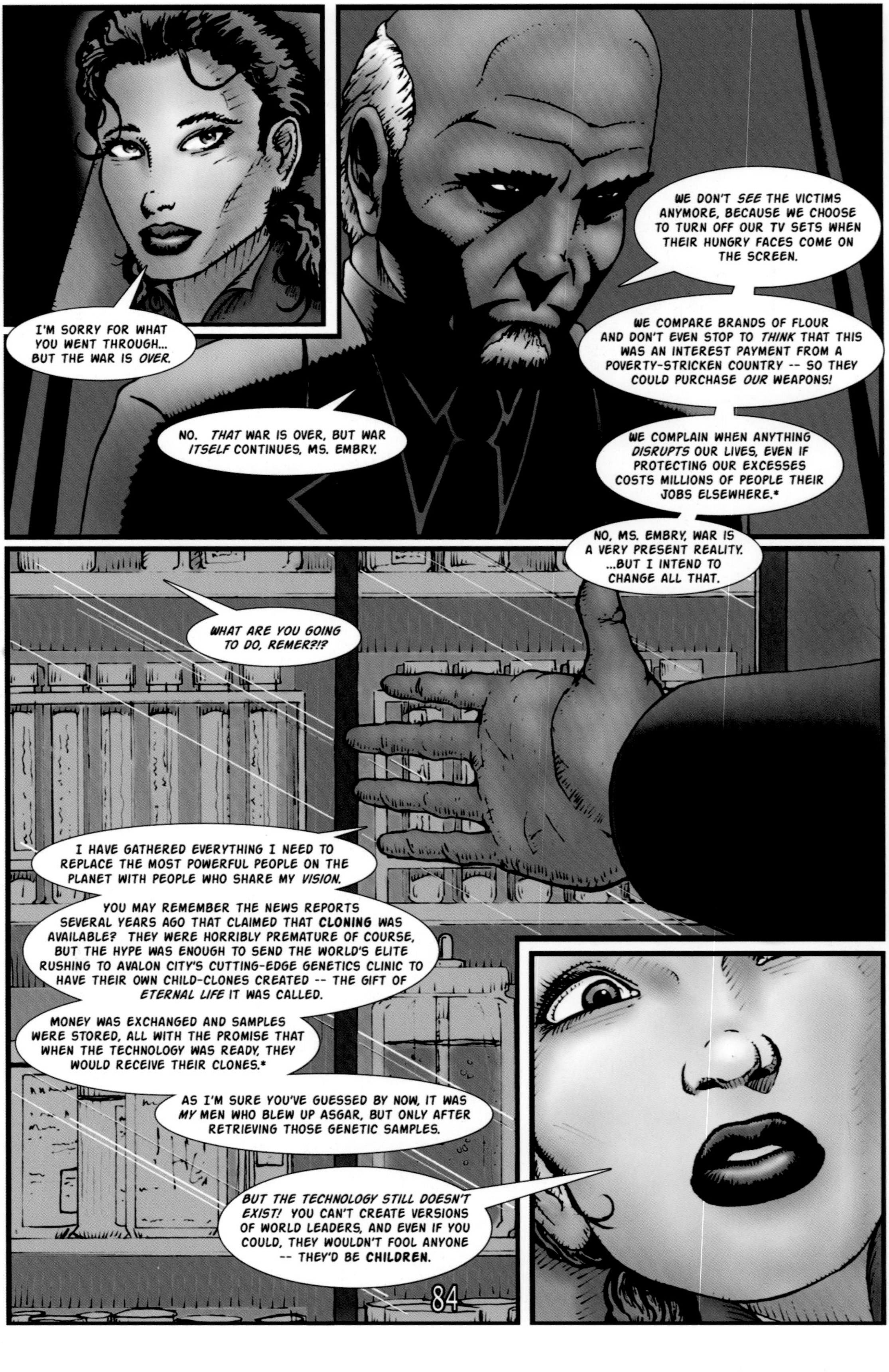
I'M SORRY FOR WHAT YOU WENT THROUGH... BUT THE WAR IS *OVER*.
WE DON'T *SEE* THE VICTIMS ANYMORE, BECAUSE WE CHOOSE TO TURN OFF OUR TV SETS WHEN THEIR HUNGRY FACES COME ON THE SCREEN.
NO. *THAT* WAR IS OVER, BUT WAR *ITSELF* CONTINUES, MS. EMBRY.
WE COMPARE BRANDS OF FLOUR AND DON'T EVEN STOP TO *THINK* THAT THIS WAS AN INTEREST PAYMENT FROM A POVERTY-STRICKEN COUNTRY -- SO THEY COULD PURCHASE *OUR* WEAPONS!
WE COMPLAIN WHEN ANYTHING *DISRUPTS* OUR LIVES, EVEN IF PROTECTING OUR EXCESSES COSTS MILLIONS OF PEOPLE THEIR JOBS ELSEWHERE.*
NO, MS. EMBRY, WAR IS A VERY PRESENT REALITY. ...BUT I INTEND TO CHANGE ALL THAT.
WHAT ARE YOU GOING TO DO, REMER?!?
I HAVE GATHERED EVERYTHING I NEED TO REPLACE THE MOST POWERFUL PEOPLE ON THE PLANET WITH PEOPLE WHO SHARE MY *VISION*.
YOU MAY REMEMBER THE NEWS REPORTS SEVERAL YEARS AGO THAT CLAIMED THAT **CLONING** WAS AVAILABLE? THEY WERE HORRIBLY PREMATURE OF COURSE, BUT THE HYPE WAS ENOUGH TO SEND THE WORLD'S ELITE RUSHING TO AVALON CITY'S CUTTING-EDGE GENETICS CLINIC TO HAVE THEIR OWN CHILD-CLONES CREATED -- THE GIFT OF *ETERNAL LIFE* IT WAS CALLED.
MONEY WAS EXCHANGED AND SAMPLES WERE STORED, ALL WITH THE PROMISE THAT WHEN THE TECHNOLOGY WAS READY, THEY WOULD RECEIVE THEIR CLONES.*
AS I'M SURE YOU'VE GUESSED BY NOW, IT WAS *MY* MEN WHO BLEW UP ASGAR, BUT ONLY AFTER RETRIEVING THOSE GENETIC SAMPLES.
BUT THE TECHNOLOGY STILL DOESN'T EXIST! YOU CAN'T CREATE VERSIONS OF WORLD LEADERS, AND EVEN IF YOU COULD, THEY WOULDN'T FOOL ANYONE -- THEY'D BE **CHILDREN**.

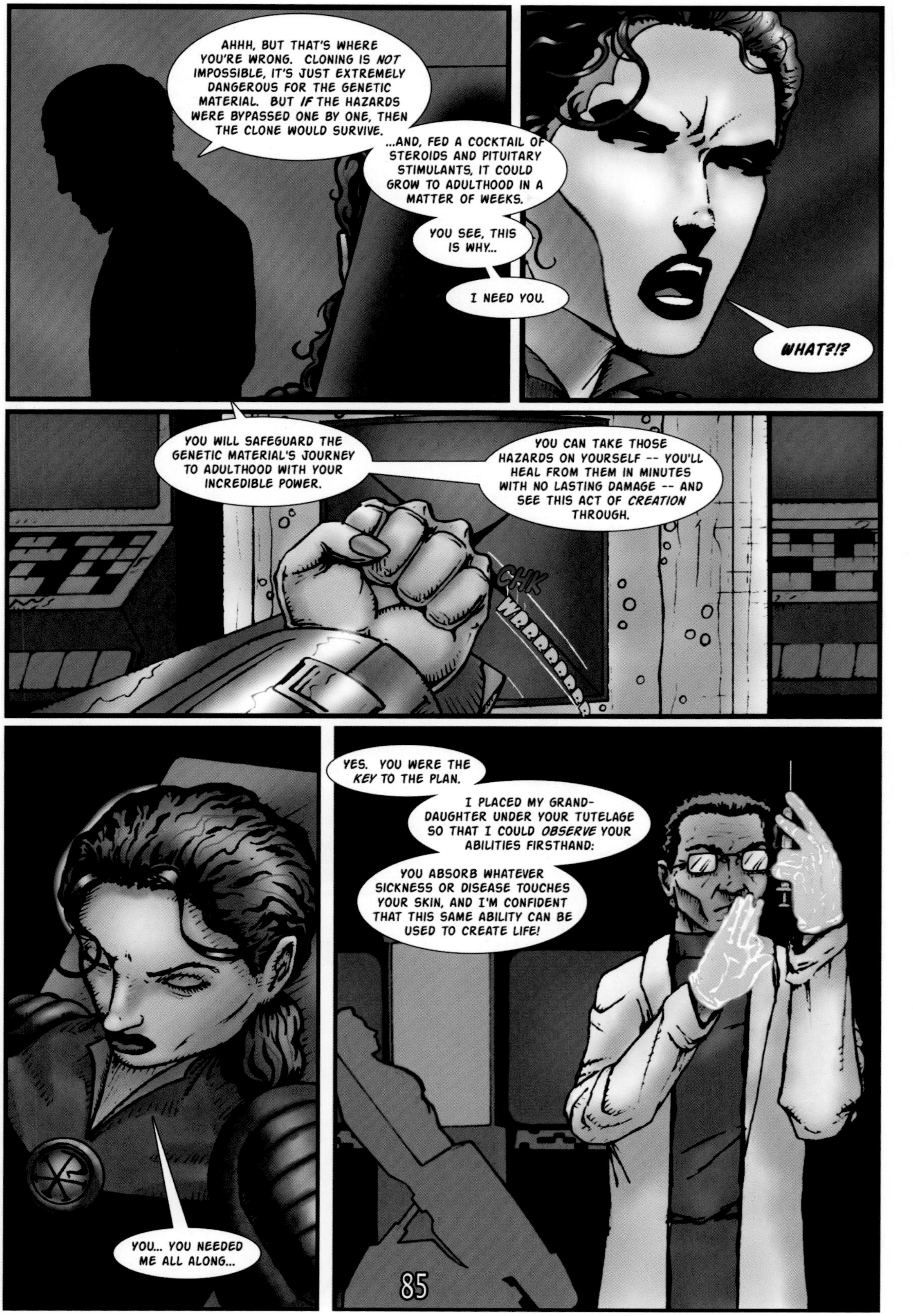
AHHH, BUT THAT'S WHERE YOU'RE WRONG. CLONING IS NOT IMPOSSIBLE, IT'S JUST EXTREMELY DANGEROUS FOR THE GENETIC MATERIAL. BUT IF THE HAZARDS WERE BYPASSED ONE BY ONE, THEN THE CLONE WOULD SURVIVE.
...AND, FED A COCKTAIL OF STEROIDS AND PITUITARY STIMULANTS, IT COULD GROW TO ADULTHOOD IN A MATTER OF WEEKS.
YOU SEE, THIS IS WHY...
I NEED YOU.
WHAT?!?
YOU WILL SAFEGUARD THE GENETIC MATERIAL'S JOURNEY TO ADULTHOOD WITH YOUR INCREDIBLE POWER.
YOU CAN TAKE THOSE HAZARDS ON YOURSELF -- YOU'LL HEAL FROM THEM IN MINUTES WITH NO LASTING DAMAGE -- AND SEE THIS ACT OF CREATION THROUGH.
CHK
WRRRRRRRR
YOU... YOU NEEDED ME ALL ALONG...
YES. YOU WERE THE KEY TO THE PLAN.
I PLACED MY GRAND-DAUGHTER UNDER YOUR TUTELAGE SO THAT I COULD OBSERVE YOUR ABILITIES FIRSTHAND:
YOU ABSORB WHATEVER SICKNESS OR DISEASE TOUCHES YOUR SKIN, AND I'M CONFIDENT THAT THIS SAME ABILITY CAN BE USED TO CREATE LIFE!

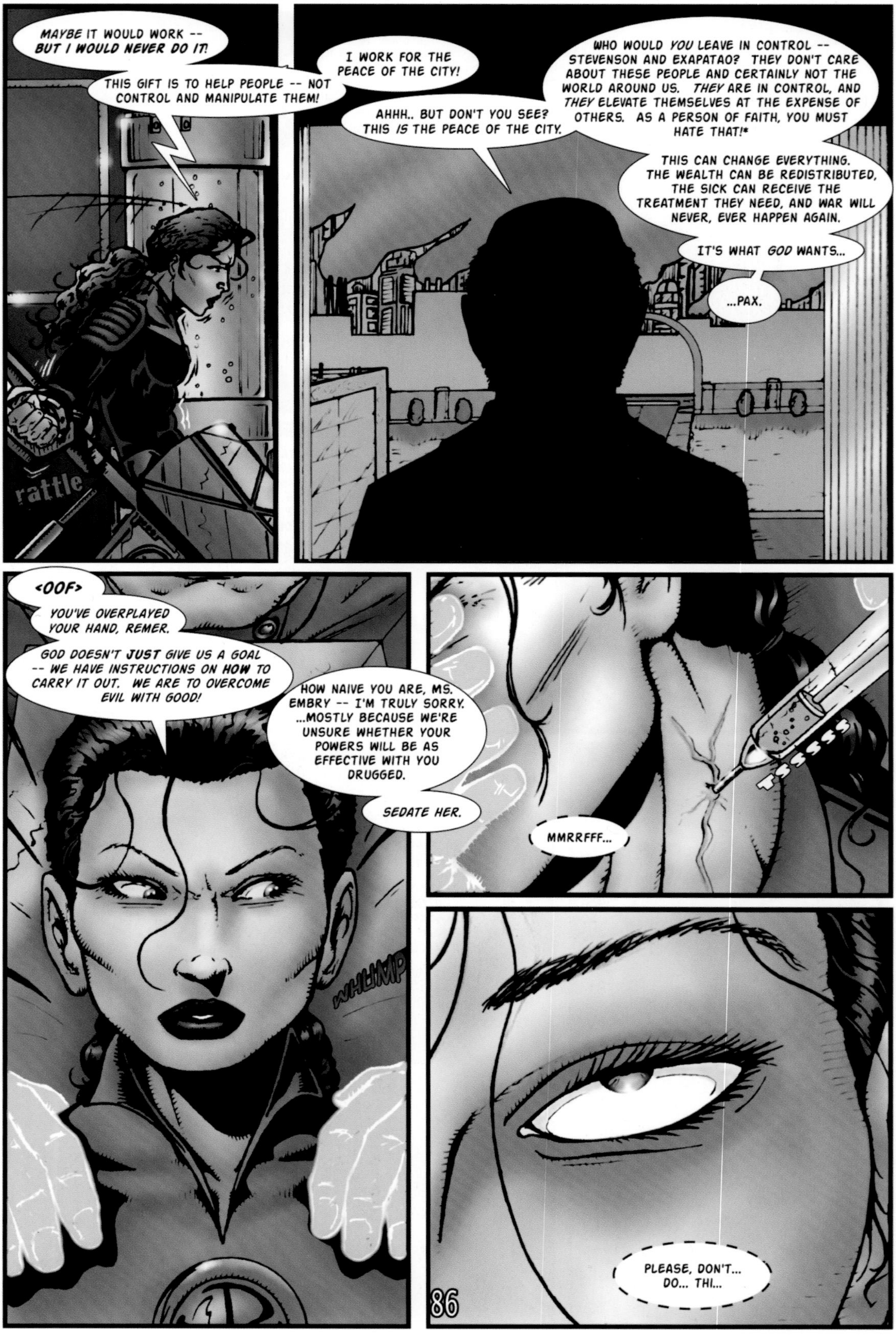
MAYBE IT WOULD WORK -- BUT I WOULD NEVER DO IT!
THIS GIFT IS TO HELP PEOPLE -- NOT CONTROL AND MANIPULATE THEM!
I WORK FOR THE PEACE OF THE CITY!
rattle
AHHH.. BUT DON'T YOU SEE? THIS IS THE PEACE OF THE CITY.
WHO WOULD YOU LEAVE IN CONTROL -- STEVENSON AND EXAPATAO? THEY DON'T CARE ABOUT THESE PEOPLE AND CERTAINLY NOT THE WORLD AROUND US. THEY ARE IN CONTROL, AND THEY ELEVATE THEMSELVES AT THE EXPENSE OF OTHERS. AS A PERSON OF FAITH, YOU MUST HATE THAT!*
THIS CAN CHANGE EVERYTHING. THE WEALTH CAN BE REDISTRIBUTED, THE SICK CAN RECEIVE THE TREATMENT THEY NEED, AND WAR WILL NEVER, EVER HAPPEN AGAIN.
IT'S WHAT GOD WANTS...
...PAX.
<OOF>
YOU'VE OVERPLAYED YOUR HAND, REMER.
GOD DOESN'T JUST GIVE US A GOAL -- WE HAVE INSTRUCTIONS ON HOW TO CARRY IT OUT. WE ARE TO OVERCOME EVIL WITH GOOD!
HOW NAIVE YOU ARE, MS. EMBRY -- I'M TRULY SORRY. ...MOSTLY BECAUSE WE'RE UNSURE WHETHER YOUR POWERS WILL BE AS EFFECTIVE WITH YOU DRUGGED.
SEDATE HER.
WHUMP
TSSSSS
MMRRFFF...
PLEASE, DON'T... DO... THI...

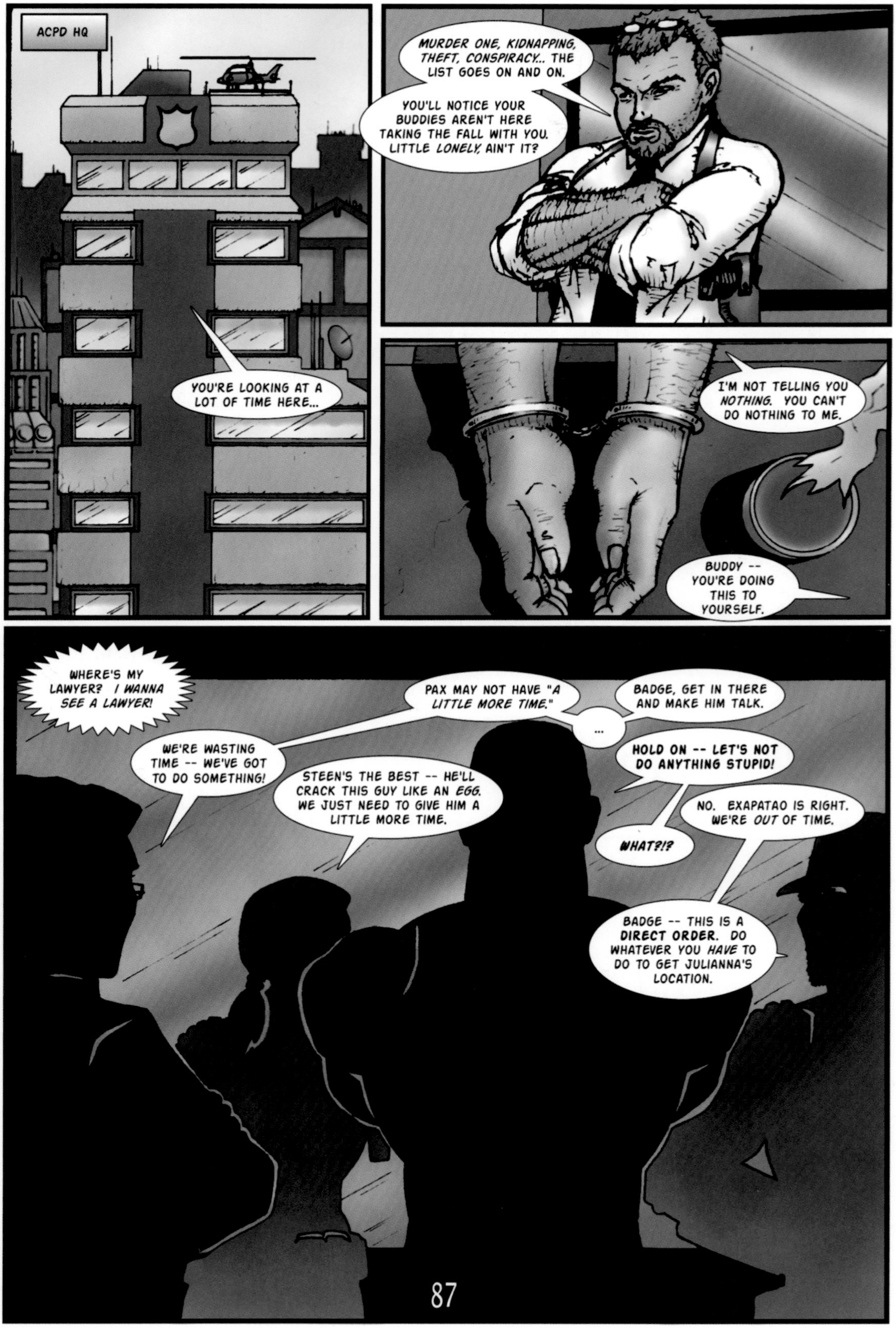
ACPD HQ
YOU'RE LOOKING AT A LOT OF TIME HERE...
MURDER ONE, KIDNAPPING, THEFT, CONSPIRACY... THE LIST GOES ON AND ON.
YOU'LL NOTICE YOUR BUDDIES AREN'T HERE TAKING THE FALL WITH YOU. LITTLE LONELY, AIN'T IT?
I'M NOT TELLING YOU NOTHING. YOU CAN'T DO NOTHING TO ME.
BUDDY -- YOU'RE DOING THIS TO YOURSELF.
WHERE'S MY LAWYER? I WANNA SEE A LAWYER!
WE'RE WASTING TIME -- WE'VE GOT TO DO SOMETHING!
STEEN'S THE BEST -- HE'LL CRACK THIS GUY LIKE AN EGG. WE JUST NEED TO GIVE HIM A LITTLE MORE TIME.
PAX MAY NOT HAVE "A LITTLE MORE TIME."
...
BADGE, GET IN THERE AND MAKE HIM TALK.
HOLD ON -- LET'S NOT DO ANYTHING STUPID!
WHAT?!?
NO. EXAPATAO IS RIGHT. WE'RE OUT OF TIME.
BADGE -- THIS IS A DIRECT ORDER. DO WHATEVER YOU HAVE TO DO TO GET JULIANNA'S LOCATION.

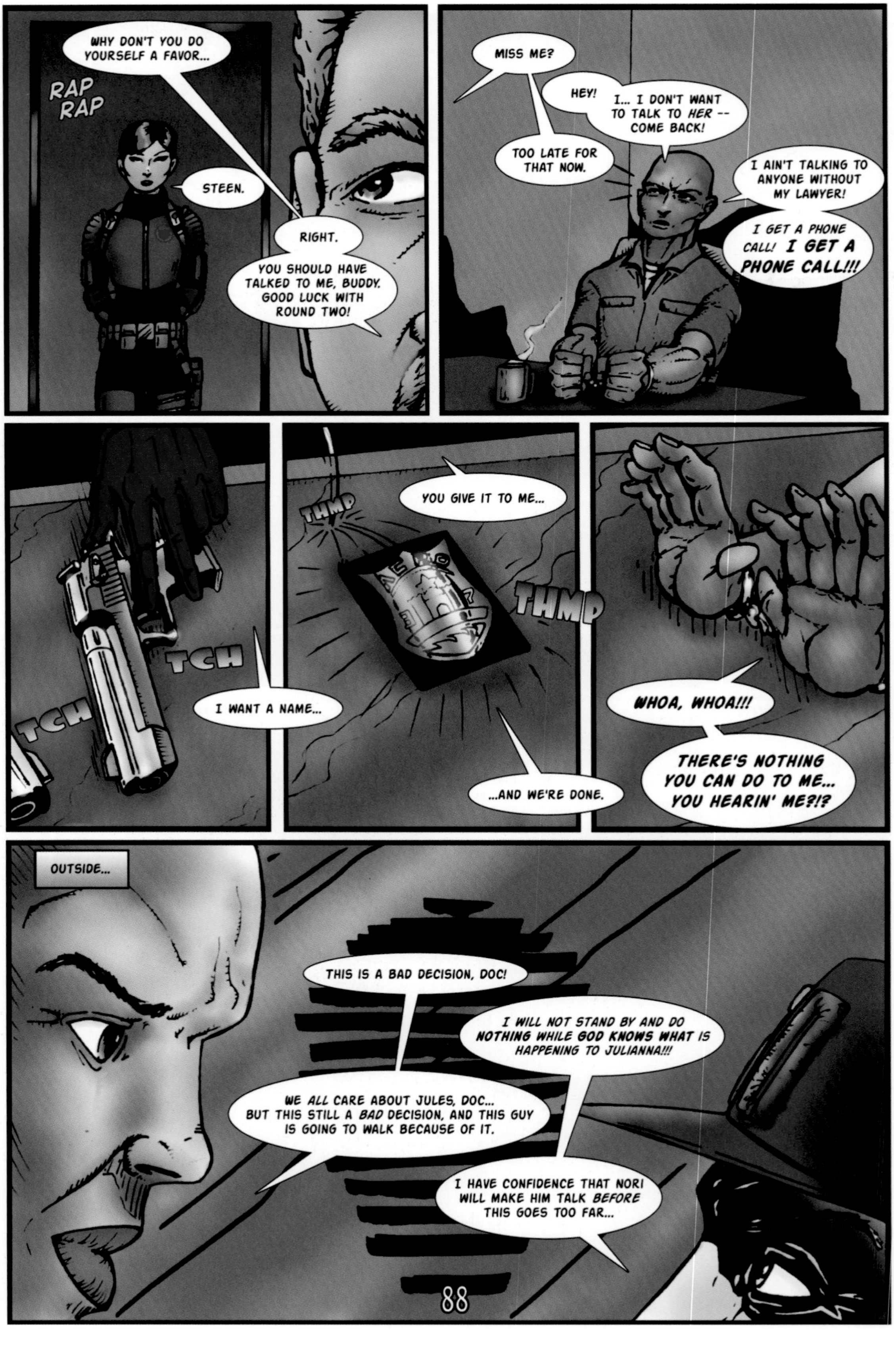
WHY DON'T YOU DO YOURSELF A FAVOR...
RAP RAP
STEEN.
RIGHT.
YOU SHOULD HAVE TALKED TO ME, BUDDY. GOOD LUCK WITH ROUND TWO!
MISS ME?
TOO LATE FOR THAT NOW.
HEY!
I... I DON'T WANT TO TALK TO *HER* -- COME BACK!
I AIN'T TALKING TO ANYONE WITHOUT MY LAWYER!
I GET A PHONE CALL! **I GET A PHONE CALL!!!**
TCH
TCH
I WANT A NAME...
THMP
YOU GIVE IT TO ME...
THMP
...AND WE'RE DONE.
WHOA, WHOA!!!
THERE'S NOTHING YOU CAN DO TO ME... YOU HEARIN' ME?!?
OUTSIDE...
THIS IS A BAD DECISION, DOC!
*I WILL NOT STAND BY AND DO **NOTHING** WHILE **GOD KNOWS WHAT** IS HAPPENING TO JULIANNA!!!*
WE *ALL* CARE ABOUT JULES, DOC... BUT THIS STILL A *BAD* DECISION, AND THIS GUY IS GOING TO WALK BECAUSE OF IT.
I HAVE CONFIDENCE THAT NORI WILL MAKE HIM TALK *BEFORE* THIS GOES TOO FAR...

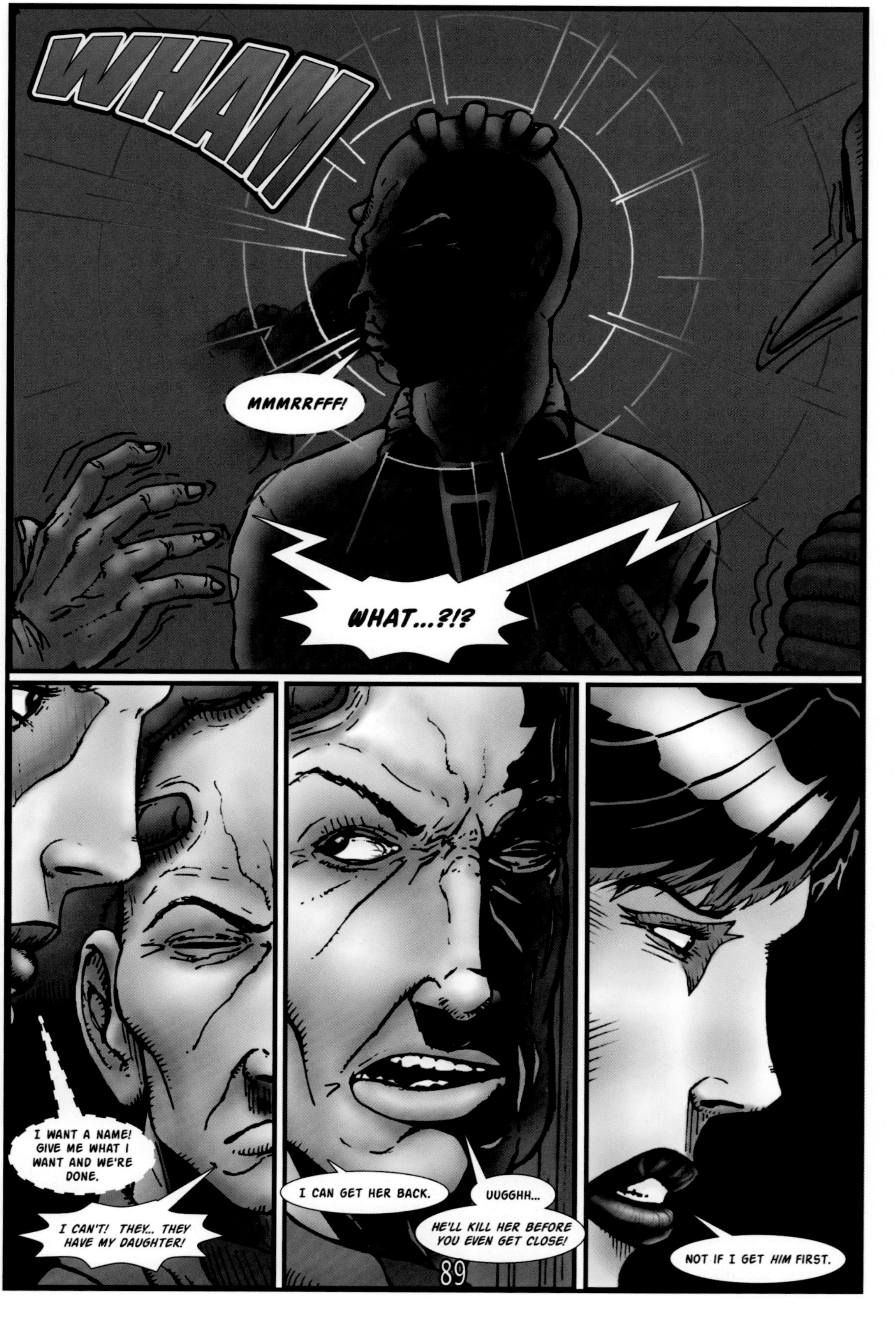
WHAM
MMMRRFFF!
WHAT...?!?
I WANT A NAME! GIVE ME WHAT I WANT AND WE'RE DONE.
I CAN'T! THEY... THEY HAVE MY DAUGHTER!
I CAN GET HER BACK.
UUGGHH...
HE'LL KILL HER BEFORE YOU EVEN GET CLOSE!
NOT IF I GET *HIM* FIRST.

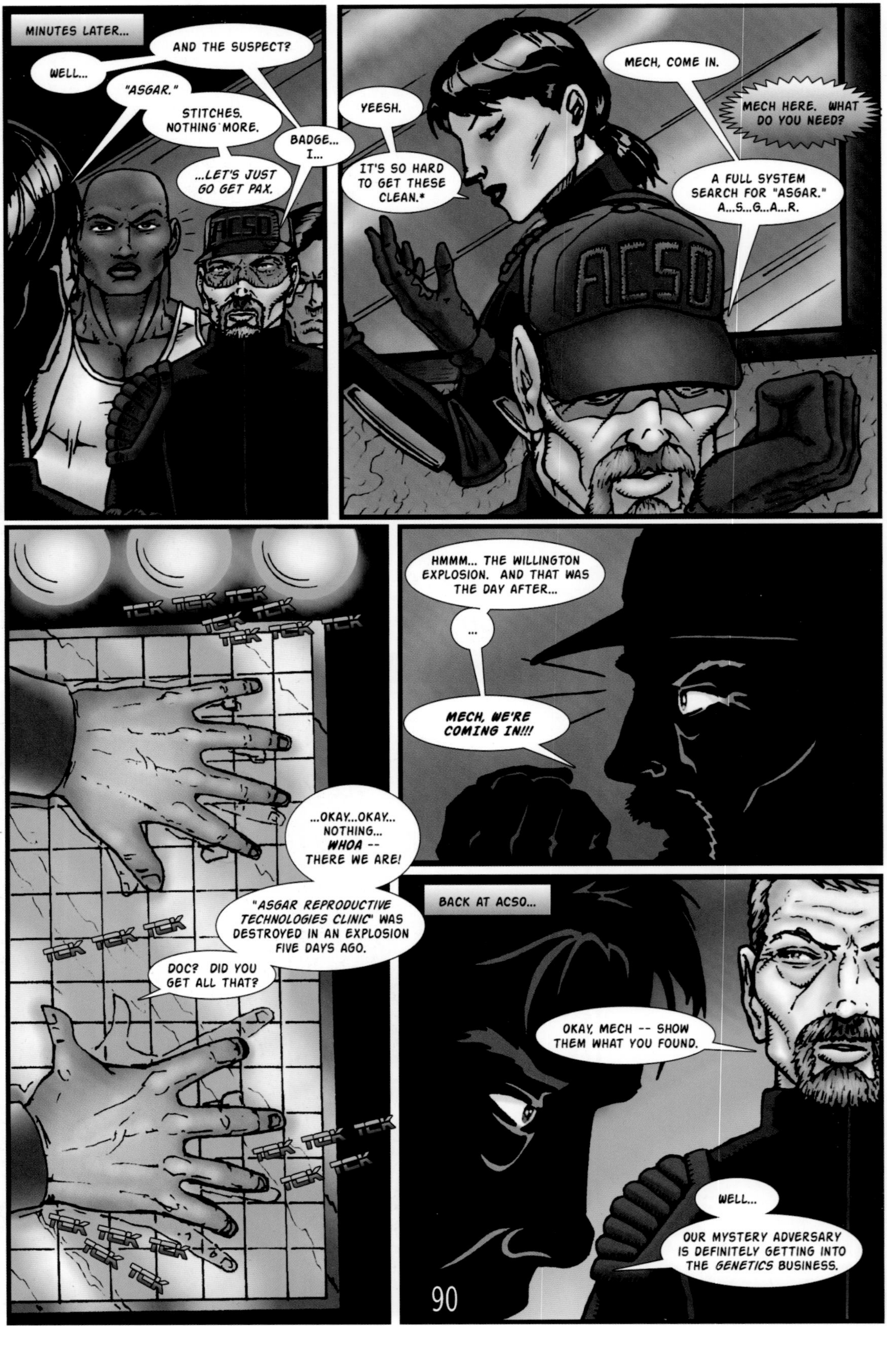
MINUTES LATER...
AND THE SUSPECT?
WELL...
"ASGAR."
STITCHES. NOTHING MORE.
BADGE... I...
...LET'S JUST GO GET PAX.
YEESH.
IT'S SO HARD TO GET THESE CLEAN.*
MECH, COME IN.
MECH HERE. WHAT DO YOU NEED?
A FULL SYSTEM SEARCH FOR "ASGAR." A...S...G...A...R.
TCK TCK TCK TCK TCK TCK TCK TCK
...OKAY...OKAY... NOTHING... WHOA -- THERE WE ARE!
"ASGAR REPRODUCTIVE TECHNOLOGIES CLINIC" WAS DESTROYED IN AN EXPLOSION FIVE DAYS AGO.
TCK TCK TCK
DOC? DID YOU GET ALL THAT?
TCK TCK TCK TCK TCK
TCK TCK TCK TCK TCK
HMMM... THE WILLINGTON EXPLOSION. AND THAT WAS THE DAY AFTER...
...
MECH, WE'RE COMING IN!!!
BACK AT ACSO...
OKAY, MECH -- SHOW THEM WHAT YOU FOUND.
WELL...
OUR MYSTERY ADVERSARY IS DEFINITELY GETTING INTO THE GENETICS BUSINESS.

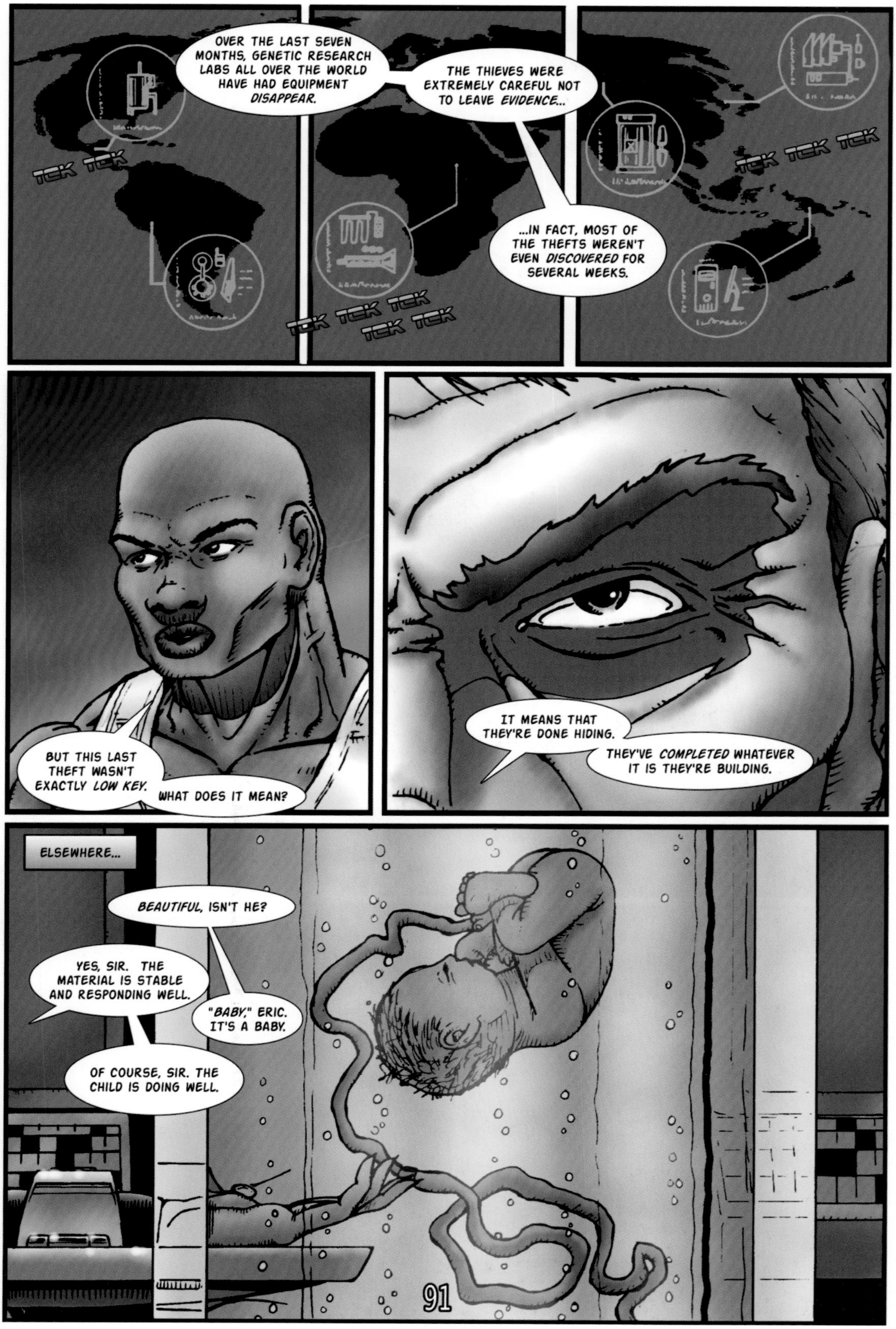
OVER THE LAST SEVEN MONTHS, GENETIC RESEARCH LABS ALL OVER THE WORLD HAVE HAD EQUIPMENT *DISAPPEAR*.
TCK TCK
THE THIEVES WERE EXTREMELY CAREFUL NOT TO LEAVE *EVIDENCE*...
TCK TCK TCK
TCK TCK
...IN FACT, MOST OF THE THEFTS WEREN'T EVEN *DISCOVERED* FOR SEVERAL WEEKS.
TCK TCK TCK
BUT THIS LAST THEFT WASN'T EXACTLY *LOW KEY*.
WHAT DOES IT MEAN?
IT MEANS THAT THEY'RE DONE HIDING.
THEY'VE *COMPLETED* WHATEVER IT IS THEY'RE BUILDING.
ELSEWHERE...
BEAUTIFUL, ISN'T HE?
YES, SIR. THE MATERIAL IS STABLE AND RESPONDING WELL.
"*BABY*," ERIC. IT'S A BABY.
OF COURSE, SIR. THE CHILD IS DOING WELL.

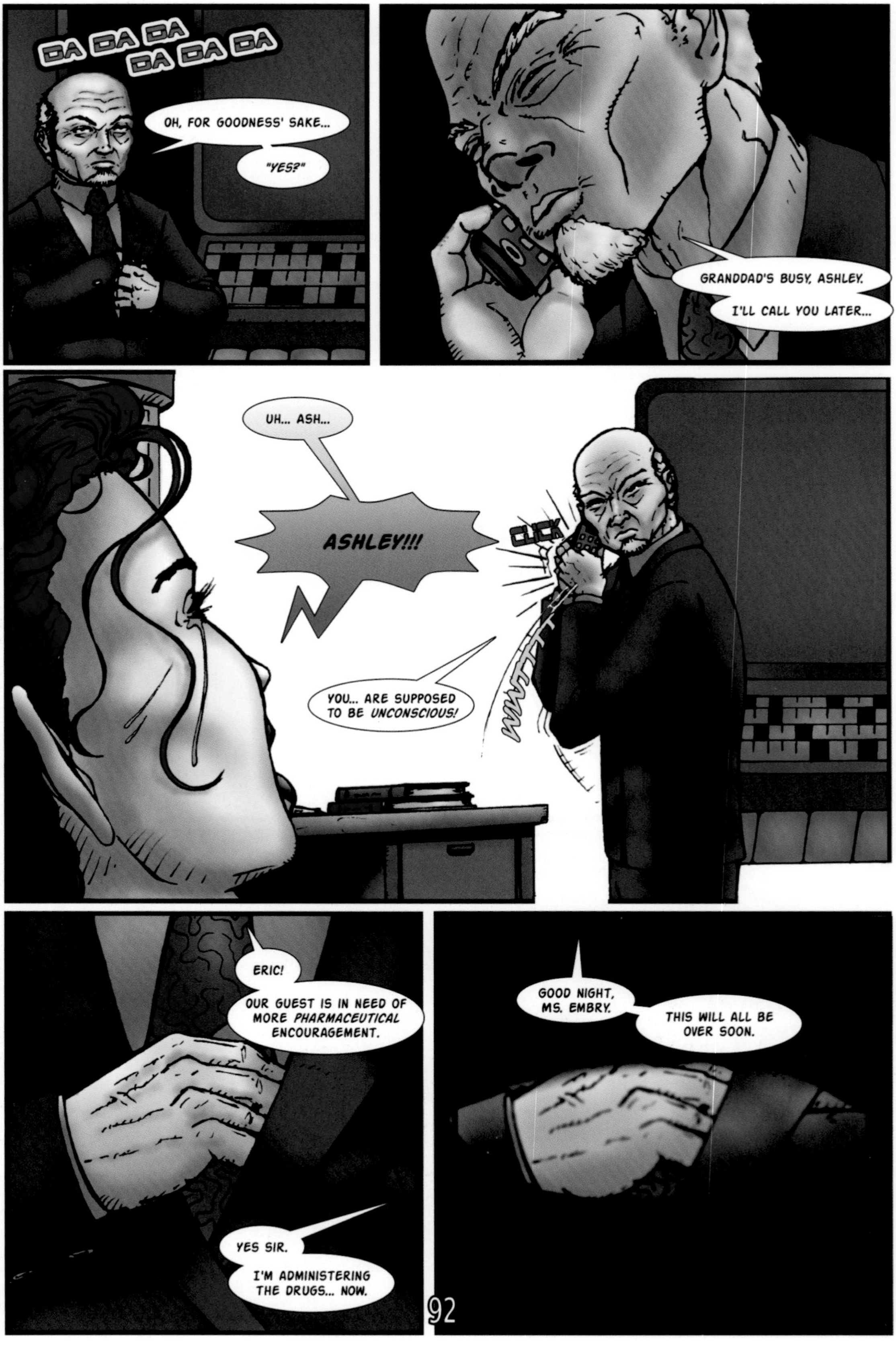
DA DA DA
DA DA DA
OH, FOR GOODNESS' SAKE...
"YES?"
GRANDDAD'S BUSY, ASHLEY.
I'LL CALL YOU LATER...
UH... ASH...
ASHLEY!!!
CLICK
YOU... ARE SUPPOSED TO BE UNCONSCIOUS!
ERIC!
OUR GUEST IS IN NEED OF MORE PHARMACEUTICAL ENCOURAGEMENT.
YES SIR.
I'M ADMINISTERING THE DRUGS... NOW.
GOOD NIGHT, MS. EMBRY.
THIS WILL ALL BE OVER SOON.

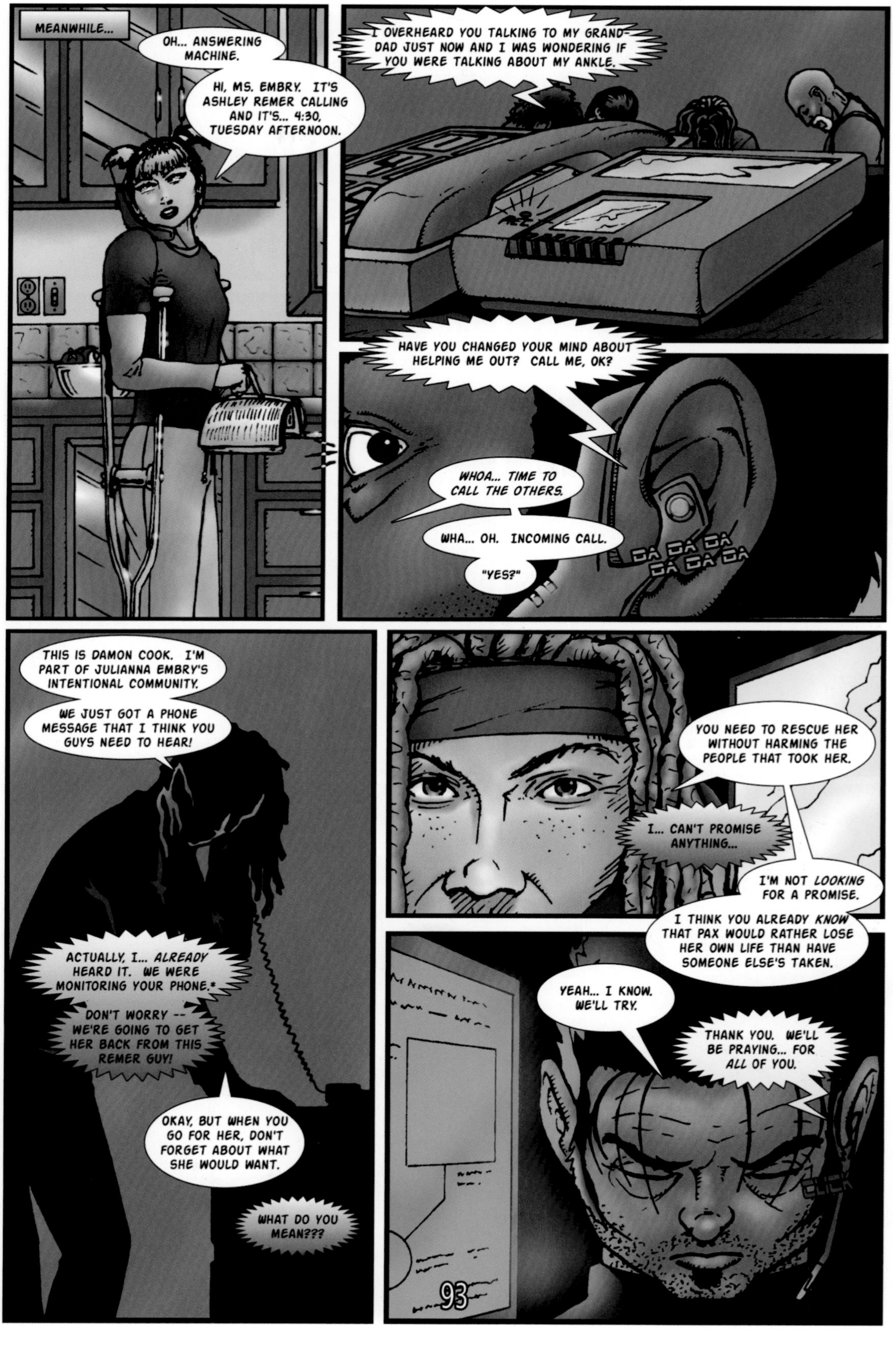
MEANWHILE...
OH... ANSWERING MACHINE.
HI, MS. EMBRY. IT'S ASHLEY REMER CALLING AND IT'S... 4:30, TUESDAY AFTERNOON.
I OVERHEARD YOU TALKING TO MY GRAND-DAD JUST NOW AND I WAS WONDERING IF YOU WERE TALKING ABOUT MY ANKLE.
HAVE YOU CHANGED YOUR MIND ABOUT HELPING ME OUT? CALL ME, OK?
WHOA... TIME TO CALL THE OTHERS.
WHA... OH. INCOMING CALL.
"YES?"
DA DA DA
DA DA DA
THIS IS DAMON COOK. I'M PART OF JULIANNA EMBRY'S INTENTIONAL COMMUNITY.
WE JUST GOT A PHONE MESSAGE THAT I THINK YOU GUYS NEED TO HEAR!
ACTUALLY, I... ALREADY HEARD IT. WE WERE MONITORING YOUR PHONE.*
DON'T WORRY -- WE'RE GOING TO GET HER BACK FROM THIS REMER GUY!
OKAY, BUT WHEN YOU GO FOR HER, DON'T FORGET ABOUT WHAT SHE WOULD WANT.
WHAT DO YOU MEAN???
YOU NEED TO RESCUE HER WITHOUT HARMING THE PEOPLE THAT TOOK HER.
I... CAN'T PROMISE ANYTHING...
I'M NOT LOOKING FOR A PROMISE.
I THINK YOU ALREADY KNOW THAT PAX WOULD RATHER LOSE HER OWN LIFE THAN HAVE SOMEONE ELSE'S TAKEN.
YEAH... I KNOW. WE'LL TRY.
THANK YOU. WE'LL BE PRAYING... FOR ALL OF YOU.
CLICK

I DON'T KNOW... IT SEEMS PRETTY QUIET.

MOSTLY AUTOMATED, I'M GUESSING.

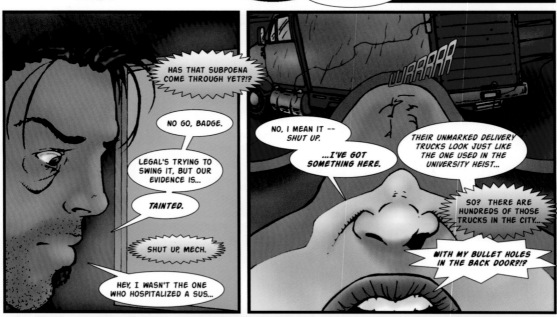

HAS THAT SUBPOENA COME THROUGH YET?!?

NO GO, BADGE.

LEGAL'S TRYING TO SWING IT, BUT OUR EVIDENCE IS...

TAINTED.

SHUT UP, MECH.

HEY, I WASN'T THE ONE WHO HOSPITALIZED A SUS...

WRRRRR

NO, I MEAN IT -- SHUT UP.

...I'VE GOT SOMETHING HERE.

THEIR UNMARKED DELIVERY TRUCKS LOOK JUST LIKE THE ONE USED IN THE UNIVERSITY HEIST...

SO? THERE ARE HUNDREDS OF THOSE TRUCKS IN THE CITY...

WITH MY BULLET HOLES IN THE BACK DOOR?!?

THAT'S ENOUGH FOR ME. BADGE, GET DOWN HERE.

BUT, DOC, THE SUBPOENA...

SUIT UP, EVERYBODY -- WE'RE GOING IN!

...I SAID, WE'RE GOING IN!

CHIK

94

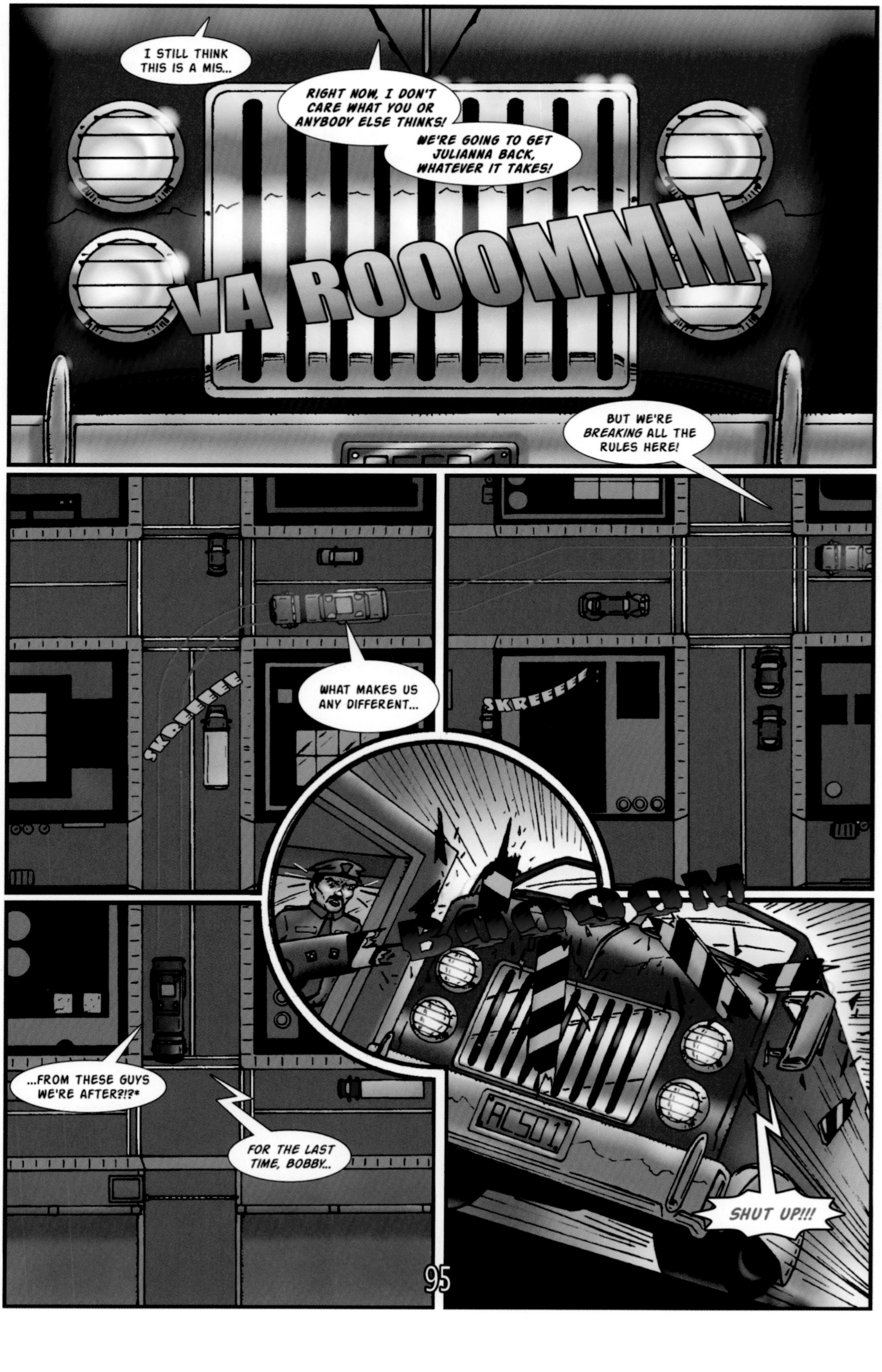

I STILL THINK THIS IS A MIS...
RIGHT NOW, I DON'T CARE WHAT YOU OR ANYBODY ELSE THINKS!
WE'RE GOING TO GET JULIANNA BACK, WHATEVER IT TAKES!
VA ROOOMMM
BUT WE'RE BREAKING ALL THE RULES HERE!
WHAT MAKES US ANY DIFFERENT...
SKREEEEEE
SKREEEEEE
...FROM THESE GUYS WE'RE AFTER?!?*
FOR THE LAST TIME, BOBBY...
SHUT UP!!!
ACSD1

CSO
OKAY -- STAY ALERT, PEOPLE...
PAX IS HERE SOMEWHERE AND WE'VE GOT A 12-YEAR-OLD FEMALE HOSTAGE THAT COULD BE NEARBY!
MECH, IS IT READY?
JUST A SECOND -- IT TAKES A MOMENT TO EXTRACT FROM STORAGE MODE...
EXPANSION COMPLETE.
SYSTEMS CHECK...
PRIMARY SYSTEMS OPERATIONAL.
ORDINANCE CHECK...
ORDINANCE AT MAXIMUM LEVELS.
OPEN OPERATOR HATCH.
OPERATOR HATCH OPEN.
OKAY... LET'S GO GET 'EM!
ACSO
TCK
TCK
WRRRRRR
IT'S A LITTLE *OVERKILL*, MECH...
BUT I THINK IT'S *EXACTLY* WHAT WE NEED RIGHT NOW.
NOW LET'S GET IN THERE!!!
WHAT HAVE WE GOT, PEOPLE?
NOTHING SO FAR, DOC...
THE PLACE SEEMS PRETTY EMPTY.
MECH HERE -- TRY THE CENTRAL ATRIUM. I'VE GOT LOTS OF HEAT SIGNATURES THERE.
WE'VE JUST REACHED IT...

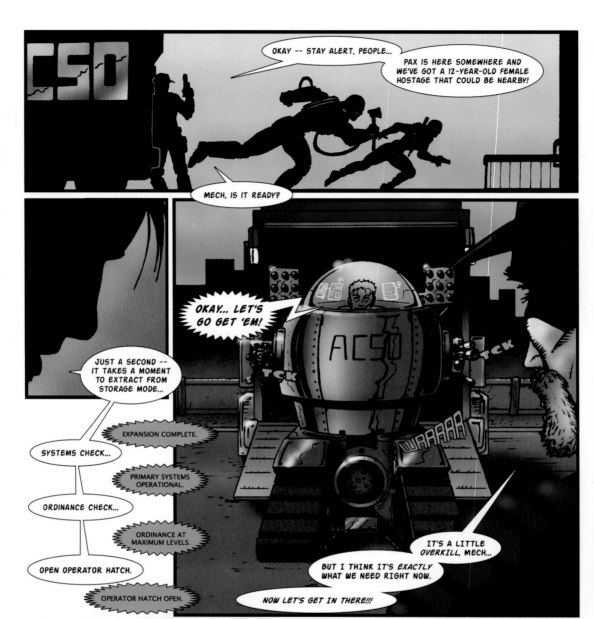

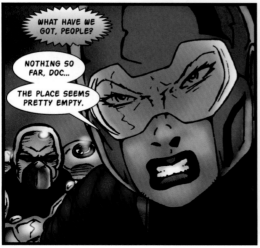

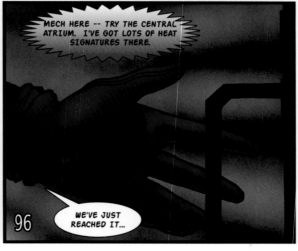

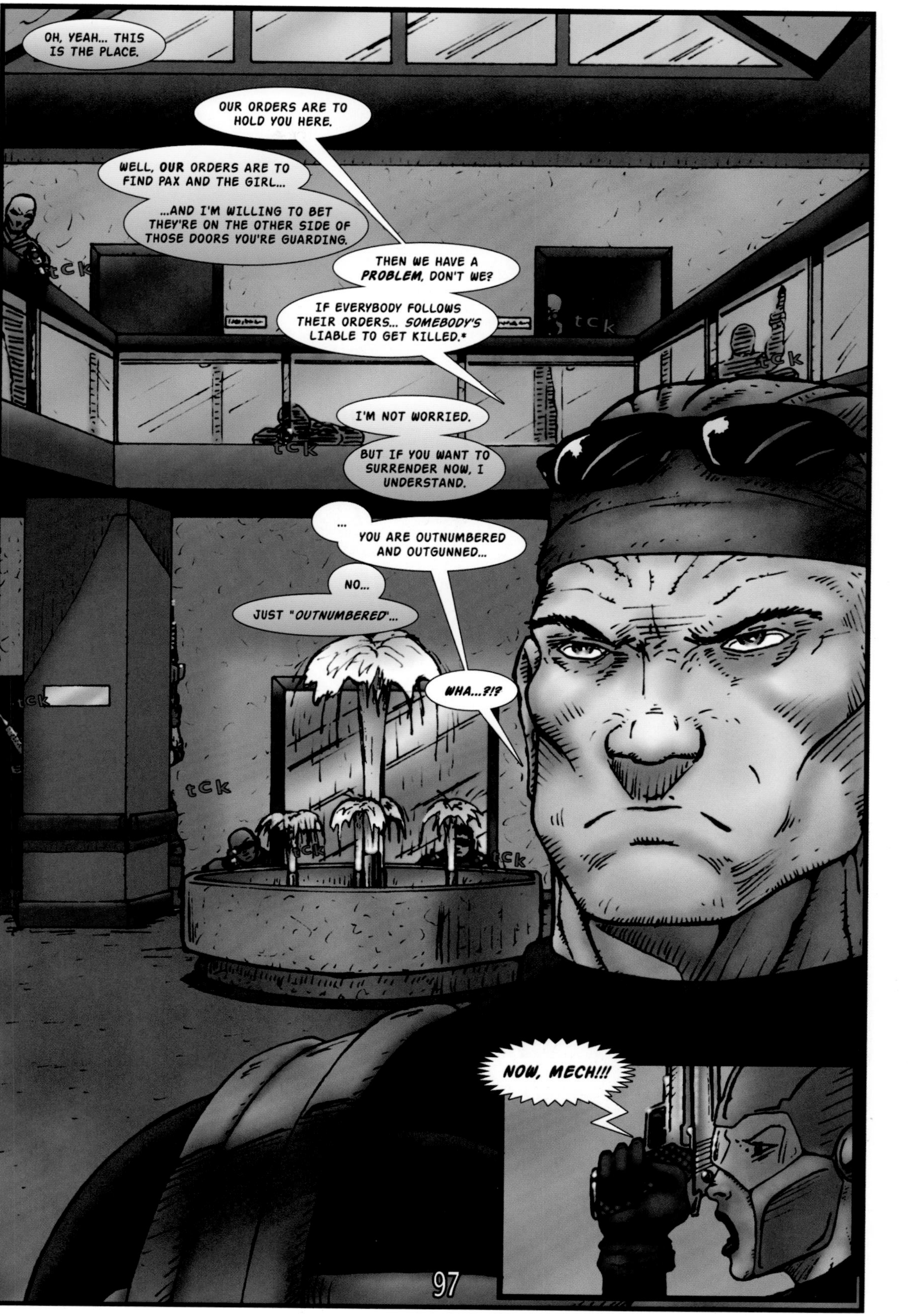
OH, YEAH... THIS IS THE PLACE.
OUR ORDERS ARE TO HOLD YOU HERE.
WELL, OUR ORDERS ARE TO FIND PAX AND THE GIRL...
...AND I'M WILLING TO BET THEY'RE ON THE OTHER SIDE OF THOSE DOORS YOU'RE GUARDING.
THEN WE HAVE A PROBLEM, DON'T WE?
IF EVERYBODY FOLLOWS THEIR ORDERS... SOMEBODY'S LIABLE TO GET KILLED.*
I'M NOT WORRIED.
BUT IF YOU WANT TO SURRENDER NOW, I UNDERSTAND.
...
YOU ARE OUTNUMBERED AND OUTGUNNED...
NO...
JUST "OUTNUMBERED"...
WHA...?!?
tck
NOW, MECH!!!

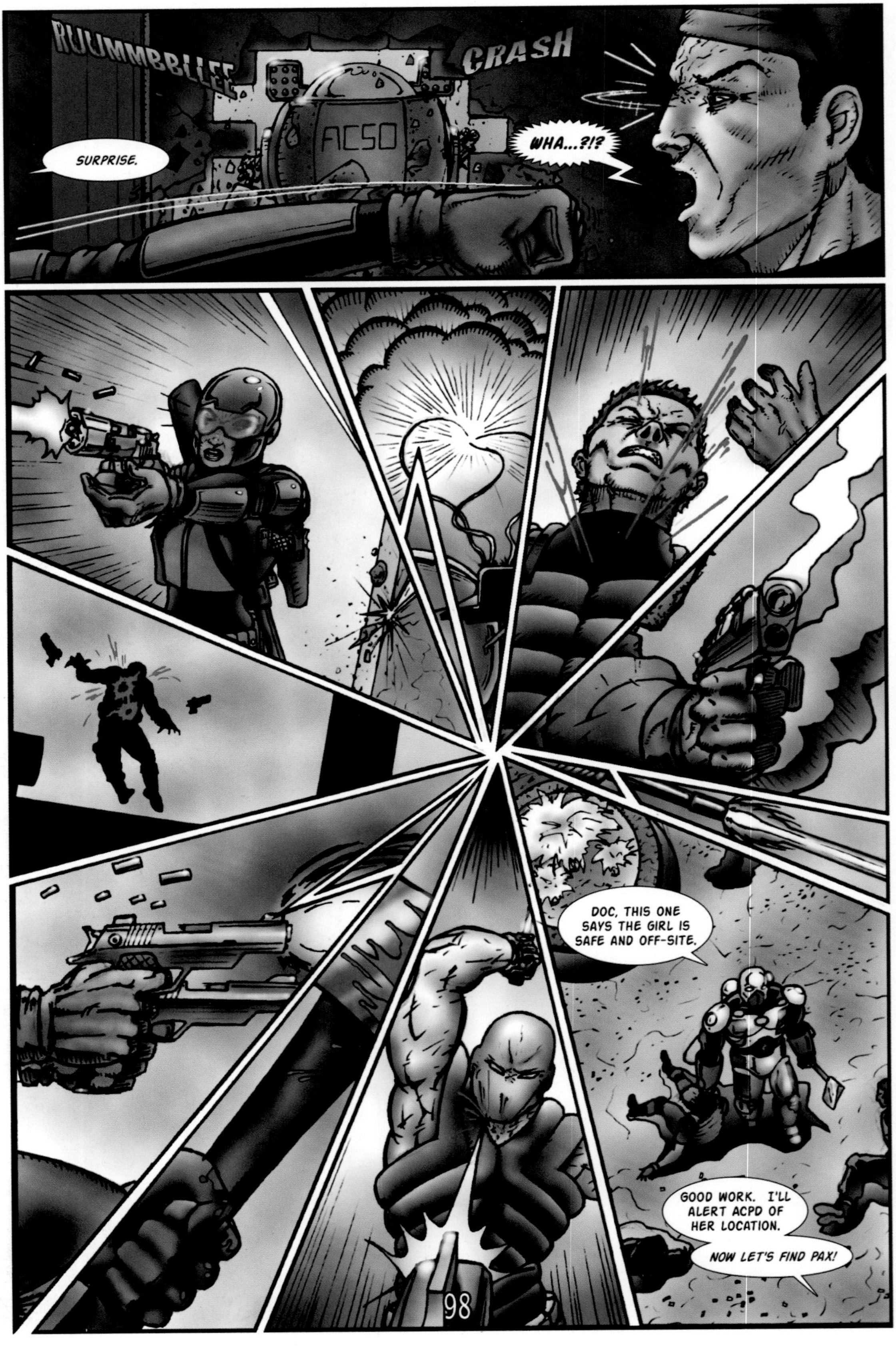
RUUMMBBLLEE
CRASH
SURPRISE.
WHA...?!?
ACSO
DOC, THIS ONE SAYS THE GIRL IS SAFE AND OFF-SITE.
GOOD WORK. I'LL ALERT ACPD OF HER LOCATION.
NOW LET'S FIND PAX!

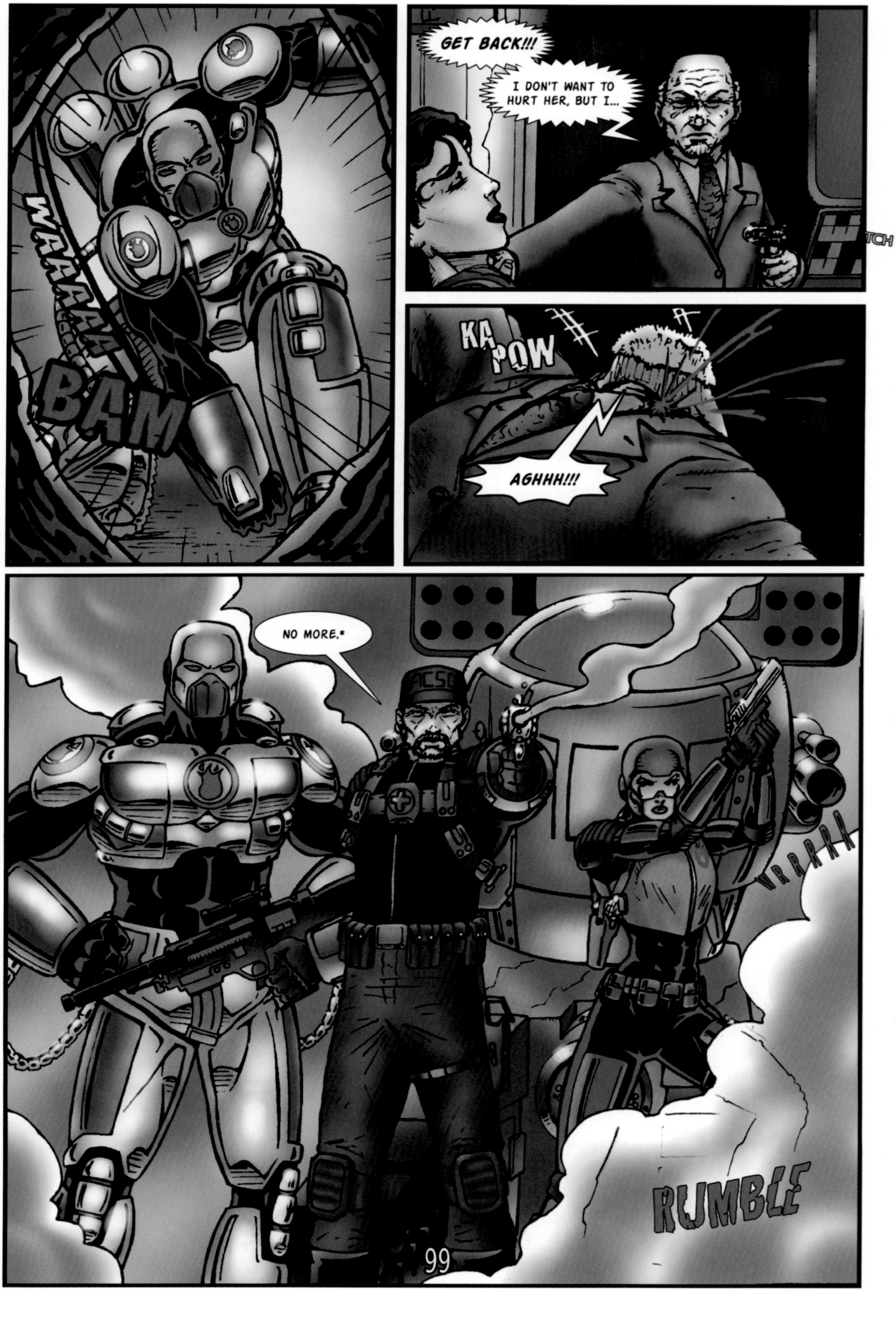
WAAAAA
BAM
GET BACK!!!
I DON'T WANT TO HURT HER, BUT I...
KA POW
AGHHH!!!
NO MORE.*
ACSO
WRRRRRR
RUMBLE

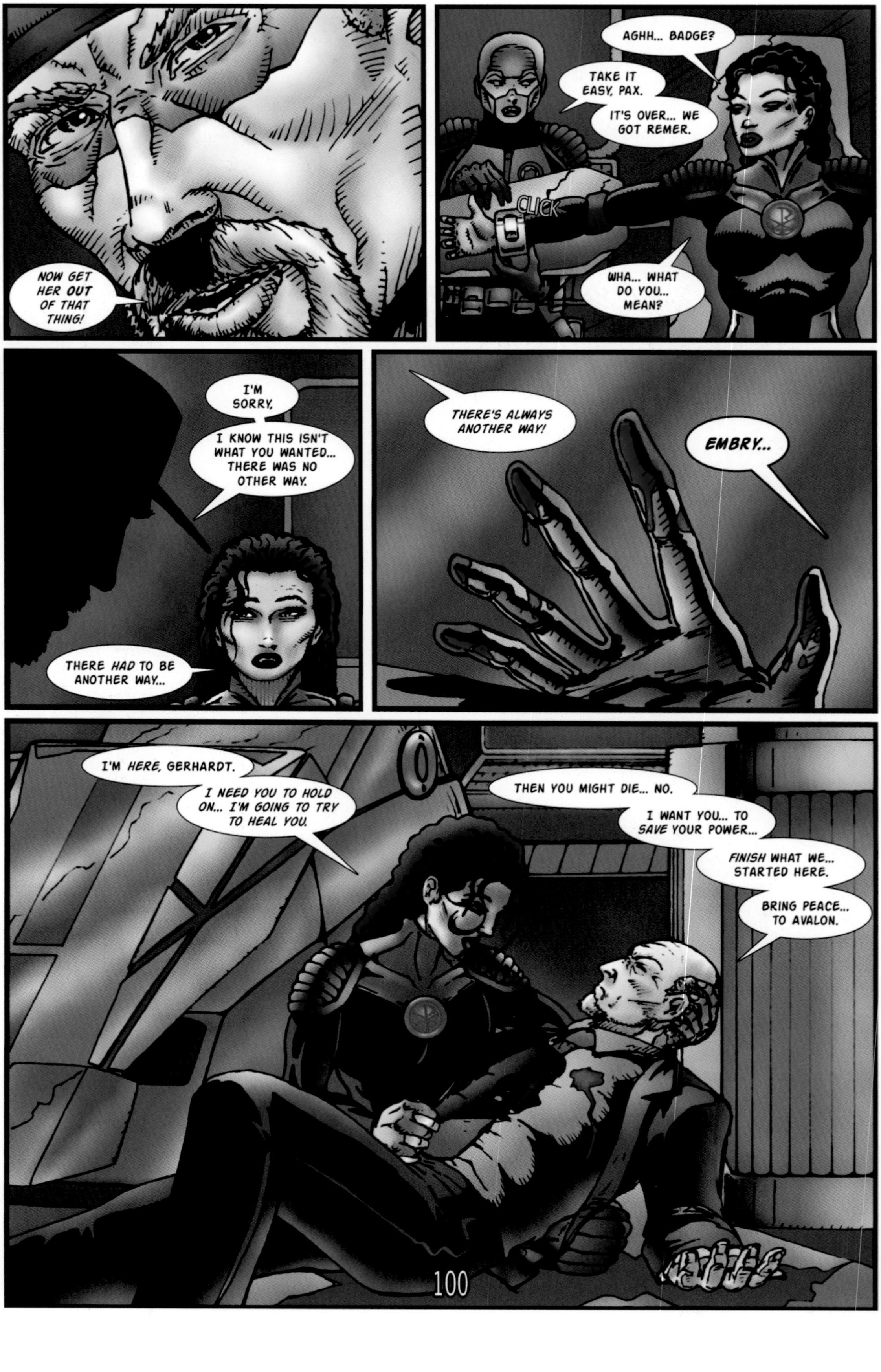
NOW GET HER OUT OF THAT THING!
AGHH... BADGE?
TAKE IT EASY, PAX.
IT'S OVER... WE GOT REMER.
CLICK
WHA... WHAT DO YOU... MEAN?
I'M SORRY,
I KNOW THIS ISN'T WHAT YOU WANTED... THERE WAS NO OTHER WAY.
THERE HAD TO BE ANOTHER WAY...
THERE'S ALWAYS ANOTHER WAY!
EMBRY...
I'M HERE, GERHARDT.
I NEED YOU TO HOLD ON... I'M GOING TO TRY TO HEAL YOU.
THEN YOU MIGHT DIE... NO.
I WANT YOU... TO SAVE YOUR POWER...
FINISH WHAT WE... STARTED HERE.
BRING PEACE... TO AVALON.

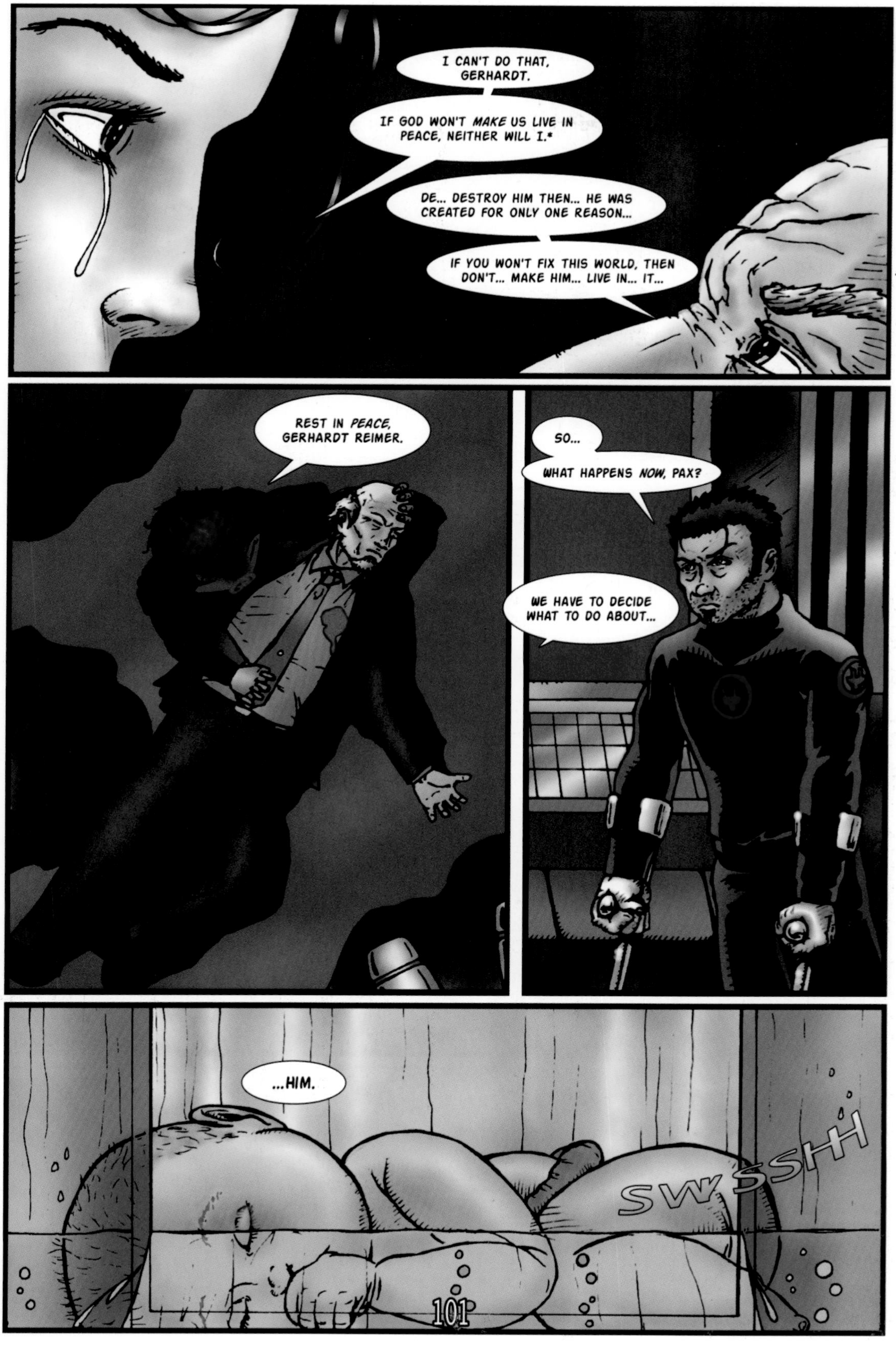
I CAN'T DO THAT, GERHARDT.
IF GOD WON'T *MAKE* US LIVE IN PEACE, NEITHER WILL I.*
DE... DESTROY HIM THEN... HE WAS CREATED FOR ONLY ONE REASON...
IF YOU WON'T FIX THIS WORLD, THEN DON'T... MAKE HIM... LIVE IN... IT...
REST IN *PEACE*, GERHARDT REIMER.
SO...
WHAT HAPPENS *NOW*, PAX?
WE HAVE TO DECIDE WHAT TO DO ABOUT...
...HIM.
SWYSSHH

AFTER A QUICK EXPLANATION...

I SAY WE LEAVE IT BE.

IF IT CAN'T SURVIVE WITHOUT OUR INTERVENTION, WE HAVE NO OBLIGATION TO SAVE IT.*

I'VE ALREADY TAKEN ONE LIFE TODAY, AND THAT WAS NECESSARY...

I DON'T KNOW THAT *THIS* IS.

THAT'S A FUNNY WORD: "NECESSARY."

GLUG GLUG

SO... WHAT ARE YOU GOING TO DO?

I JUST DON'T KNOW...

THIS ISN'T THE SORT OF THING WE'RE PREPARED FOR.

WE?

THE FOLLOWERS OF GOD. WE'VE GOTTEN INTO THE HABIT OF NOT *DEALING* WITH STUFF UNTIL IT'S TOO LATE... WE'RE NOT PREPARED TO DEAL WITH A CLONED BABY.

I HAVE NO IDEA WHAT TO DO!

GOD, I JUST DON'T KNOW...

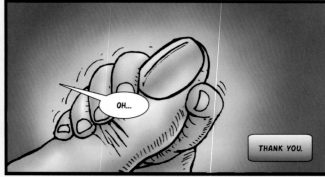

OH...

THANK YOU.

...

I'M RESPONSIBLE FOR MY CHOICES, *NO MATTER WHAT* THE CIRCUMSTANCES ARE.

YOU MAY BE THE RESULT OF ONE MAN'S MISTAKES, BUT THAT DOES NOT MAKE YOU A MISTAKE.

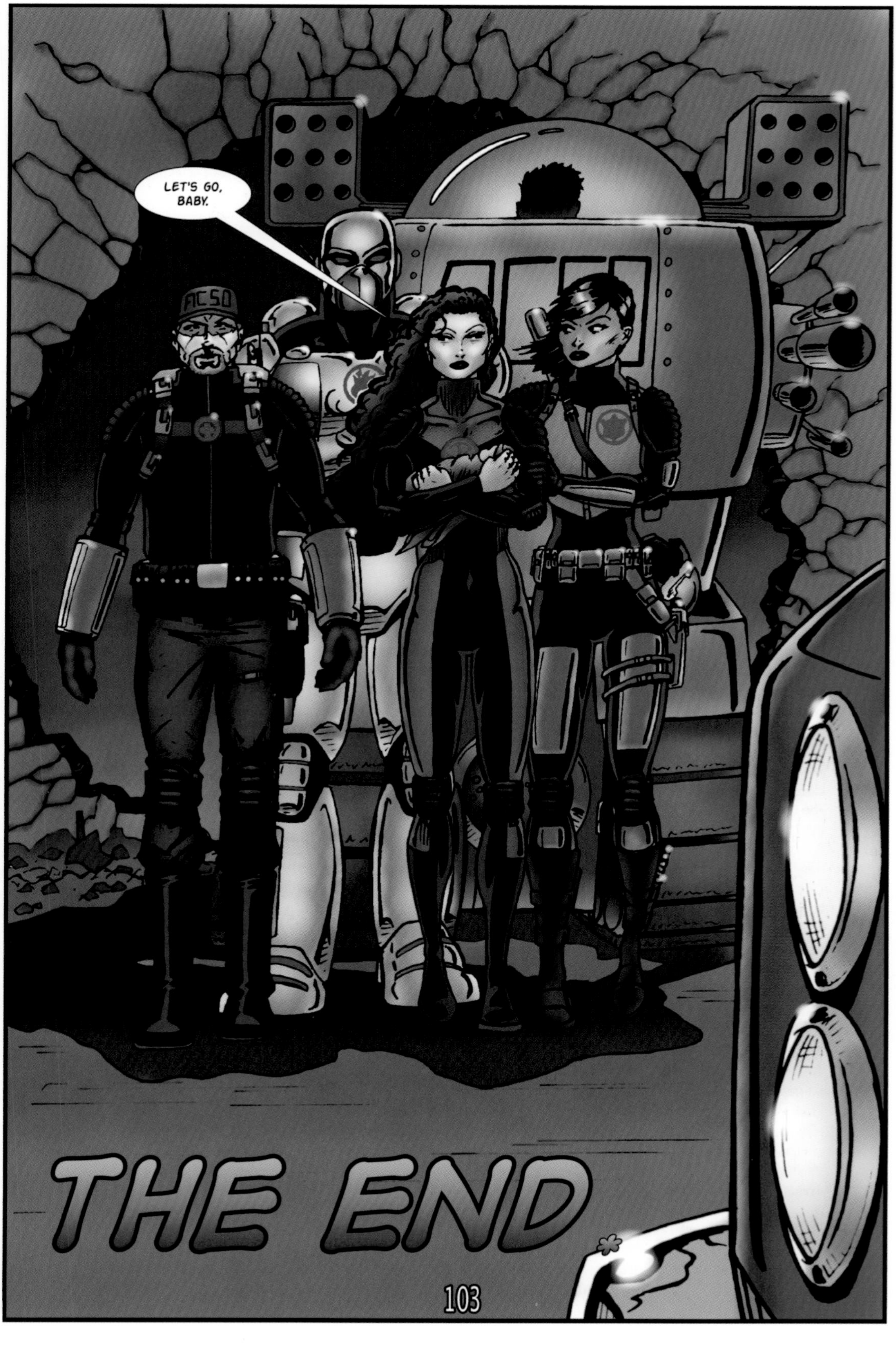
LET'S GO, BABY.
ACSO
THE END

THINKING IT THROUGH

*7 - What do you think the TV special was trying to accomplish? Considering how this man responded, how is it actually coming across to the people of Avalon City? How did seeing the production notes (in green ovals) change how this came across to you?

*10 - Why do you think Pax insisted on this alteration to her equipment? Is she being unreasonable?

*12 - Given how seriously this man is injured, why does Pax want to know his name? How does that change what you expect her to do for him? How does knowing any person's name change how you relate to them?

*19 - Does this system seem fair to you? What would motivate Pax to operate this way?

*22 - How do you feel about getting personal knowledge about these gunmen? How does it affect the way you look at them? Do you think it would change how ACSO would confront them?

*24 - Do you think Exapatao is right? What would you sacrifice to look good? What should others sacrifice?

*25 - Do you think Pax is making a bad decision in refusing to heal celebrities? What do you think are her reasons for this choice? How are these reasons causing her to clash with Exapatao and the mayor?

*31 - Why is Badge so frustrated with Mech? How would you react in her situation?

*36 - According to Pax, she got the impulse to attack the gunman from watching a movie. Is this a realistic conclusion? What, if any, connection do you see between "watching" and "doing"?

*37 - How would the other members of ACSO have handled Pax's situation? Why does Pax refuse to engage the gunman? Do you think it's fair for her to threaten to leave the team if their priorities change?

*50 - If the world is "designed," as Pax puts it, how come there are so many problems? Does Fireguard's conclusion that his lack of control shows the absence of a higher power make sense to you? Why or why not?

*53 - What do you think Pax might mean by "entanglements"? Is she being unrealistic? How would this play out in our world?

*57 - How do you think the rest of ACSO would have handled this confrontation? How might the outcome have been different?

*61 - How many people do you think died in this explosion and the fire that followed? Noting that the team seemed unconcerned (since it wasn't their problem), do you think their reaction would be different if they saw the faces of those people who died?

*64 - Is it unfair for Pax to refuse to heal Ashley now when she was willing to the first time? How would you feel in Ashley's shoes?

*66 - What would allow a Buddhist like Nori to take on a job that might require her to kill?

*67 - Pax lives in an intentional community -- a group of people who choose to live together because of common philosophical or religious beliefs. There are many reasons to try this: to live cheaply, to build friendships, to reduce waste, to celebrate common ideas, to make a statement, etc. You can find out more about intentional communities at www.thesimpleway.org or by reading Shane Claiborne's book, *The Irresistible Revolution* (Zondervan), for the inside scoop. For more info on living simply, check out Richard Swenson's book, *Margin* (Navpress). Anyway, from what you've learned about Pax, why do you think she lives this way? Why does Pax want to meet Remer instead of just refusing the money?

*69 - French philosopher Jacque Ellul has some thought-provoking ideas about progress and efficiency. His book, *Perspectives on Our Age* (Anansi Press), is definitely worth a read. Do you agree with Remer's comment about "the quickest path"?

*72 - Why doesn't Pax just go ahead and heal the athlete? Is she being too critical of Exapatao's motives? Where does her decision leave the children's home?

*77 - Mech is used to playing games where things get blown up... so why is he so frustrated here?

*79 - The Omega gunmen wear masks over their entire face, as opposed to the other team. Does it make you think differently about them? Why?

*83 - Who is the victim in Remer's story? Who is the enemy? What is the problem with assigning those titles to specific people?

*84 - How aware are you of the circumstances behind your lifestyle? What are some of the consequences of digging deeper?
   - Cloning is not a futuristic moral dilemma. What do you think about genetic research? How much research should be allowed? What are some of the consequences of a world with multiple "you's"?

*86 - What is Remer's argument here? Why does Pax oppose his plan to force people into peace? For insight on the ethical implications of freedom and change, check out Mark Baker's book, *Religious No More* (InterVarsity Press).

*90 - What is the significance of Badge's comment? Would you have done what she did? Why did Doc give this order?

*93 - Where did the tip about Pax's location actually come from? Was it really necessary for ACSO to tap the phone line? Are they justified in breaking the rules? Who decides which rules are okay to break?

*95 - How do we tell the "good guys" from the "bad guys"? What happens when that distinction gets blurred? How does this relate to the idea of bullying?

*97 - What do you think of this comment about "orders"? Is it strange that the gunman is the one making it? What is actually going on here?

*99 - Were you suprised that it was Doc who pulled the trigger and not Badge? Why did he do it?

*101 - Do you agree with Pax that God won't make us embrace peace? Why or why not?

*102 - Following Fireguard's logic, a person would have to observe the baby to find out if it could survive on its own. Is there a moral dilemma involved in an "observation only" response to problems?

*103 - What do you think Pax should do with the baby now?

AFTERMATH - The team attacked Remer's factory without orders or a warrant and killed several people there, including Remer himself. Given that police officers are held accountable for every shot fired (and must appear before a review board that weighs the circumstances and passes judgment on those actions), what do you think will happen to Doc and the rest of ACSO now?

Visit **WWW.PAXAVALON.COM** and join the conversation!

PAX IN PROGRESS

BADGE

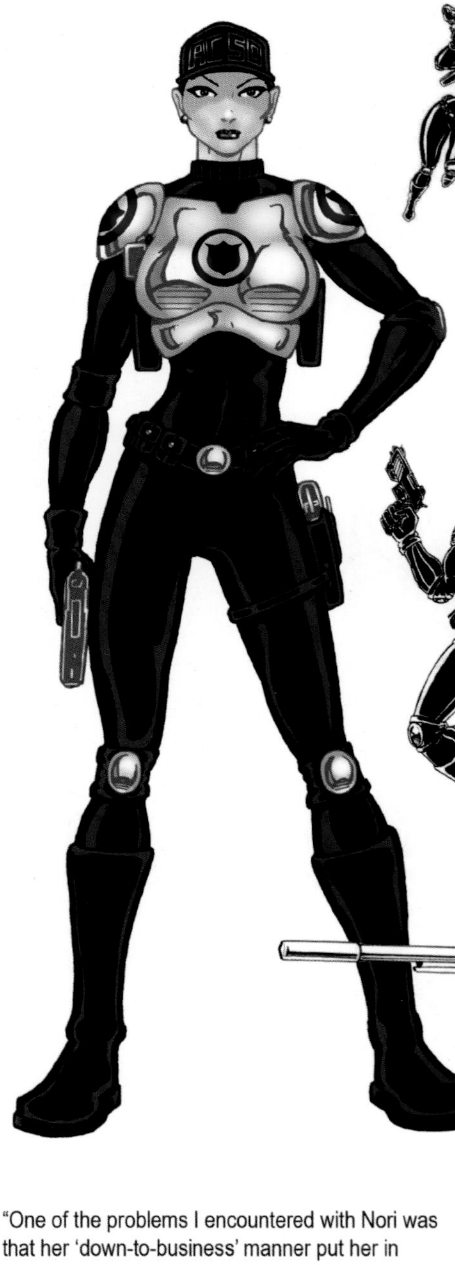

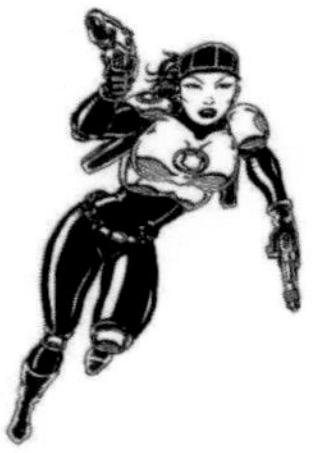

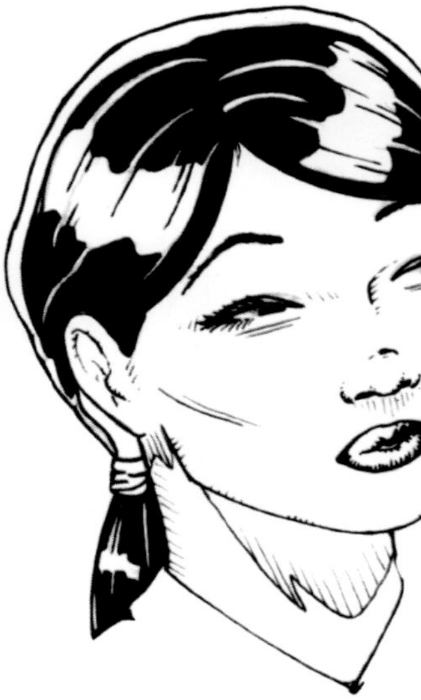

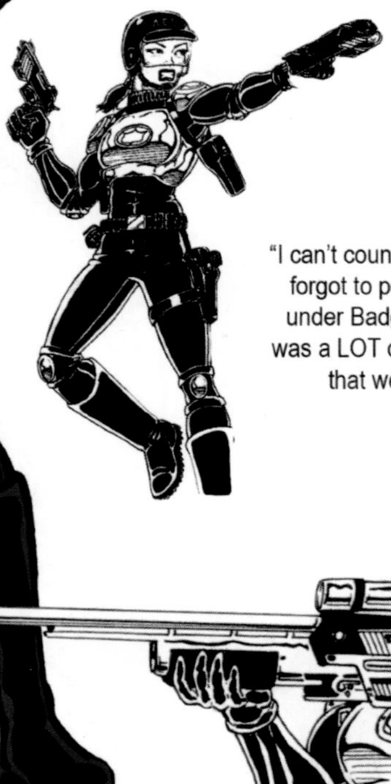

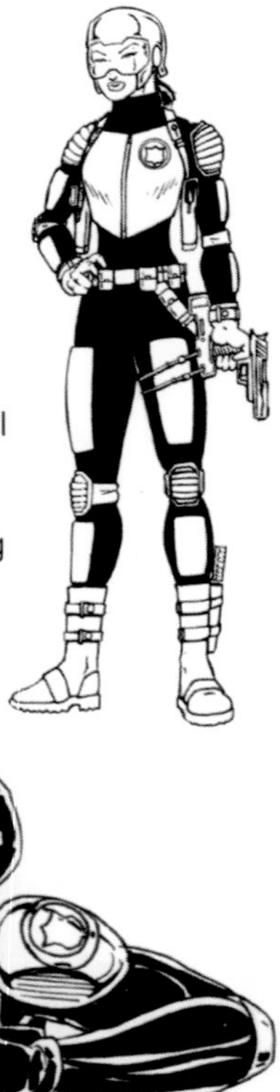

"I can't count how many times I forgot to pencil the holsters under Badge's arms... there was a LOT of computer editing that went on there."

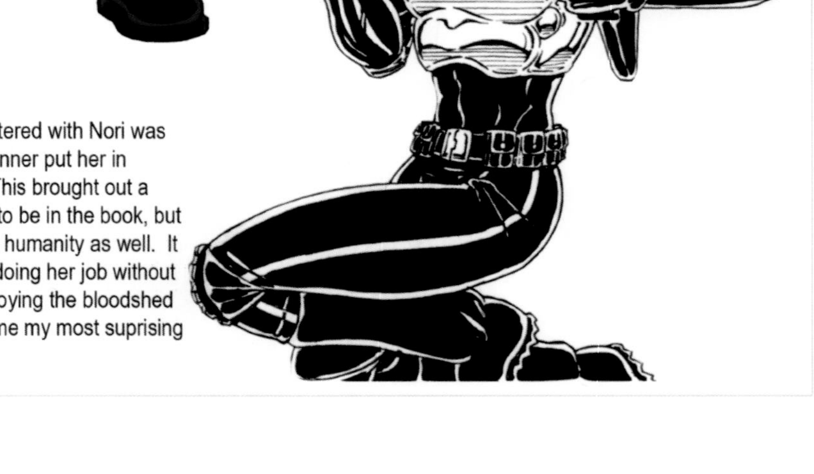

"One of the problems I encountered with Nori was that her 'down-to-business' manner put her in constant conflict with Bobby. This brought out a sarcasm that I never intended to be in the book, but perhaps it injected a little more humanity as well. It was also difficult to pencil her doing her job without making it look like she was enjoying the bloodshed at a personal level. She became my most suprising source of pithy remarks."

DOC

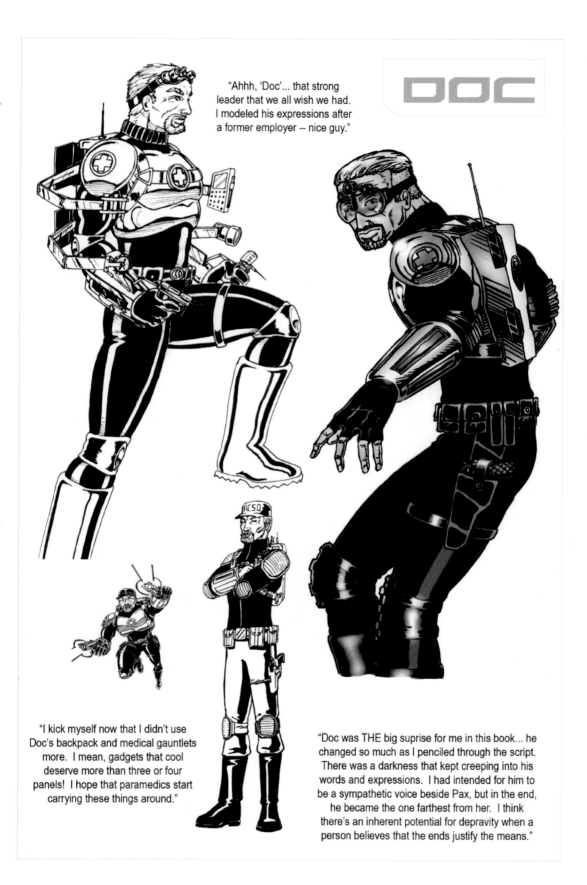

"Ahhh, 'Doc'... that strong leader that we all wish we had. I modeled his expressions after a former employer -- nice guy."

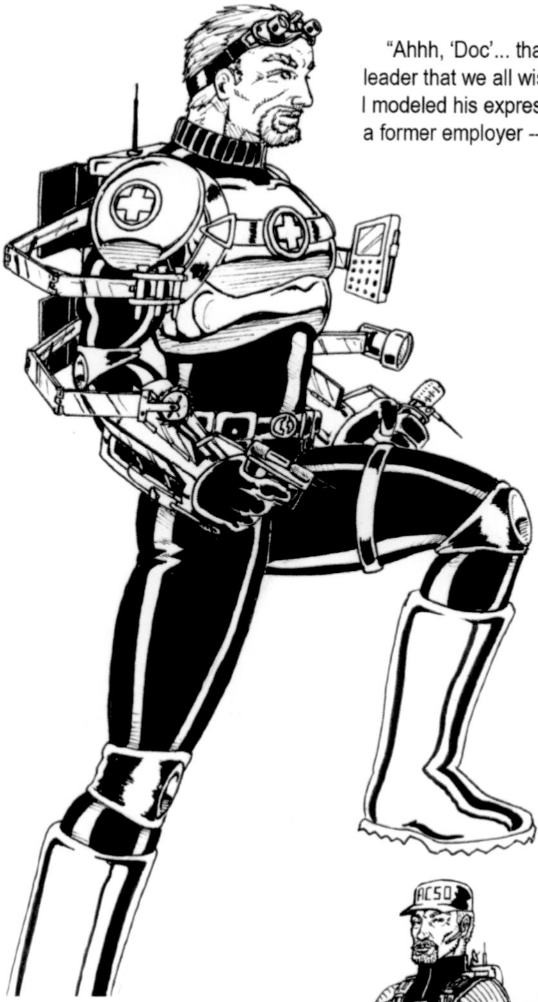

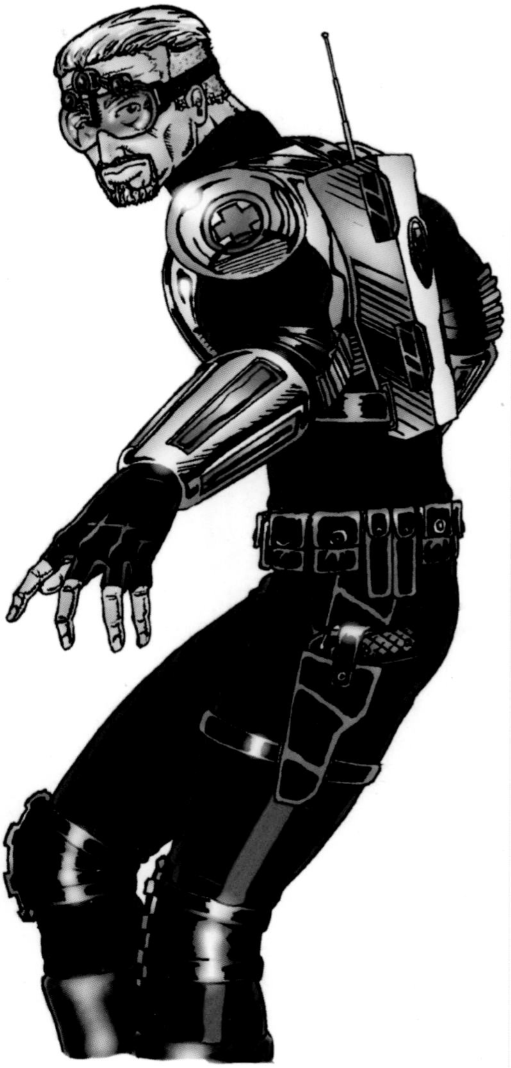

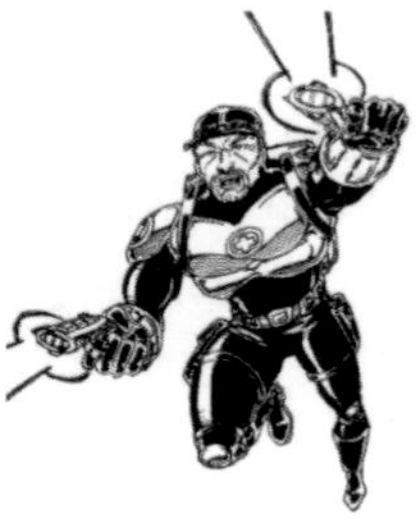

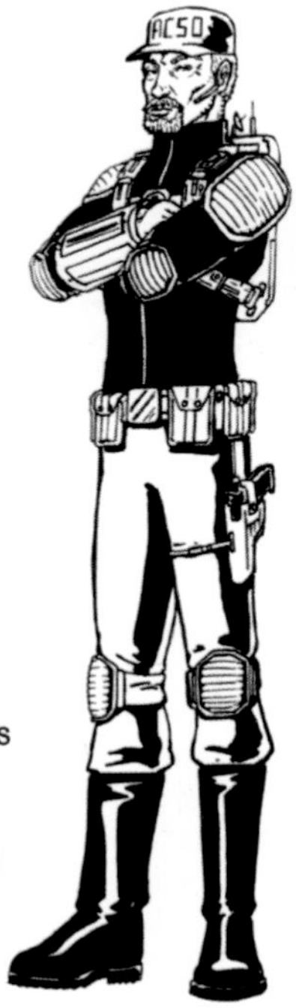
ACSO

"I kick myself now that I didn't use Doc's backpack and medical gauntlets more. I mean, gadgets that cool deserve more than three or four panels! I hope that paramedics start carrying these things around."

"Doc was THE big suprise for me in this book... he changed so much as I penciled through the script. There was a darkness that kept creeping into his words and expressions. I had intended for him to be a sympathetic voice beside Pax, but in the end, he became the one farthest from her. I think there's an inherent potential for depravity when a person believes that the ends justify the means."

PAX

"The trick in comic books is to use words sparingly and communicate details to the reader with pictures as much as you can. That's a little easier to do when you want to show power and destruction, and a lot more difficult when you have a character like Pax, who is supposd to be graceful and athletic without being intimidating."

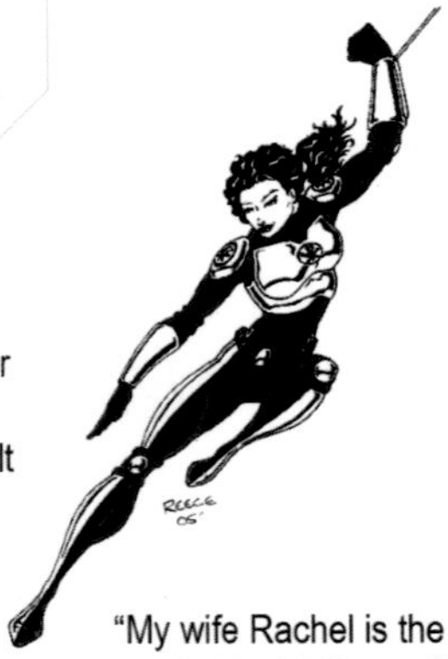

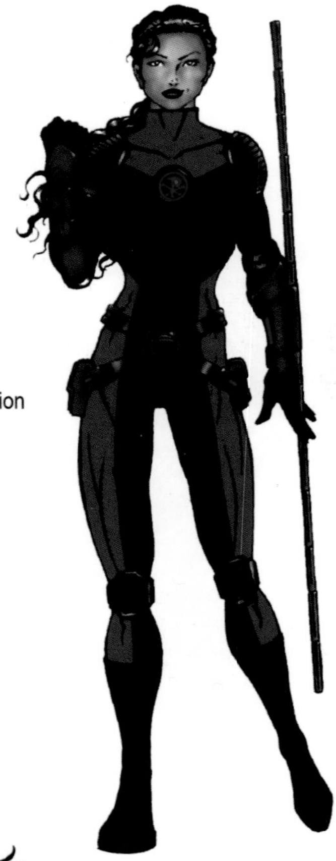

"My wife Rachel is the inspiration behind Julianna Embry."

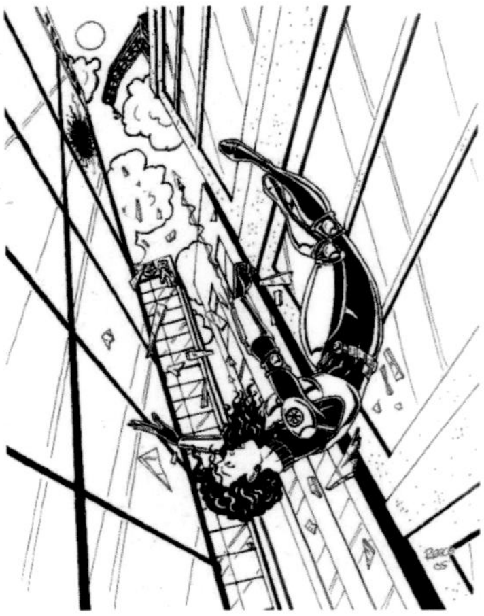

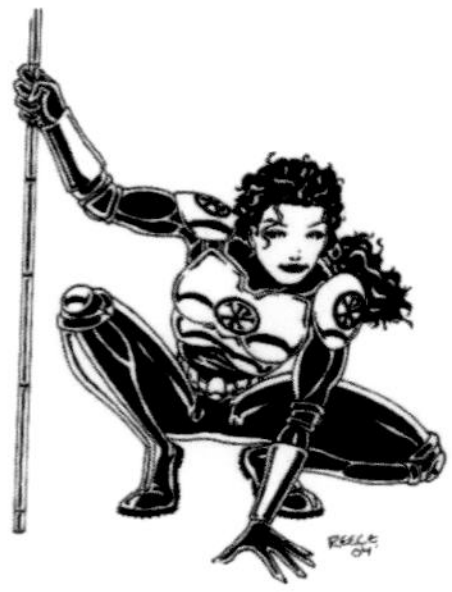

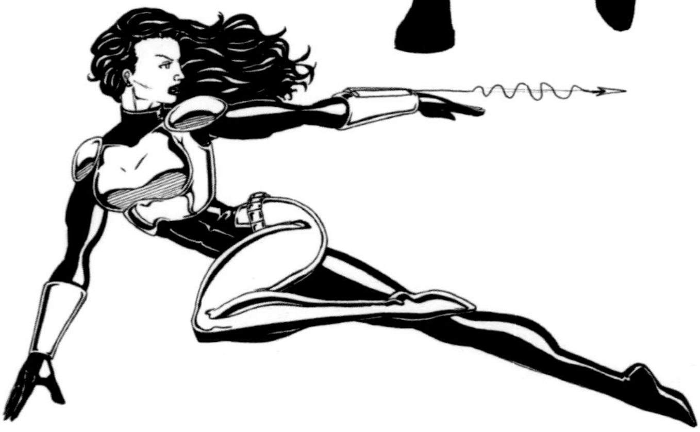

"Each of the team sports a symbol that identifies their main area of responsiblity. In making her shield the *Chi-Rho* (the symbol for Christ in the ancient Roman world), Pax declares herself to be dedicated to an ideal beyond her function or capabilities. She does not define herself primarily as a healer -- that is what she does, not who she is."

"Readers sometimes wonder why some of the team get new uniforms partway through the book. It goes against the norm of comics (keep the recognizable and comfortable elements consistant) and can be a little confusing. There are two reasons for the change: 1. I felt a little uncomfortable with the metal chestplates that some of the team were sporting. While this is pretty standard in comic books, it did distract from their faces (and put large white spaces into otherwise dark frames). 2. I got bored with the uniformity and lack of detail of the original costumes. From a distance, Pax and Badge looked a lot alike -- so I redesigned the outfits and wrote it into the script that Exapatao was getting ideas for change from the television ratings."

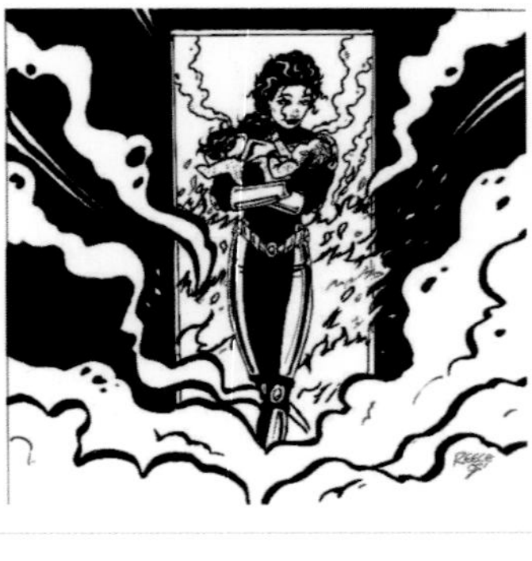

FIREGUARD

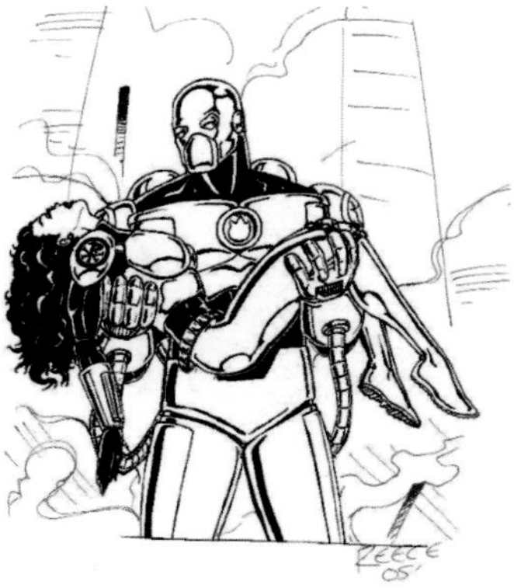

"There were so many subtle changes to the armor throughout the book. Sometimes they were deliberate improvements... and sometimes I just flat out forgot stuff."

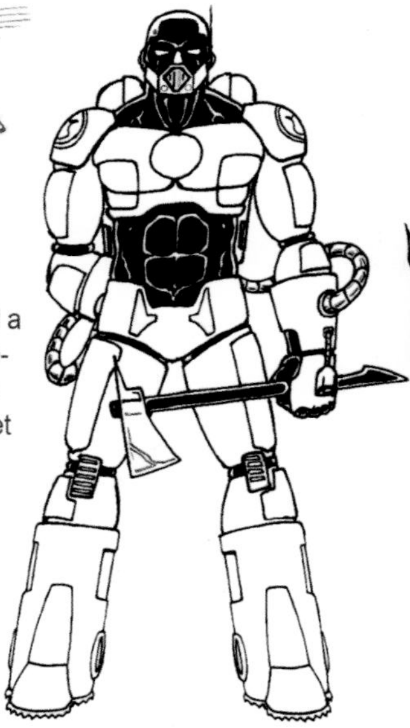

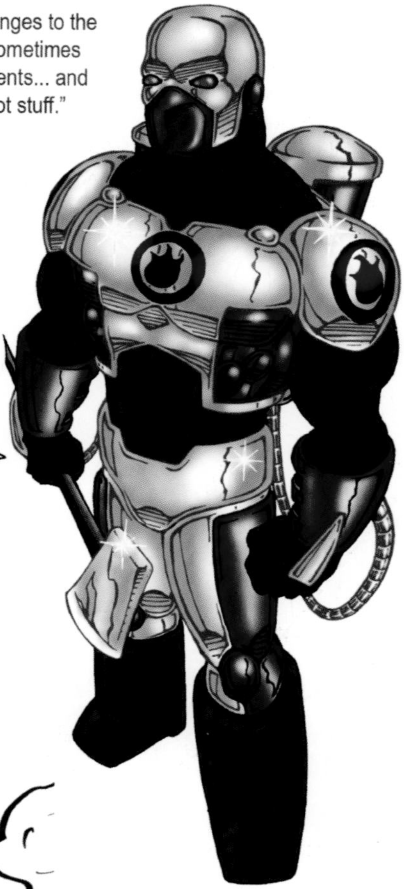

"Some of my proofreaders suspected a little romance between Pax and Fireguard... nothing intentional but who knows where things will go if they get on the same page some day."

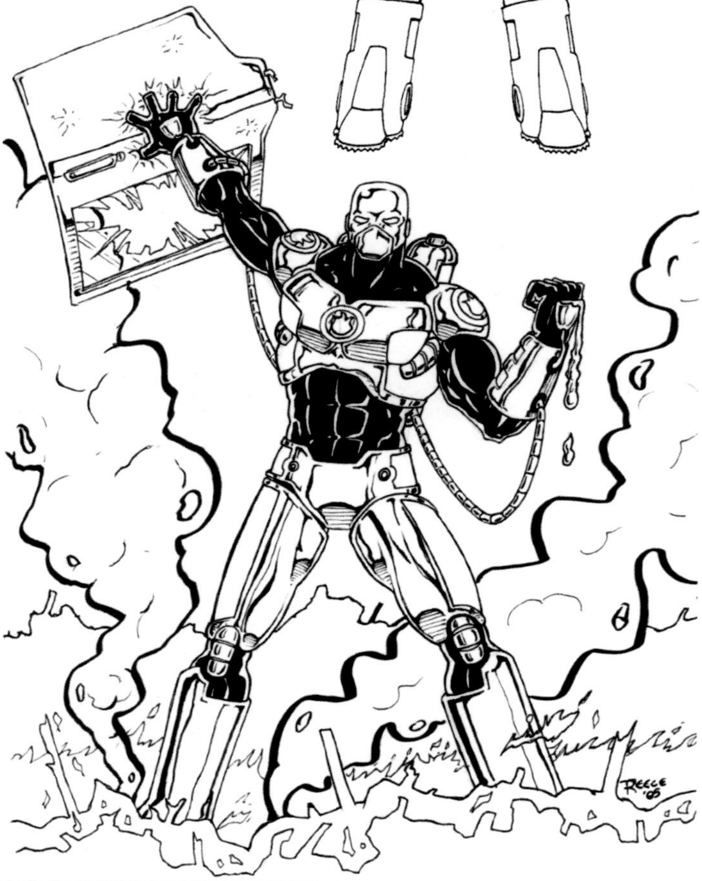

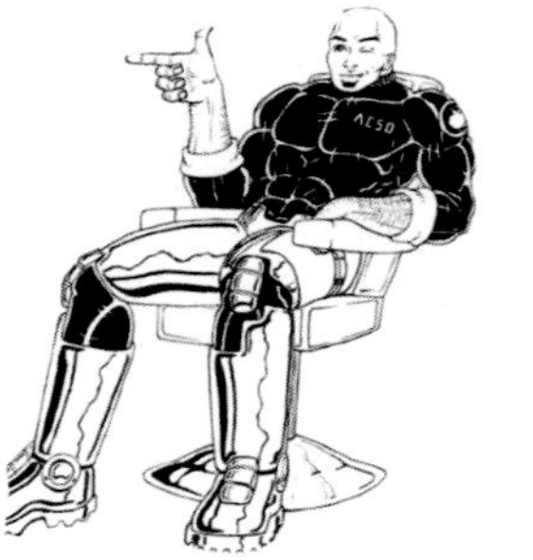

"Tyson had so much more potential than I explored in this book. Apart from a 'poker' reference and the occasional joke, he just seemed like the stereotypical strong, silent type. I was also hoping to develop more of a 'buddyship' between him and Bobby -- something light but with that fierce loyalty that often suprises us."

"Okay, confession time... I modeled Bobby after myself. It's not that we look that much alike (I never could grow much for facial hair), but his natural tendency toward violence as entertainment and his flippancy toward life in general have been constant thorns in my side as I've journeyed through the idea of seeking peace on God's terms. His sarcastic words were often my own first reaction to the situations he encountered, and the way the team responded to him... well, I've heard all those things more than a few times. Even though he reminds me of the worst parts of myself, I take heart in the thought that he really is a good guy, and in the end... well, you almost think he's starting to get where Pax is coming from."

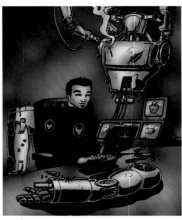

"Words cannot describe the frustration of trying to fit somebody in a wheel-chair into panels with other standing characters! There were so many times that I wimped out and went with a close-up face shot or silhouette because I didn't want to work around the height difference. I'm reminded though, that any frustrations I might have in drawing a wheelchair do not come close to actually being in one."

"Originally I planned to have many different robots at Bobby's disposal. They would all incorporate the same Hammerhead lenses (allowing Bobby to see things in 3-D) but would have various functions. I modeled some of these after various construction vehicles, but in the end, only the Hammer-head prototype and the Warmachine made it in. Part of the problem was the space that these things would take up in the ACSO mobile unit... the other problem was the space they took up in panels."

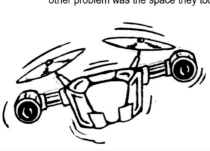

A.C.S.O.

"Pax Avalon didn't start out as a team concept. Originally I was going to tell a story about a single man who had the ability to heal people and refused to resort to violence. The problem was that, the more people I bounced this idea off, the harder I had to work to make it sound interesting. 'So, what's actually going to happen in this book?' they would ask me, and I would try to explain the inner conflict that he faced. The problem, of course, is that comics are a visual medium, and when you want to demonstrate inner conflict, you usually parallel it with an external one. But I didn't want to create another simplistic 'bad guys' and 'good guys' comic book... that doesn't challenge us to do anything except flip the page. So the team concept was born. Five people with radically different ways of solving problems, dealing with problems. They want to get along, but they don't necessarily understand each other -- and that's something that most people can relate to."

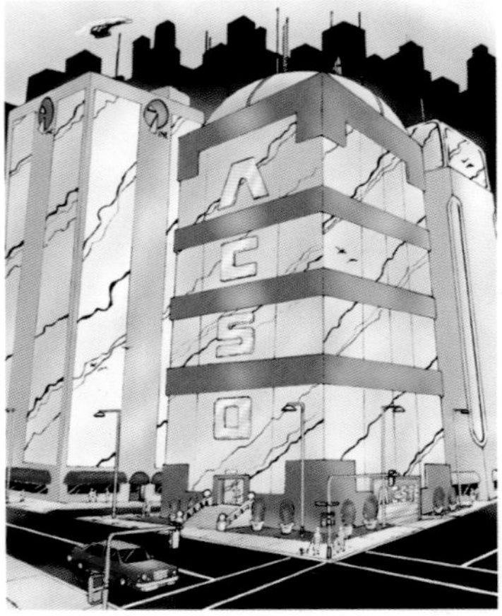
ACSO

THE REST

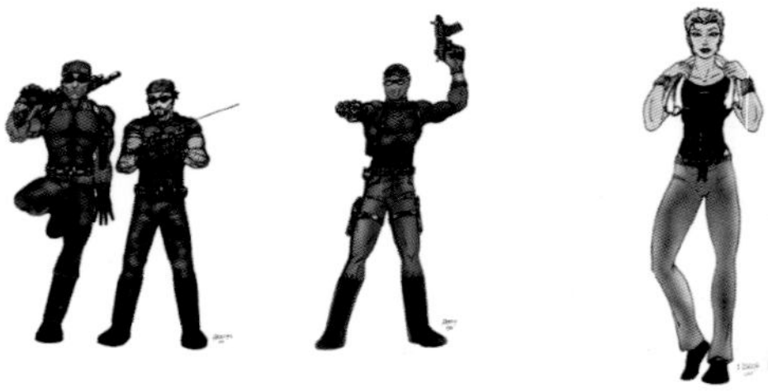

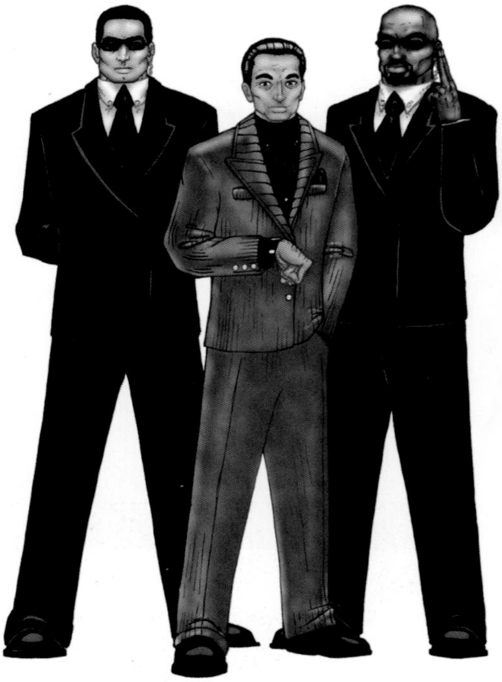

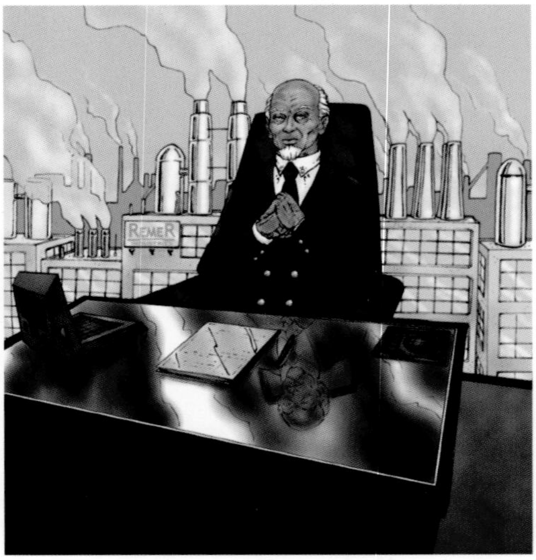

"It's a little sad designing characters that are only going to make it onto one or two pages. So to avoid feeling like I was condemning these 'people' to obscurity, I based most of them on friends of mine. This way, their lives go on and I don't have to figure out how to fit them into every script!"

"The ACSO mobile unit almost didn't make it into existence. I've never really enjoyed drawing transports (absolute creative block in this area), but a friend of mine suggested combining features from exisiting vehicles. So I found pictures of different fire and dump trucks (and a 1960's-era milk truck) and combined them."

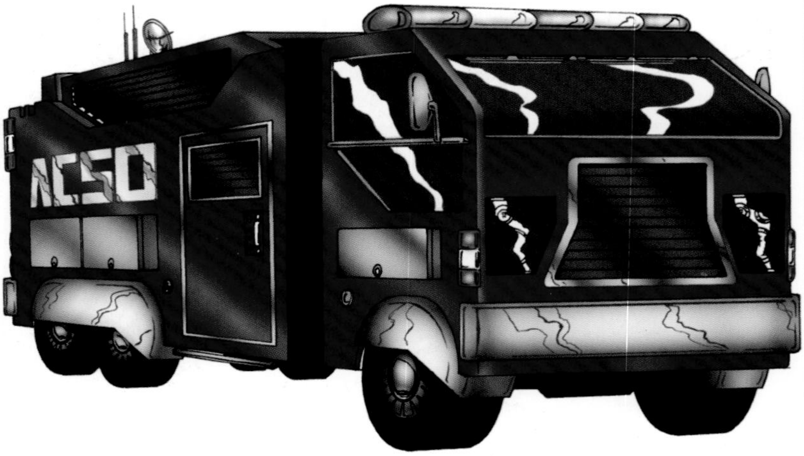
ACSO

COMING SOON

Pax Avalon

- BIRTHRIGHT -

"It's important to me that each book doesn't start with a reboot -- a separate story with all the characters and circumstances independent from previous stories. No, the actions of these characters have consequences, and this needs to be reflected in the continuity. This said... there are going to be a lot of changes to the world of Pax Avalon in ***BirthRight***. Some new characters, new problems, and a completely different context for Pax's mission in her beloved city."

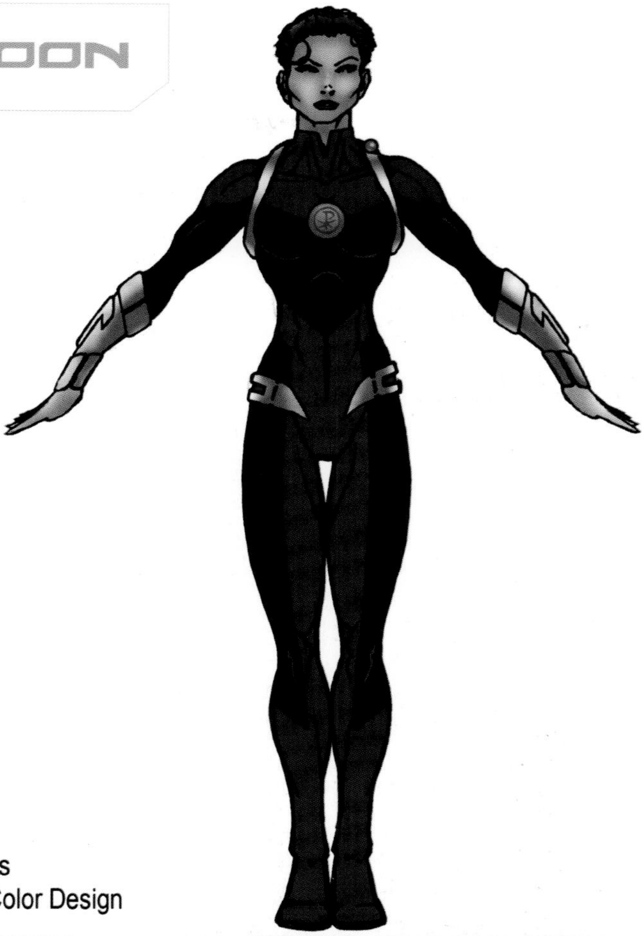

Right: Initial *Pax* Costume Alterations
Bottom: Initial *KnightHood* Ink and Color Design

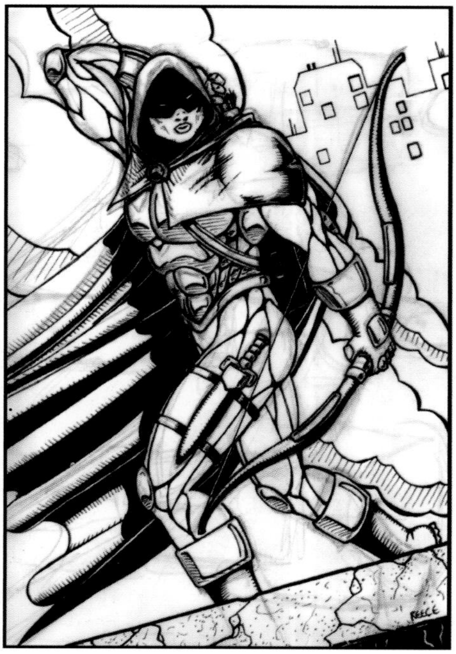

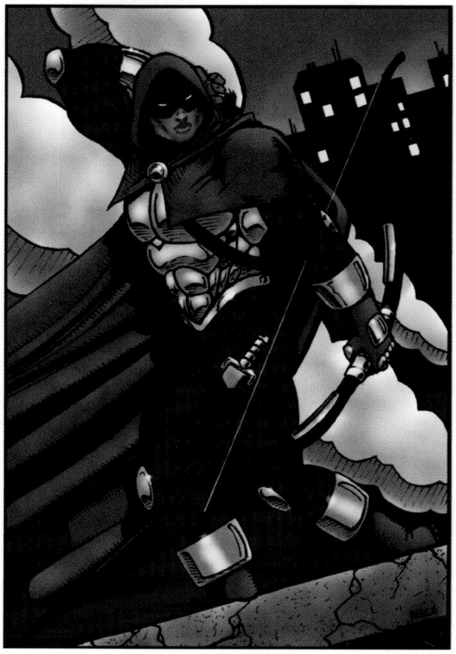

THE AUTHOR

This book is dedicated to my wife, Rachel.
It's a joy living with a heroine every day.

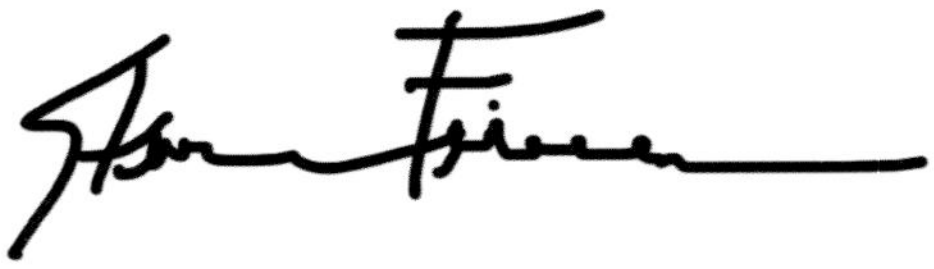

Steven "Reece" Friesen wears a lot of hats! He's worn youth pastor hats (goofy) and associate pastor hats (respectable) at churches in British Columbia and Saskatchewan, and a whole bunch more during his years studying at Columbia Bible College and doing missions with Venture Teams International.

These days, he's sporting a hardhat with his carpenter dad while pursuing a Masters of Theology mortarboard at Canadian Mennonite University. He's even been known to wear a baseball cap to cover up the hair he's losing from raising three daughters, Abigail, Laureli, and Cariana, with his wife, Rachel, in Calgary, Alberta.

Friesen was born in Swan River, Manitoba, but he remembers very little about the event (though his mother claims to remember it vividly).

If he could pick any superpower, it would be flight.